AMERICA'S FAILING EXPERIMENT

AMERICA'S FAILING EXPERIMENT

How We the People Have Become the Problem

Kirby Goidel

ROWMAN & LITTLEFIELD
Lanham • Boulder • New York • London

Published by Rowman & Littlefield
A wholly owned subsidiary of The Rowman & Littlefield Publishing Group, Inc.
4501 Forbes Boulevard, Suite 200, Lanham, Maryland 20706
www.rowman.com

Unit A, Whitacre Mews, 26-34 Stannary Street, London SE11 4AB

British Library Cataloguing in Publication Information Available

Library of Congress Cataloging-in-Publication Data
The hardback edition of this book was previously catalogued by the Library of Congress as follows:

Goidel, Robert K., 1967–
America's failing experiment : how we the people have become the problem / Kirby Goidel.
pages cm
Includes index.
1. Democracy—United States—Citizen participation. 2. Political participation—United States. 3. Political culture—United States. 4. United States—Politics and government—21st century. I. Title.
JK1764.G66 2014
320.973—dc23
2013031601

ISBN 978-1-4422-2650-0 (cloth : alk. paper)
ISBN 978-1-4422-4750-5 (pbk. : alk. paper)
ISBN 978-1-4422-2651-7 (electronic)

Printed in the United States of America

CONTENTS

ACKNOWLEDGMENTS

This book would have been unthinkable without the influence of two professors, very different in style, but both incredibly impactful. Neither bears responsibility for any of the conclusions drawn here. Indeed, I imagine (and hope) each would take issue with the arguments put forward in this text.

I had the good fortune to stumble into Tony Eksterowicz's American government course as a directionless but intellectually curious psychology major circa 1986. After a handful of lectures, I was hooked. His probing questions about the effectiveness of democratic governance, the responsibilities of democratic citizenship, and the possibilities for reform have been a constant refrain in all of my teaching and research.

Don Gross similarly saved me from law school when he called and offered a teaching assistantship at the University of Kentucky in 1989. I gladly accepted. Don is a talented quantitative scholar, but he relishes asking difficult, often uncomfortable, and frequently unanswerable questions.

I also owe special thanks to Adrienne Moore, the former director of the Reilly Center for Media & Public Affairs at Louisiana State University. Adrienne continues to believe that scholarship should be about big ideas and real-world consequences. Adrienne supported this project from its inception, read various drafts along the way, and offered timely words of encouragement.

Thanks are also due to Johanna Dunaway, Ashley Kirzinger, Jason Turcotte, Tony Eksterowicz, and Keith Gaddie for reading earlier drafts of the manuscript and offering suggestions, corrections, and criticisms. The mistakes that remain are my own. My neighbor and friend Andy Redpath similarly agreed to read an early draft and offered suggestions for improving the book's appeal beyond academic audiences.

My greatest thanks are, of course, reserved for my family. My parents, Don and Lou Goidel, always encouraged political debate and discussion, igniting a lifelong interest in politics. They taught me to carefully weigh evidence and reach independent decisions. My wife, Beth, tolerated my sabbatical with good humor and patience (though she also vowed that I am never allowed to retire). Most of all, this book is for my kids, Hannah and Spencer, who have learned to deal with my distractions and obsessions. I hope it makes them proud.

INTRODUCTION

We Are the Problem

This is a book about the failure of American democracy. And, let's be honest, American democracy is failing. We are unable to address our most pressing problems, unwilling to plan, think, or invest beyond the next election cycle, and seemingly unable or unwilling to correct our current course. This is not *just* a problem of our elected officials. They are not, as is commonly believed, out of touch. If anything, they are too responsive to public opinion and interest group pressures. Nor are they intellectually or morally inferior to the elected officials of the past. They are no more incompetent than our elected representatives from the 1950s, 1920s, 1890s, or 1800s. Indeed, they are likely less corrupt, better educated, and more professional than politicians in the past. Tip O'Neill, a former speaker of the House who served in Congress from 1952 to 1985, captured the problem elegantly when asked about the differences between the Congress when we he began his career in the 1950s relative to the Congress when he ended his career in the 1980s. "The people are better," O'Neill explained. "The results are worse."

It is a widely held misconception that if we could simply throw out all the bums and start all over, our politics would be purified and cleansed. An NBC/*Wall Street Journal* poll conducted in August 2011, for example, found that 54 percent of Americans would vote to defeat and replace every single member of Congress, including their own representative.[1] The problem, according to this view, is not the system but the people who run it. In a milder form, this misconception is expressed in support of replacing professional politicians and their expertise with regular people with everyday common sense: the citizen legislator idealized by reformers advocating term limits and campaign finance reform. More subtly, it influences how politicians portray themselves and cast their opposition. George W. Bush, a graduate of Yale University and the Harvard Business School, portrayed Harvard graduates Al Gore and John Kerry as elitists. Sarah Palin's everywoman appeal was similarly an embodiment of a deeper public sentiment for leadership from everyday people with core values. In contemporary politics, there is a palpable desire for "commonsense" solutions and a price to be paid for appearing too smart.

Oddly, and perhaps ironically, the deep disaffection from the current crop of elected officials hardly affects public support for the "political system" more broadly defined. Tea Party adherents give the U.S. Constitution nearly religious reverence even as they hold public officials (especially Democrats and moderate Republicans) and politics in great disdain. The failures of contemporary politics, according to this view, are rooted in departures from our original constitutional design and a lack of fidelity to the original intent of the Founding Fathers. If we return to our constitutional origins—so the thinking goes—all will be well. Such thinking, of course, ignores the actual history in favor of mythology. Historical accounts illustrate the Founding Fathers were of not like minds at the time of the Constitution's drafting, as they disagreed strongly on many of the Constitution's key provisions. James Madison, often described as the Constitution's chief architect, altered his interpretations as the political context shifted from the early drafting of the Constitution and the Washington administration to his alliance with Thomas Jefferson and the formation of the Democratic-Republican Party.[2]

Arguing that we have simply lost our way has an inherent and intuitive appeal, full of religious and political symbolism. Indeed, I will make a similar, though more nuanced, argument. But the problem is not politicians' promiscuity with constitutional intent—the problem is us, the American public. Our politicians are, by and large, doing what we have asked them to do. "We the people" are simply not up to the task of self-governance; we are easily misled and controlled by corporate power and interest group campaigns. In truth, we never have been up to the task, but, for a variety of reasons, our failings are more evident, more troublesome, and more dangerous in contemporary politics.

Democracy requires citizens that are informed, tolerant, and engaged. We are none of those things. Survey research routinely shows a public woefully misinformed about the basics of American government.[3] More Americans, for example, can name all the members of the Simpsons family than can name their First Amendment freedoms.[4] Nearly three-quarters of Americans (74 percent) can name the Three Stooges, while only 42 percent can correctly identify the executive, legislative, and judicial branches of government.[5] The challenge for public opinion pollsters isn't uncovering isolated pockets of ignorance—that requires no real effort or creativity—but rather discovering where the public has meaningful political attitudes rooted in an accurate understanding of issues or candidates.[6]

Public ignorance is easy fodder for late-night comedians, but it is no laughing matter when it comes to democratic governance. It undermines one of the central pillars of democratic governance—an informed public capable of making meaningful decisions about community, policy, and politics. But public ignorance is nothing new. Indeed, based on formal education alone, one might expect that knowledge about the fundamentals of American government should be higher now than at any time in our history. An increasing number of high school and college graduates should, in theory, translate into better-educated citizens. Unfortunately, this is too simplistic. Education is increasingly justified as worker training; recently adopted accountability standards have emphasized the fundamentals (reading, writing, and mathematics) as opposed to civic education, and the teaching of American history and politics has become increasingly politicized. Even civics courses are of questionable value when it comes to increasing political knowledge. Without wading too deeply into these waters, this much seems clear: formal education does not necessarily or easily translate into greater understanding or factual knowledge of our political system.[7] As a point of comparison, Michael X. Delli Carpini and Scott Keeter found that while formal education remains the single best predictor of political knowledge, knowledge levels of college graduates today are equivalent to those of high school graduates in the 1940s.

On the other hand, there is little reason to believe that public ignorance is more troubling today than ten, twenty, or one hundred years ago. H. L. Mencken writing in the 1920s observed, "Democracy is a pathetic belief in the collective wisdom of individual ignorance." Winston Churchill is widely quoted as saying that "democracy is the worst form of government except all those other forms that have been tried from time to time," but he also opined that the "best argument against democracy is a five-minute conversation with the average voter." Novelist Oscar Wilde described democracy as "the bludgeoning of the people by the people for the people."

If public ignorance is not new, it is more troubling because it is more consequential. The American political system has long protected itself from too much public input—first, through a brilliantly conceived constitutional design and, second, through political organizations like political parties. The public spoke, but its voice was heavily filtered. In today's politics, we suffer from too few filters, too few gatekeepers, and an oversupply of information. As a result, the public speaks loudly but incoherently.

It isn't that politicians are ignoring the public, but rather that they are listening too closely, and even worse, they are acting on incoherent, inconsistent, and unstable public preferences. Their reward is often an unappreciative public and declining trust in government. The Iraq War is an excellent example. When the war began, it was widely supported by both the public and elected officials. Public opinion turned when the war lasted longer and cost more than originally anticipated. Whether the public was intentionally misled by the Bush administration about the purposes or commitment required or whether the media or the opposition party dropped the ball by not voicing objections loudly enough in light of favorable public opinion polls is not particularly relevant for this point. A politician following the voice of the public would have supported both the initial invasion of Iraq *and* the withdrawal of troops just months later.

Budgetary politics highlight the problem as well. Convinced that budgets can be balanced simply by eliminating waste, the public demands both lower taxes and higher government spending. Government responds with short-term deficits and long-term debt. The public then demands deficit reduction but does not support the necessary tax increases or spending cuts in big-ticket government programs to make serious debt reduction possible. This is not coherent policy. Indeed, it appears to be logically possible only through wholesale misconceptions about the amount of waste inherent in government bureaucracies. This is problematic for several reasons. First, waste is not only in the eye of the beholder but also inevitable in any large organization. All large corporations "waste" money, as does any large government agency.[8] Second, there is not enough waste to reconcile the competing demands for increased government spending and reduced taxes. Third, Americans dislike spending much more in the abstract than in specific big government programs, like Medicare, social security, or defense spending.[9] The politicians closely attuned to public opinion would vote to reduce taxes *and* to either increase government spending or protect big-ticket entitlement programs from any offsetting cuts.

The larger problem is not that the politicians are not sensitive to public opinion broadly defined but rather that they are hypersensitive to pressures of organized groups and special interests. Political scientists have long taught that the American political system is a pluralistic rather than a majoritarian democracy. Pluralism is defined in this context by multiple points of access and public involvement focused around narrowly defined private interests. Farmers, for example, are more involved in agricultural policy, corporations in tax law, and manufacturers in industrial policy. But while pluralism accounts for the gaps between democratic theory and the realities of an uninvolved and apathetic public, its fatal flaw has been a decided bias in favor of moneyed interests. In 1960, E. E. Schattschneider famously wrote, "The flaw in the pluralist heaven is that the heavenly chorus sings with a strong upper-class accent." [10] Schattschneider's quote reflects the realities of pluralism: the people who join groups and participate in politics are wealthier, better educated, and better equipped to command resources for effective communication and policy influence. The more pluralistic the society, the greater the upper-class bias.

For many observers, U.S. government is best described in terms of not just pluralism but also hyperpluralism, in which group activity becomes so dominant that policy gridlock results. Writing in 1994 in the *New Republic*, Jonathan Rauch described what he called the "hyperpluralism trap," whereby populist rhetoric leads to greater interest group control: "Activists and reformers who think the answer to democracy's problems is more access for more of the people need to wake up. Uncontrolled access only breeds more lobbies. It is axiomatic that 'the people' (whatever that now means) do not organize to seek government benefits; lobbies do." [11] This situation has been magnified in contemporary politics. The exponential growth of digital media has expanded the opportunities for communication and feedback, the gap between rich and poor has expanded, and the middle class has dwindled.

We can blame corruption, capitalism, lobbyists, special interest politics, the mainstream media, failing public schools, or the demise of the two-parent household for this sorry state of affairs, but there is no mistaking our collective failure as citizens. We get the government we deserve so we are governed poorly. Or rather, we are governed by private interests rather than the public good—ironically, not because government does not listen to us but because it listens to us too closely and what we have to say is contradictory, uninformed, and nonsensical. Organized political interests step into the void.

If public ignorance didn't matter, this would be nothing more than fodder for late-night television. Jay Leno's "man in the street" interviews show a public that is laughably ignorant of the very basics of American civic life. But public ignorance, as stated before, is no laughing matter, and for the reasons outlined in the following chapters, it matters now more than ever before. First, the public is increasingly asked to pass judgment not just on the direction of the country but also on the details of health care reform, foreign affairs, and tax policy. A definable public opinion lurks beneath the surface that fairly reflects true public preferences, but what too often passes as public opinion—aggregated survey responses—is highly sensitive to question wording and issue framing.[12] Second, changes to our political system, our communication infrastructure, and society at large have made public opinion more important and more dangerous. In short, we have become more participatory, we have increased the avenues available for immediate and interactive public feedback, and our politicians have become more narrowly attuned to short-term public preferences and interest group pressures. In the process, we have put our political system at risk by making it more susceptible to demagogues who promise simple, but unworkable, solutions to complex problems and/or solutions that require stepping outside of our constitutional framework.

Watching contemporary politics, it is difficult to escape this depressing and demoralizing thought: Perhaps the ancient philosophers were correct. Perhaps democracy does inevitably lead to tyranny. Perhaps the American political experiment—which has balanced carefully between a republican structure and a democratic ethos—has nearly run its course. Democracy, at least as we have practiced it, appears to be faltering. In the following pages, I explain how we got to this point and outline some suggestions for how we can reform—and hopefully save—our political system. The first step to recovery is admitting that we have a problem and that the problem is rooted in our democratic impulse. We are the problem.

BUT IS THE POLITICAL SYSTEM REALLY BROKEN?

Books written by ivory tower academics sounding the warning bells of political system failure are hardly new. Students of American politics have long expressed concerns about the fragility of American democracy, the lack of knowledge and apathy of the American public, and the corruption and self-serving nature of political elites.[13] Despite such dire warnings, we have somehow managed to muddle our way through the Civil War and the Great Depression, as well as the social, political, and economic upheaval associated with rapid industrialization during the nineteenth century. The skeptic can take a quiet comfort in this: we have endured far worse.

The cyclical nature of American political history in which social and economic progress occurs in rapid spurts in the wake of crises similarly offers a reason to counsel patience rather than reform. Political change often lags behind broader changes in the social and economic context. Indeed, this is often a defining characteristic of political crisis. So do we really need a recovery plan or do we need the patience to wait until the dust settles and a more productive and less partisan era emerges? It is perhaps worth recalling that the political system has not remained constant but has shaped—and been shaped by—each of these crises. Or perhaps, stated differently, the question is not whether we will change, but when and how.

It is also tempting to see our contemporary morass entirely in budgetary terms, the failure of our political system to live within its means, and the reluctance of voters to pay the short-term costs of deficit reduction. It is equally tempting to see the problem solely as the province of elite partisanship, a deep polarization that makes compromise and consensus nearly impossible, and that is nearly absent in the great mass of citizens who make up our democracy. Yet if budgetary politics and elite polarization serve as great examples of our political dysfunction, they are more symptom than cause. The problems are deeply rooted in the inherent pathologies of democratic governance. To remain politically solvent, democratic governance requires filters and mid-course corrections. It requires leadership that can translate shortsighted democratic demands into the best possible long-term policy decisions.

Our contemporary political system fails this important test. Across a range of issues, we are unwilling to make short-term sacrifices for long-term gains. Long-term problems—climate change, budget deficits, social security—do not get addressed because we are unwilling to pay the costs. Importantly, this not simply a problem of U.S. national politics; it runs to the core of democratic governance. States and municipalities across the country have proved fiscally irresponsible; they are unable (or unwilling) to address unfunded liabilities in their retirement systems, and unable (or unwilling) to pay for critical government services, and there is a race to the bottom in terms of the provision of government services and the reduction of taxes. State governments fail to adequately fund public schools while simultaneously providing tax breaks to large employers. Public education may suffer, but at least we have a Bass Pro Shop. Collectively, we are kicking the can down the road. But it is not just about budgets and debt: we are unwilling to make the long-term investments—in roads and infrastructure, in science and education—that will yield a stronger and healthier society over the next several decades.

If the mounting stack of unresolved issues sitting on our collective desk worries me deeply, I worry even more about the solutions we will offer to fix these problems. Surveying this landscape, the common refrain is the Al Gore solution: to complain that our democracy has been "hacked" by special interests.[14] This is perhaps true, but it alleviates democratic responsibility, the culpability of the average citizen in creating and maintaining our current dysfunction. The system can be hacked because it lacks the firewall of an informed citizenry assumed by democratic and participatory theorists. Here is the paradox of democratic governance: by opening the door even wider to citizen input, democratic reforms unintentionally empower the special interests to "hack" the political process by giving the most intensely partisan voices more levers to influence the political process. More democracy won't solve this problem. Indeed, it will likely make it worse.

Before going further, let me make an important caveat. I am not arguing that people should not have the right to vote or that we should repeal the Fifteenth, Seventeenth, Nineteenth, or Twenty-Sixth Amendments. [15] Every American citizen should have the right to participate in the political process. This, however, begs the more important questions: (1) How much influence should the public have, particularly over everyday policy matters? (2) What form should that influence take? Currently, public influence takes shape in forms that blur lines of political accountability and that make effective leadership more difficult. Instead, public opinion should enhance accountability and empower leadership. This is a system-level failure and can only be fixed with structural changes.

One of the central premises of this book is that for reform to work, it must begin with an understanding of individual psychology. Decades of psychological research have cast doubt on the "Enlightenment model of reasoning" underlying contemporary faith in democratic political systems. Individuals are simply not wired to think rationally or objectively. Instead, they reason backward from conclusion to evidence, from emotion to cognition. Yet the history of American political reform is almost entirely immune to an understanding of the cognitive limitations and biases inherent in individual decision-making. Reformers often assume—either implicitly or explicitly—an Enlightenment model of reasoning: a rational and reasoning voter capable of sorting and evaluating unlimited quantities of data. Political scientists have long recognized that this is not the case, but they have adopted the unfortunate fallback position that voters are doing "well enough" without adequately answering the question of what "well enough" actually means. Under what circumstances, if any, might we fairly say that voters are not doing well enough? [16] Given all that we have learned about individual psychology, what is the "best" system to enable reasonably informed decision-making? Is there a way to design the system such that the system-level requirements for citizen participation match what we understand about individual cognitive processing?

Curiously, James Madison seemed to understand this in devising the U.S. Constitution. His design created an important but limited role for public opinion, balancing the need for public input and elite control. This is the balance we must seek to regain before our republican government fails us. Or rather, before we fail it.

NOTES

1. The poll was conducted August 27–31, 2011, and included one thousand respondents, including two hundred reached by cell phone. Specific question wording is as follows: "If there was a place on your ballot that allowed you to vote to defeat and replace every member of congress, including your own representative, would you do this or not?" http://online.wsj.com/article/SB100014240531119045374045765540300058990252.html?mod=WSJ_hp_LEFTTopStories (accessed September 9, 2012).

2. Andrew Burstein and Nancy Isenberg, *Madison and Jefferson* (New York: Random House, 2013).

3. Michael X. Delli Carpini and Scott Keeter, *What Americans Know and Why It Matters* (New Haven, CT: Yale University Press, 1996).

4. "Americans' Awareness of First American Freedoms," *McCormick Tribune Freedom Museum*, 2006, http://www.forumforeducation.org/node/147 (accessed May 23, 2013).

5. Cited in Brit Hume, "Zogby Poll: Most Americans Can Name Three Stooges But Not Three Branches of Government," *Fox News*, August 16, 2006, http://www.foxnews.com/story/0,2933,208577,00.html (accessed May 23, 2013).

6. David W. Moore, *The Superpollsters: How They Measure and Manipulate Public Opinion in America* (New York: Four Walls Eight Windows, 1995).

7. Ricard Niemi and Jane Junn, *Civic Education: What Makes Students Learn* (New Haven, CT: Yale University Press, 1998).

8. The definition of waste is subjective. Google, for example, provides "nap pods" for employees, a perk that arguably enhances innovation and creativity, but imagine a federal or state government agency with nap pods. Google, similarly, provides free food for employees. Outside of Google, golf trips and resort vacations are often seen as a cost of doing business in major corporations and a reward for a job well done.

9. According to a 2013 survey conducted by the Pew Research Center for the People & the Press, the public showed little support for cutting specific programs. See "As Sequester Deadline Looms, Little Support for Cutting Most Programs," Pew Research Center for the People & the Press, February 22, 2013, http://www.people-press.org/2013/02/22/as-sequester-deadline-looms-little-support-for-cutting-most-programs/1/ (accessed May 23, 2013).

10. E. E. Schattschneider, *The Semi-Sovereign People: A Realist View of Democracy in America* (New York: Holt, Rinehart, and Winston, 1960).

11. Jonathan Rauch, "The Hyperpluralism Trap," *New Republic*, June 6, 1994, 22–25.

12. This is not intended as a criticism of contemporary survey research, which attempts to measure public preferences. The measurement tool is not the problem, nor is the effort to understand public opinion broadly defined. The problem is in the structure of public opinion, the issue-based content, and its sensitivity to framing and context.

13. One may fairly argue that our contemporary political dysfunction is rooted in the realization of the American Political Science Association's call for more responsible political parties in the 1950s. See *Toward a More Responsible Two-Party System* (New York: Rinehart, 1950); Thomas Mann and Norman Ornstein, *It's Even Worse Than It Looks: How the American Constitutional System Collided with the New Politics of Extremism* (New York: Basic Books, 2012).

14. Al Gore, *The Future: Six Drivers of Global Change* (New York: Random House, 2013).

15. Though I am tempted by arguments to repeal the Seventeenth Amendment.

16. If we think of this as a hypothesis, short of revolution, there is no test powerful enough to reject the null that the system is working well enough.

I

CONSTITUTIONAL DESIGN
AND DEMOCRACY

A republic, if you can keep it.

—Benjamin Franklin

This quote is well known, widely cited, and poorly understood. Like most of the Founding Fathers, Benjamin Franklin was wary of the democratic impulse, describing democracy as "two wolves and a lamb voting on what to have for lunch." John Adams similarly observed, "Democracy never lasts long. It soon wastes, exhausts, and murders itself. There is never a democracy that did not commit suicide." While it is a mistake to believe that the Founding Fathers held singular views regarding democracy, these statements were broadly reflective of the sentiments of the time, well rooted in political philosophy and practical experience, and well evidenced in *The Federalist Papers* and the U.S. Constitution. Democracy was never the intent.

Long before Adams and Franklin, Plato observed that "democracy passes into despotism." Cynical about the capacity of individual citizens to rule themselves, Plato advocated a republic ruled by philosopher kings, men motivated by wisdom. The structure of the U.S. Constitution owed more to Plato's student Aristotle, who shared a healthy skepticism about the capacity of democracy—

which he defined as a rule by the needy and susceptible to dema-gogues—but found the idea of a political system built around phi-losopher kings impractical in the real world of governance. In practice, Aristotle argued, the best possible system combined fea-tures of a democracy and oligarchy in a polity defined first and foremost around the rule of law.

James Madison, the chief architect of the U.S. Constitution, also drew heavily from the French philosopher Baron de Montes-quieu, who advocated separation of power as a mechanism for checking against the abuse of power within a democratic system of government.[1] "When the legislative and executive powers are united in the same person, or in the same body of magistrates," Montesquieu wrote, "there can be no liberty." We also find in Montesquieu's writings warnings about the limitations of demo-cratic governance. "The tyranny of a prince in an oligarchy," he observed, "is not so dangerous to the public welfare as the apathy of a citizen in a democracy."

Fear of democracy is deeply rooted in our constitutional de-sign. The urgency for a Second Constitutional Convention was sparked by a popular uprising, Shays' Rebellion (1786), in which a group of Massachusetts farmers attempted to seize the federal arsenal in Springfield, Massachusetts, to end bank foreclosures on their properties. Many of the men engaged in the rebellion, such as Daniel Shays, were Revolutionary War veterans who had not been fully paid for their military service but found themselves in court for nonpayment of their debts. Shays' Rebellion was a demo-cratic uprising aimed at elite control of a financial system that put the interests of wealthy merchants above the interests of the com-mon man. The common man, the military veteran and farmer, lost the battle. Thomas Jefferson famously quipped in the rebellion's aftermath, "I hold it, that a little rebellion, now and then is a good thing," while adding, "The tree of liberty must be refreshed from time to time with the blood of patriots and tyrants." Jefferson thought the participants in Shays' Rebellion were misguided but well meaning, and that such rebellions served as useful checks on the power of government.

Most of the Founding Fathers, however, found the rebellion and the ineffective response disconcerting and clear evidence of the need for a stronger central government. The initial effort at revising the Articles of Confederation held in Annapolis had failed miserably: only five states bothered sending representatives. Shays' Rebellion created a sense of urgency to the need for revision that made the Second Constitutional Convention in Philadelphia a success. Writing in this context, Elbridge Gerry opined that "the evils we experience flow from an excess of democracy. The people do not want virtue but are dupes of pretend patriots." George Washington similarly cautioned that "we are fast verging to anarchy and confusion!" Washington described the rebellion as "a triumph for the advocates of despotism." Notably, even before the rebellion, Washington had expressed concerns about democratic governance generally and the effectiveness of the Articles of Confederation specifically: "Experience has taught us that men will not adopt and carry into execution measures best calculated for their own good, without the intervention of a coercive power."

James Madison was no less pessimistic about human nature or democracy. In *The Federalist Papers*, James Madison, Alexander Hamilton, and John Jay presented the case for the U.S. Constitution in a series of letters to the editor as part of the campaign for ratification in New York. In *Federalist No. 10*, James Madison warned that *majority* factions were the single most significant threat to democratic governance. "Pure democracies," he argued, "have in general been as short in their lives as they have been violent in their deaths." His brilliant design left only the fingerprints of democracy on an otherwise republican form of government, defined by representative government, internal checks against the consolidation of power, divisions of executive, legislative, and judicial powers, and the logistical difficulties of organizing over such a large territory.

Put simply, the American Constitution was designed to thwart, rather than encourage, majority rule and democratic governance. Even Thomas Jefferson, the most democratic of the Founding Fathers, believed that governments worked best under the direction of a natural, rather than an artificial, aristocracy. As historian Charles Merriam concluded in a 1902 exploration of Jefferson's political philosophy, Jefferson "wanted aristocratic rulers democratically chosen."[2] Walter Lippmann credits Jefferson with convincing the American public that an undemocratic constitutional design was intended to empower direct popular rule. As Lippmann observed,

> The American people came to believe that their Constitution was a democratic instrument, and treated it as such. They owe that fiction to the victory of Thomas Jefferson, and a great conservative fiction it has been. It is a fair guess that if everyone had always regarded the Constitution as did the authors of it, the Constitution would have been violently overthrown, because loyalty to the Constitution and loyalty to democracy would have seemed incompatible. Jefferson resolved that paradox by teaching the American people to read the Constitution as an expression of democracy.[3]

We have believed in a façade of democracy and tied that faith to our founding documents—the Declaration of Independence, the U.S. Constitution, and *The Federalist Papers*—without recognizing the inherent contradictions built into a revolutionary Declaration of Independence and the inherently elitist governing principles found in the U.S. Constitution. Consent of the governed was necessary to form a government and to give government its legitimacy but not for deciding specific policy decisions. That task was better left to knowledgeable elites.

In Madison's constitutional scheme, only the U.S. House of Representatives was directly elected by the "people." The right to define the people was intentionally left to the states and was not included as part of the Constitution. Throughout the founding period, the right to vote was generally limited by the states to white male property owners. This was to ensure that voters had a "stake in society" out of fear that poor citizens would band together and vote to redistribute property. Writing in the 1920s, historian Charles Beard made the controversial assertion that the

Founding Fathers were driven primarily by base economic incentives rather than more noble considerations of self-governance. While the thesis was overstated, it captured a very real concern.[4] Left unchecked, the people, inflamed by passion and empowered by majority rule, would threaten the public interest by redistributing wealth.

The U.S. Senate, as originally designed, was elected by state legislatures and was not directly elected until the Seventeenth Amendment. The Senate, it was thought, would embody enough wisdom and experience to cool and refine any democratic passions that might arise in the House of Representatives. As George Washington explained the necessity of the Senate to Thomas Jefferson, he said, "we pour legislation into the senatorial saucer to cool it," meaning that legislation arising in the people's branch, the House of Representatives, would be tempered by the slower-moving and more aristocratic Senate. Perhaps stated differently, popular ideas would not become law without careful consideration by the more aristocratic Senate.

Similarly, the American president would be kept at a distance from public opinion by a convoluted electoral process that involved selection first through the Electoral College and then the House of Representatives. If the system worked as designed, presidential elections would be decided by the House of Representatives and the president would be two steps removed from popular opinion. The process has rarely worked as designed, as most presidential elections are decided by Electoral College majorities. Curiously, unusually close elections, like the 2000 *Bush v. Gore* decision, are treated as constitutional crises rather than as vindications of the Founding Fathers' brilliance in constitutional design.[5] Writing in January 1980, for example, constitutional scholars Laurence Tribe and Thomas Rollins imagined the possibility of John Anderson's independent candidacy throwing the Reagan-Carter election into the House of Representatives and noted the irony that most Americans were unaware that this was how the Founding Fathers intended the Electoral College to work.[6] Similarly, in July 1992, Ross Perot cited concerns about the possibility that his candidacy might throw the election into the House of Representatives as a reason for dropping out of the presidential race. As Perot observed,

> As you know, if we cannot win in November the election will be decided in the House of Representatives, and since the House of Representatives is made up primarily of Democrats and Republicans, our chances of winning would be pretty slim.
>
> Now that the Democratic Party has revitalized itself, I have concluded that we cannot win in November and that the election will be decided in the House of Representatives. Since the House of Representatives does not pick the President until January, the new President will be unable to use the months of November and December to assemble the new government.
>
> I believe it would be disruptive for us to continue our program since this program would obviously put it in the House of Representatives and be disruptive to the country. . . . So therefore I will not become a candidate.[7]

Perot rejoined the race in October, saying his real reason for dropping out involved the possibility that Republican dirty tricks would disrupt his daughter's wedding. But imagine the possibility and ensuing controversy of a contemporary presidential election being decided by the House of Representatives. Were the Constitution to function as intended, the result would be a sharp decline in public trust and calls for political reform.

Despite this original intent, the history of American politics has reflected a mostly continuous growth in executive power as the link between presidents and popular will has grown. Particularly during times of crisis, the public expects and demands presidential action, and a president's historical greatness is largely determined by his aggressive use of presidential authority. In 1973, Arthur Schlesinger Jr. outlined the pathologies inherent in these institutional arrangements and described them as "the imperial presidency." Confronted with a recalcitrant legislature, a crisis, and the need to act, presidents are tempted to step outside constitutional boundaries to act decisively. Indeed, presidential greatness is determined in large part by the expansion of executive power.

The advent of modern polling and daily tracking of presidential approval ratings further linked presidential action with public opinion in an ongoing and continuous referendum of public support. Virtually every presidential action is evaluated in the context of overnight polls and shifting approval ratings. Notably, polling did not create this problem; it only magnified it. Constitutional scholar Bruce Ackerman traces "the rise of the plebiscitary presidency" to its origins in the election of 1800 and the election of Thomas Jefferson. The gradual erosion of constitutional intent was made possible by the failure of the Founding Fathers to anticipate the development of political parties and the close and growing relationship between presidents and public opinion.[8] Before George Gallup fielded his first opinion poll, the link between presidents and public opinion was firmly entrenched.

The staggered terms of our elected officials are further evidence of a deep democratic distrust among the Founders. The House of Representatives, elected to two-year terms, would be the repository of public opinion and, in theory, subject to much tumult and turnover. The more aristocratic Senate would be appointed by state legislatures to six-year terms. As a further check on the democratic impulse, only a third of the Senate would be selected every two years, ensuring that senators would arrive under unique and fracturing political pressures. The president would, for similar reasons, be elected to a four-year term. The Supreme Court, the final arbiters of constitutional meaning, would be furthest removed from public opinion, selected by the president and confirmed by the Senate for lifetime appointments.

Under Madison's carefully constructed design, the path to majority rule would be heavily and intentionally obstructed. History and our cultural commitment to democratic governance, however, would prove to be more powerful than the institutional structures (separation of powers and checks and balances) created by the U.S. Constitution.

THE CONSTITUTION'S OPPONENTS

Often forgotten in contemporary discussions of the Constitution are the Anti-Federalists, the loosely defined opposition to ratification. Where they do merit mention, it is generally in the context of the addition of the Bill of Rights rather than more fundamental questions about the threat of an overly intrusive national government or the role of the people in the proposed constitutional order. Perhaps ironically, Tea Party advocates may have more in common with the Anti-Federalists than the Federalists, as the Anti-Federalists were deeply suspicious of a centralized national government while the Federalists were seeking to expand federal authority to deal with the crisis created by a weak and ineffective national government.

Included among the Anti-Federalists were patriots such as Patrick Henry, who famously proclaimed "give me liberty or give me death" during the American Revolution but also said that he smelled "a rat" at the Second Constitutional Convention in Philadelphia. He was correct in his suspicions. The Philadelphia Convention met in secrecy to avoid accusations of treason, went far beyond their authorization to "revise" the Articles of Confederation by scrapping the existing government in its entirety, and fundamentally changed the rules of the game to make ratification easier. The Second Constitutional Convention has often been described as a bloodless coup, moving the newly formed American republic away from its more radical democratic impulses and toward the stability and status quo of a new constitutional order.

The Anti-Federalists, for their part, also expressed greater faith in the capacity of the "people" relative to the institutional maze created by Madison's constitutional structure as the central mechanism for ensuring government responsiveness and accountability. In *Federalist No. 51*, Madison observed,

> If men were angels, no government would be necessary. If angels were to govern men, neither external nor internal controls on government would be necessary. In framing a govern-

ment which is to be administered by men over men, the great difficulty lies in this: you must first enable the government to control the governed; and in the next place oblige it to control itself. A dependence on the people is, no doubt, the primary control on the government; but experience has taught mankind the necessity of auxiliary precautions.

In contrast, the Anti-Federalists described the proposed government as a "despotic aristocracy among freemen."[9] The same Elbridge Gerry who proclaimed that Shays' Rebellion flowed from an excess of democracy wrote that his central objection to the proposed constitution was that "there is no adequate provision for a representation of the People."[10] George Mason, often referred to as the father of the Bill of Rights, similarly voiced his concern that "in the House of Representatives there is not the substance, but the shadow only, of representation, which can never produce proper information in the legislature, or inspire confidence in the people."

Both the Federalists and the Anti-Federalists saw the need for a stronger central government and both groups had reservations about the capacity of democratic governance. They differed in their views of accountability. The Federalists placed greater faith in the capacity of institutional structures relative to the people as a check on government power, while the Anti-Federalists placed greater faith in the people. The ratification of the Constitution was a victory for institutions and the rule of law over democracy and majority rule.

This debate did not end in 1787 but instead carried over into the first party system and the divisions between the Federalists led by Washington, Hamilton, and Adams and the Democratic-Republicans led by Jefferson and Madison. Indeed, it has been a recurring theme throughout the history of American politics. Do we live in the republic created by the Constitution or in the democracy that forms the basis of the American political creed?

REDEFINING THE REPUBLIC:
HOW AMERICA BECAME A DEMOCRACY

Despite its controversial origins, the framing of the Constitution has achieved mythical status, as if its wisdom had been handed down on tablets carved in stone. Americans may not like their government very much, but they adore what they perceive are the constitutional foundations upon which it rests. In reality, most Americans are woefully ignorant of the Constitution. A survey conducted in 2011 by ABC News, for example, found that substantial majorities did not know the term for a U.S. senator (61 percent), the number of Supreme Court justices (63 percent), or the size of the House of Representatives (86 percent).[11] Each year, the First Amendment Center tests public knowledge of Americans' First Amendment Freedoms. The results from the 2012 survey revealed that 65 percent could name freedom of speech, 28 percent freedom of religion, 13 percent freedom of the press, 13 percent the right of assembly, and 4 percent the right to petition government. Remarkably, the 28 percent for freedom of religion is the highest number on record since the First Amendment Center began collecting this data in 1997.

It is perhaps no small irony that the modern-day Tea Party, which extols "constitutional" values, is exactly the sort of faction that Madison and the other Founding Fathers feared: impassioned rather than enlightened, motivated by emotion rather than reason. Factual concerns about Obama's citizenship would not have been unexpected, nor would they have surprised the Founders (and neither would the Tea Party's misguided beliefs about constitutional intent).[12] As John Adams observed, "public information cannot keep pace with facts." The solution for the Founding Fathers was to keep the public at arm's length from meaningful and substantive governance, a fact lost among the Tea Party's constitutional purists.

More generally, given the Founders' profound distrust of democratic governance, it is curious to live in a time when democracy has taken on such positive connotations worldwide. It is a one-word justification for international conflict, revolution, and re-form. It has resonance across political cultures, social classes, and religious identities. There is scarcely a group, individual, or politi-cal party—no matter how authoritarian or elitist—that does not claim the mantle of democracy. To be "democratic" is to be virtu-ous and good.

Perhaps this has always been the case. Writing in 1946 in "Poli-tics and the English Language," George Orwell observed, "In the case of a word like democracy, not only is there no agreed defini-tion, but the attempt to make one is resisted from all sides. It is almost universally felt that when we call a country democratic we are praising it: consequently the defenders of every kind of regime claim that it is a democracy, and fear that they might have to stop using that word if it were tied down to any one meaning. Words of this kind are often used in a consciously dishonest way."[13] As Or-well observes, not only is "democracy" poorly defined but its vagueness is also rooted in its usefulness to political movements, governments, interest groups, and political parties. To call a government democratic is to defend it against criticism. Successful (and unsuccessful) reform movements craft their messages in the language of democracy. And successful political parties campaign in populist hues and tones.

There is a curious disconnect between our civic religion—an enduring and unwavering commitment to democratic govern-ance—and our daily functioning as a constitutional republic.[14] Our constitutional republic was designed to allow limited public influ-ence while entrusting decisions in the hands of those who could exercise more reasoned and nuanced judgment. It was to be a government of elites and experts influenced, but not swayed, by public passions and capable of operating on behalf of the public interest. Its saving grace would be that its elites would not be selected via a landed aristocracy or right of birth (as was the case in Europe) but on the basis of a political meritocracy. For Thomas Jefferson, this was the distinction between a "natural aristocracy" based on a merit and an "artificial aristocracy" based on wealth and birthright.

Aside from its considerable normative and symbolic value, there is little reason to believe that pure or direct democracy works particularly well. Indeed, the mechanisms of direct democracy—the initiative and referendum—are often used to limit the policy-making flexibility of elected officials, empower interest groups, and restrict minority rights.[15] California initiative campaigns are dominated by interest group organizations and money, and the California state government, handcuffed by the results, has been sliding toward insolvency.[16] The progressive levers of direct democracy have made effective governance in California virtually impossible as voters opt for simplistic but ineffective solutions to complex problems. State governments, more generally, have raced to the bottom by cutting state government services, reducing taxes, and providing tax breaks to large corporations.

Even representative democracy appears capable of becoming too democratic and devoid of the leadership necessary to move policy forward. Such is the case of contemporary American government, which suffers from too much—not too little—democratic input. The consequence is a government incapable of addressing long-term problems, such as budget deficits or a looming social security crisis, and overly fixated on the next election cycle. Paralyzed by contradictory democratic impulses, the system lurches slowly—but surely—toward crisis. The problem with democracy is too much democracy.

This is not a new thesis. British political scientist Anthony King observed that the failings of American government are almost always rooted in too much—rather than too little—democracy.[17] American politicians, he observed, were "running scared" despite remarkably high reelection rates and, subsequently, were overly responsive to public demands. As a result, elected politicians become incapable of solving long-term problems. Similarly, in their review of public opinion toward American political institutions, John Hibbing and Elizabeth Theiss-Morse concluded that the public wants a smaller (rather than larger) role in public policy and recoils from democratic processes and procedures.[18] As a result, our least democratic institution—the U.S. Supreme Court—is our most revered, while our most democratic institution—the U.S. Congress—is our most reviled. Congressional approval ratings are often in the teens, occasionally falling into the single digits, while Supreme Court approval ratings have historically hovered between 50 and 60 percent. More recently, political scientist Thomas Brunell has argued that citizens are happier when elections are uncompetitive and prefer voting for the winner over a healthy and competitive election campaign.[19] Yet reform movements almost always prescribe more democracy—no matter the ill—and political crises almost always yield to more public input. The result is a cycle that inevitably leads to greater paralysis and frustration. As King explains,

> The paradox that has resulted is obvious and easily stated. Recent history suggests that when large numbers of Americans become dissatisfied with the workings of their government, they call for more democracy. The more they call for more democracy, the more of it they get. The more of it they get, the more dissatisfied they become with the workings of their government. The more they become dissatisfied with the workings of their government, the more they call for more democracy. The cycle endlessly repeats itself.[20]

The pattern has repeated itself from the very foundations of American government. The first challenge arose from Thomas Jefferson, who embodied a more democratic conception of the Constitution and the presidency; he opposed the limited executive defined by the Constitution and, thanks to a budding two-party system, connected the presidency to popular will.[21] Jefferson's victory in the 1800 election featured the first transfer of power from the ruling party to the opposition party, the beginning of the first party system, and the first crisis caused by a constitutional defect: an Electoral College tie between Thomas Jefferson and his vice-presidential running mate Aaron Burr. The result was a significant step toward a more organized "grassroots" party system, forestalled by the "Era of Good Feeling," a brief period of one-party dominance from 1817 to 1825. An additional consequence was the adaption of the Twelfth Amendment separating presidential and vice-presidential voting in the Electoral College.

The tension between our republican constitutional design and the democratic impulse has been evident in American politics ever since. President Andrew Jackson, for example, saw himself as the democratic challenge to the existing aristocracy. Denied the presidency in 1824 despite receiving the most popular and Electoral College votes (and amid allegations of a corrupt bargain that elevated Speaker of the House Henry Clay to secretary of state in exchange for his support of John Quincy Adams), Jackson secured even greater popular support in 1828 and developed the first grassroots political party. Historians offer mixed reviews of Jackson's legacy, but there is little question that his election was made possible by and expanded the democratic underpinnings of American government, including extending suffrage to include "property-less" white males and movements within states to tie their electoral votes more closely to the popular vote.

There is also little doubt that Andrew Jackson saw himself as the embodiment of the public will aligned against an aristocratic and entrenched federal government. One consequence was the spoils system, put in place to be sure supporters were administering Jackson's policy preferences and not undermining his administration. The spoils system assisted in creating strengthened political parties, the key mechanism for participatory democracy, while also opening the door to greater political corruption. More broadly, Jackson's populist appeal strengthened the executive branch relative to the legislature and further cemented the connection between public opinion and presidential leadership.

From 1828 onward, democracy was practiced through the political parties. The development of the modern political party is often noted as an oversight by the Founding Fathers. James Madison had warned about the mischief of factions in *Federalist No. 10*, observing that "a zeal for different opinions concerning religion, concerning government, and many other points, as well of speculation as of practice; an attachment to different leaders ambitiously contending for pre-eminence and power; or to persons of other descriptions whose fortunes have been interesting to the human passions, have, in turn, divided mankind into parties, inflamed them with mutual animosity, and rendered them much more disposed to vex and oppress each other than to co-operate for their common good."

The irony that Madison helped form one of the first political parties is not lost on historians, though the formation of early political parties during this period—the Federalists led by George Washington and Alexander Hamilton and the Democratic-Republicans led by Thomas Jefferson—was thought to be temporary and necessary only to compete against the opposition. Once the opposition was vanquished, the political parties would cease to exist. In his Farewell Address, George Washington warned of "the baneful effects of the spirit of party." Washington recognized the inevitability of political organizations, but he also believed the "spirit of party" should be discouraged, as it represented a danger to the common good. In a letter written to Jonathan Jackson in 1780, John Adams similarly observed that "there is nothing which I dread so much as a division of the republic into two great parties, each arranged under its leader, and concerting measures in opposition to each other. This, in my humble apprehension, is to be dreaded as the greatest political evil under our Constitution."

In forming the opposition to the Federalist Party led by Alexander Hamilton, Jefferson and Madison began organizing the framework for a grassroots political party. This development was forestalled by their success and the "Era of Good Feeling." However, it didn't last long. The highly divisive election of 1824 and the subsequent success of Andrew Jackson in 1828 introduced the first modern grassroots political party, fundamentally moving the American political system away from its republican foundations and toward more democratic and participatory politics. To be sure, participation remained limited and Jackson's democracy excluded women and African Americans, but there is little question that it was more "democratic" than what came before. In this respect, Jackson furthered the Jeffersonian democratic challenge to our republican constitutional design. The Constitution may have set tight boundaries around democratic governance, but the American creed and the American public celebrated participatory politics and a democratic and egalitarian ethos. That democratic spirit was transforming the American political system beyond the narrow boundaries of the Constitution and in ways unimagined by the Founding Fathers.

Jacksonian democracy also serves as a reminder of the limitations of participatory democracies, for it opened the doors to widespread political corruption and the creation of urban party machines. The spoils system initiated by Jackson to ensure that his supporters controlled the levers of government gave political parties tangible incentives to reward political support and engage in voter mobilization. Likewise, control of nominations guaranteed political parties a powerful role in determining who ran for office under the party label. In localities without effective opposition, securing the nomination was the key to winning elections and controlling local government. Notably, this was also a period of heightened partisanship and political activity. Voter turnout in presidential elections often exceeded 70 percent of the voting-age population. More than any other period, this "Golden Age of Political Parties" perhaps best reflected the tenets of participatory democracy.

The rampant corruption that also defined the era, however, cried out for reform. As is so often the case, the cure for democratic excess was more democracy. The Progressive movement targeted party machines by advocating for the Australian ballot, direct primaries, nonpartisan elections, and a merit-based civil service system. In each instance, reformers moved power that was centralized in the political parties and placed it in the hands of voters. Perhaps ironically (though also intentionally), empowering voters to take control of political parties weakened the central mechanism of participatory politics. Indeed, a reform movement aimed at weakening political parties—the single most important instrument for voter mobilization—necessarily weakened democratic political participation. Democratizing the political parties

made them less democratic and led to a decrease in voter participation.

Progressive reforms also empowered individual candidates and
helped to cement a defining characteristic of American politics for
the next one hundred years—its candidate-centered focus. Only
loosely bound by party labels, candidates were able to define their
candidacies to fit the needs of local constituencies. The result was
political parties that were ideologically amorphous. Southern
Democrats provided a conservative base to the Democratic Party
but would often vote with the Republican Party. Northeastern
Rockefeller Republicans often sided with more progressive and
liberal Democrats. In 1964, for example, President Lyndon Johnson relied on substantial support from liberal northern Republicans to push the Civil Rights Act through Congress. In the 1980s,
President Ronald Reagan effectively governed with a conservative—but not a Republican—majority.

Changes in the media landscape also developed a more direct
and personal link between presidents and public opinion. Radio
allowed Franklin Delano Roosevelt to speak directly to the people
in fireside chats, fundamentally changing the nature of presidential communication and defining the U.S. president as the "voice
of the people" fighting against entrenched economic interests.
The presidency as an institution subsequently became less party
centered and more centered around the individual occupant in the
White House. The rise of the so-called rhetorical presidency is
perhaps best documented by political scientist Jeffrey Tulis, who
argues that presidents were increasingly called upon to lead
through rhetoric—not as part of formal constitutional design but
as a result of changing practices and expectations.[22] Speech increasingly served as a substitute for actual governance.[23] A key
element in this shift was the changing media landscape.

These changes were not without consequence. Where presidents once communicated at college reading levels, today they
communicate at an eighth-grade reading level and in more con-
versational tones.[24] This democratization of presidential rhetoric
reflected an alarming "dumbing down" of American politics made

possible by the growing link between presidential action and popular approval and a growing cadre of communication consultants
field testing every utterance, statement, and policy.

Television did not create but rather cemented these trends,
adding an even more compelling and personalized visual component. With television, John F. Kennedy could lose a presidential
debate based on spoken words while winning the debate—and the
presidency—through image. In a broadcast era, style was at least
as important as substance. Having learned the lessons of the 1960
campaign, Richard Nixon returned in 1968 repackaged by a team
of media professionals such as Roger Ailes, Harry Treleaven, and
Frank Shakespeare.[25] As the prescient Marshal McLuhan observed in 1964, "Politics will eventually be replaced by imagery.
The politician will be only too happy to abdicate in favor of his
image, because the image will be much more powerful than he
could ever be."[26]

McLuhan was right only to a point. Imagery did not replace
politics—it defined politics. Tracking the use of White House polling, Lawrence Jacobs and Melanie Burns found a departure from
issue polling to personality-based polling during the Reagan administration: as Reagan pushed for policies that were not politically popular he sought reassurance that his personal likeability remained strong.[27] Likeability trumped policy and party.

Bill Clinton similarly survived a series of scandals that would
have felled a lesser politician because of his ability to emote empathy and caring. And while George W. Bush may have been easily
caricaturized as a bumbling know-nothing president by Will Ferrell (and others), he also maintained a sense of good humor and
likeability throughout his term that served his administration well.
Bush, rather than Gore in 2000 or Kerry in 2004, was described as
the candidate you wanted to have at your house for barbeque and
beer. Similarly, President Barack Obama benefited from a "coolness" factor in 2008 that allowed him to upset Democratic frontrunner Hillary Clinton and beat Republican nominee John
McCain in the general election. In sizing up the 2012 election,
Washington Post columnist Ruth Marcus observed that, since

1984, the more likeable candidate of the two major party nominees has won the presidency in each election.[28] In 2012, Republican nominee Mitt Romney struggled to overcome a likeability gap and questions about whether he was likeable enough to win. An ABC News poll conducted in September 2012, for example, found that voters preferred President Barack Obama over challenger Mitt Romney as the candidate they would most like to have dinner with (by a 52–33 margin) or who would make a more loyal friend (by 50–36 margin).[29] Informed and engaged voters may fairly ask whether likeability should matter: Do we want candidates we like or candidates who will solve our most pressing problems? In the abstract, we would unquestionably say candidates who solve problems. As a practical matter, likeability is the winner.

Changes in the nomination process, the growth of political polling, and the rise of political consultants also helped to transform American politics into a permanent political campaign. The 1968 Democratic Convention in Chicago, marred by riots, protests, and violence, serves as one of the pivotal events, as it greatly extended the presidential election season.[30] Amid the assassinations of Martin Luther King Jr. and Robert Kennedy and at the height of the Vietnam War and anti-war protests, Vice President Hubert Humphrey secured the Democratic nomination despite not competing in the Democratic primaries. Instead, Humphrey focused his attention on securing delegates in nonprimary states and winning the support of the party establishment at the expense of the party's highly vocal and mobilized anti-war base. Rioting in Chicago and the heavy-handed tactics of Chicago mayor Richard Daley in attempting to squelch the riots proved to be an embarrassment for the Democratic Party, and they also damaged Humphrey's chances at winning the presidency.

As a consequence, the Democratic Party decided to change its rules, via the McGovern-Fraser Commission, to ensure that a nominee's delegate count was reflective of their political support within the party base and to provide adequate representation of women, minorities, and young voters at the national convention. The practical effect—all in the name of a more democratic process—was to increase the importance of presidential primaries and caucuses in determining the nomination while minimizing the role of party regulars. George McGovern, who chaired the commission, won the 1972 Democratic nomination in large part because he better understood the implications of the rules changes. He was soundly defeated by Richard Nixon.

Perhaps even more important was the decision by former Georgia governor Jimmy Carter to go all in on Iowa in 1976. Carter, at the time, had little national name recognition, but his victory in Iowa propelled him to the Democratic nomination. Prior to Carter's run, little attention was focused on Iowa, a small, unrepresentative state of little consequence to the total delegate count. After Carter, Iowa and New Hampshire became critical to a nominee's success and—equally important—expanded the presidential campaign season as Iowa and New Hampshire jealously guarded their first-in-the-nation status and as other states moved earlier in the process to have greater impact over presidential nominations. The result is a presidential selection process that no rational human being would have ever devised, created largely by happenstance, and that has proved remarkably resistant to change.

When Kentucky senator and Republican leader Mitch McConnell vowed that the "single most important thing we want to achieve is for President Obama to be a one-term president," he was simply codifying the nature of contemporary American politics as a permanent campaign. The phrase "permanent campaign" has its roots in Sidney Blumenthal's 1980 book of the same name and was used by political consultant Pat Caddell in a strategy memo for the 1976 Jimmy Carter presidential campaign.[31] In the book, Blumenthal documents how the decline of political parties and party machines forced politicians to campaign continuously in order to achieve their policy objectives, a lesson that eluded President Barack Obama during his first term. As President Obama explained, the mistake of his first term "was thinking that this job was just about getting the policy right. And that's important. But the nature of this office is also to tell a story to the American people that gives them a sense of unity and purpose and optimism, especially during tough times."[32] The separation between campaigning and governance, never very thick in American politics, is thinning to a point at which it can no longer be recognized.

While political parties have experienced a resurgence over the last several decades and are playing an increasingly important role in election campaigns, the nature of American politics as a permanent campaign has become deeply rooted. Worse, the campaign is not only permanent but also increasingly polarized along partisan lines, and that polarization extends to nearly every aspect of governance.

Much of the blame for this state of affairs resides with Newt Gingrich,[33] the mastermind of the 1994 Republican Revolution. Prior to Gingrich's ascent, the Republican minority leader, Robert H. Michel, operated under the quaint idea that the minority party had a responsibility to work with the majority to solve problems and to forge compromises (where possible) to further the national interest. Gingrich operated under a very different model that saw the path to majority control as strewn with obstructionist and partisan tactics, including regular charges of ethical misconduct by Democratic leaders.

Gingrich's Republican Party more resembled political parties in parliamentary systems—tightly controlled, hierarchically organized, and ideologically rooted—than traditional American political parties, which were generally defined as loose coalitions of like-minded individuals organized to win elections. Gingrich, who was masterful as an opposition leader, proved to be less effective once Republicans achieved majority status. His decision to force a shutdown of the federal government and to impeach a sitting president proved central in Bill Clinton's political recovery following the 1994 Republican Revolution. Like Icarus, the Greek mythological figure who flew too close to the sun, Gingrich's hubris proved to be his undoing. Even so, his impact continues to reverberate throughout the American party system.

Gingrich's model for governing provided the playbook for Republicans in the wake of President Barack Obama's historic 2008 election, modifying it only to ensure even less compromise. The lesson learned by congressional Republicans from the Clinton era was not that the obstructionist tactics failed but, rather, that compromises in the wake of the government shutdown allowed President Clinton to co-opt Republicans on important issues (e.g., welfare reform) and to build a "small ball" record of policy success. As Brookings Scholars Thomas Mann and Norman Ornstein describe in *It's Even Worse Than It Looks*, the willingness of Republicans to risk the U.S. credit rating to score political points on deficit reduction brought politics to a cynical and dismal new low. "For the first time," Mann and Ornstein observe, "major political figures, including top congressional leaders and serious presidential candidates, openly called for default or demanded dramatic and unilateral policy changes in return for preserving the full faith and credit of the United States."[34]

Contemporary politics has maintained the characteristics of a permanent campaign that have defined the American political system for well over three decades while adding a level of partisan polarization that makes the entire political system less governable and more dysfunctional. For Mann and Ornstein, the root cause is a mismatch between ideological parliamentary-style political parties and a political system built on separation of powers, checks and balances, and built-in advantage for defensive politics. They pay less attention to the responsibility of the citizenry in these arrangements, but do note that "the public is perpetuating the source of its discontent, electing a new group of people who are even less inclined to or capable of crafting compromise or solutions to pressing problems."

We can be more definitive here. The root cause of our dysfunctional politics is a public that finds politics built around unworkable oversimplifications of complex problems appealing. This is not a partisan statement. Voters electing President Barack Obama in 2008 had unrealistic expectations about what could be accomplished during his first term and about the capacity of his historic candidacy to transform the fundamentals of American politics. In a political system built around the idea that democratic majorities are dangerous, a committed minority can (and will) obstruct policy change. This is not a failure of our political system as designed but rather how the system was intended to work with one important exception: public opinion was supposed to be further removed from the policy-making process so that elected officials could act as public trustees.

Dysfunctional politics is further rooted in a public that holds contradictory beliefs about government policy. Voters spurred to action in 2010 by rising deficits, for example, were misinformed, uninformed, or disingenuous if they believed deficits could be reduced without significant cuts in entitlement and military spending *and* tax increases. While the Mann and Ornstein book focuses mostly on Republican obstructionism, it is worth noting that President Barack Obama would have likely had a mini-revolt within the Democratic Party over his willingness to put entitlement programs on the negotiating table to make significant deficit reductions.[35] Moreover, if Republicans are guilty of oversimplifying tax issues, Democrats are guilty of demagoguery on entitlement spending. The larger issue is that both parties are appealing to a public that wants fewer taxes and more government spending. Rather than educate the public or engage in serious dialogue over the long-term consequences of policy choices, the political parties are content to engage in short-term manipulations of public preferences. The reason is quite simple: voters are unlikely to reward serious discussions, particularly if it involves any sacrifice on their part.

The Budget Sequestration of 2013 fits perfectly into this narrative. Sequestration was created as part of the Budget Control Act of 2011 to force both sides to the negotiating table on spending cuts and tax reform with the threat of automatic across-the-board cuts. The theory was that the cuts would be too severe for either side to let sequestrations actually happen. The theory was wrong, and automatic cuts began on March 1, 2013. While it is easy to cast partisan stones on the issue, the reality is that, in reaching this point of dysfunction, both President Barack Obama and congressional Republicans have fairly represented the preferences of their base supporters and have carefully calculated how voters will attribute blame. Neither side moves when it believes not only that it holds the winning hand but also that the other side has more to lose. The casualty is declining trust in the political system and public policy driven by auto-pilot rather than by careful consideration for what government services should be protected and what services should be cut. More broadly, as long as voters reward this type of dysfunction, it will endure. As long as voters hold contradictory beliefs, policy will continue to reflect these contradictions, and long-term issues will continue to go unsolved.

WHAT ABOUT POLITICAL ELITES?

So far we have said little about the culpability of elected officials and other political elites. In the introduction, we noted that elected officials are—contrary to conventional wisdom—no worse than politicians from the past. Indeed, they are more educated, more professional, and less corrupt than politicians from the "Golden Age" of American politics.

There is certainly a case to make that our elites have failed us, as does MSNBC television host Christopher Hayes in his thoughtful and provocative book, *Twilight of the Elites*.[36] Employing Robert Michels's "iron law of oligarchy"—"who says organization, says oligarchy"—Hayes illustrates how elites have grown corrupt and incompetent and, in the process, have rigged the game in their favor. In the language of the Wall Street bailout, they became too big to fail. The result is a crisis of authority in which average citizens no longer trust the experts or elected officials to produce fair processes or results, to provide accurate and factual information, or to solve problems. Seen in this light, the frustration of the Tea Party and the Occupy Wall Street movement may be aimed at very different targets but they are rooted in the same source of discontent: a political process that no longer appears to be serving their interests.

While Hayes's general thesis is compelling, it misses on three important points. First, it is never clear why it took so long for

American meritocracy to succumb to Michels's iron law. According to Michels, leaders are corrupted by their selection as leaders and by the incentives to remain in leadership positions. Ultimately, those incentives create social distance between leaders and followers—for example, when union leaders are no longer able to deliver the vote or use organizational structures for personal gain rather than to improve the welfare of their members. If this is inevitable, why does the iron law become pathological at this particular point in history? Why are elites more socially distant today than in the 1980s or 1990s?

Second, Hayes overstates our collective commitment to meritocracy. While it is true that Americans express a greater tolerance for inequality than other cultures, the application of that principle is at best uneven. Consider conservative populism that rails against northeastern intellectual elites who supposedly control the news media, Hollywood, and university campuses. More generally, in contemporary conservative politics, there is a penalty for appearing too smart—as if advanced knowledge evaporated good old-fashioned common sense. If conservatives are suspicious of intellectual merit, liberals are equally suspect of economic success. In the historic 2008 election, one of the most important side issues was the number of houses John McCain owned, supposedly a signal that McCain was out of touch with the travails of the common man. In 2012, Mitt Romney's personal fortune became a leading campaign issue—both in the Republican primaries and in the general election—not as a testament to his business acumen or leadership skills but as a question of his suitability to be president. Was Mitt Romney too successful to understand the struggles of the average American? The fact that these questions arise suggests a strong democratic and populist ethos.

In its worse form, this ethos takes shape as a barbeque and beer analysis: the candidate who gets elected is the candidate you would most want to have over for a backyard barbeque. George W. Bush, despite his fractured syntax and frequent verbal missteps, had endearing personal qualities that indicated he had a good sense of humor and an irascible Tom Sawyer quality. Bill

Clinton, with his insatiable gregariousness, filled whatever room he entered with energy and charm.[37] Barack Obama far outpaced Mitt Romney in terms of likeability. Americans may value achievement, but when it comes to elections they want candidates who are enough like them to empathize with their daily concerns and struggles.

Third, the thesis misses the increased responsiveness of the system to outside political pressures. One can argue about whether these external pressures are democratic in nature or whether they reflect the capture of policy by entrenched political interests, but there is little question that the system is more open to outside influence today than four or five decades ago. Thanks to the advent of digital media, communication channels are more open and less controlled by centralized gatekeepers than at any time in our past. Gone are the days when the big three networks held the capacity to legitimize (or delegitimize) specific points of view. A single individual with a tablet PC or smartphone, fairly minimal Internet skills, and enough commitment can express opinions instantly and to fairly wide audiences. Unauthorized YouTube videos can influence the course of a campaign. The impact of this type of communication—because it often originates from a trusted source—may be more powerful (though also more limited in reach) than traditional media.

Smart campaigns, like the 2008 and 2012 Obama campaigns, are increasingly tapping into the power of social media to communicate directly to supporters. As news stories break, these campaigns emphasize positive story lines or communicate counterframes to unfavorable news, minimizing the impact of potentially damaging information. A number of campaigns now strictly limit their access to traditional media, opting to run their entire operations with little (or no) unfiltered interactions with traditional news organizations.

Related, elected officials now have better tools (and specialized consultants) for gauging, understanding, and manipulating public preferences. Micro-targeting allows campaigns the ability to narrowly target messages to specific types of voters based on voting history, demographics, location, and purchasing habits, and communicate fundamentally different messages to different segments of the electorate. Looking at the evidence broadly, it is difficult to sustain the charge that the public has too little influence. Perhaps they are being misled and voting against their self-interest, or perhaps they are misinformed or uninformed because of elite lies and distortions, but they are unquestionably influential. More to the point, the public bears much of the responsibility for our current democratic malaise. Elite manipulation occurs because the democratic ideal of an engaged and informed citizenry falls far short of reality. Or perhaps stated differently, our elites may be failing, but it is because they have learned to appeal more effectively to democratic passions, to manipulate democratic input, and to be rewarded not for solving problems but for being on the right side of political issues.

Reasoned judgment has been the casualty.

CONCLUSION

Returning to Benjamin Franklin's famous quote, we have not maintained our republic but have instead moved toward a more democratic and more dysfunctional political system. The result is declining trust and confidence in government and a slow spiraling toward crisis. If history is prologue, our next wave of reform will move us even further toward democratic governance and we will be no more satisfied with the result. The reason is quite simple: policy responsiveness is not a solution to what ails us. What we believe we want (more democracy) and what we actually want (more responsible and more accountable governance) are worlds apart.

The Second Constitutional Convention met in secret for a reason. Had they met publicly, the work of "revising" the Articles of Confederation would have been difficult, perhaps impossible, to accomplish. James Madison understood this tension well and subsequently proposed a political system that allowed for distance between the public's passions and the reasoned judgment of political elites. Despite Madison's design, American politics has moved slowly away from its republican origins and toward greater democracy. Democracy has not, however, solved our problems. Indeed, one can fairly argue that it has made our problems worse while decreasing citizen trust and confidence. Consider, once again, the problem of budget deficits: Wouldn't significant deficit reduction be easier if policymakers met in secret beyond the purview of the 24/7 news media and lazy eye of public attentiveness?[38] Is the appeal of nonpartisan commissions (e.g., Simpson-Bowles)—even when they fail—an implicit acknowledgment that democracy isn't working very well?

NOTES

1. Curiously, Montesquieu is not particularly well known despite his profound influence on the Founding Fathers, especially Madison. In *The Spirit of Laws*, Montesquieu articulated his theory of the separation of powers and constitutional governance, and advocated for the ending of slavery.

2. Charles Merriam, "The Political Theory of Thomas Jefferson," *Political Science Quarterly* 17 (1902): 24–45.

3. Walter Lippmann, *Public Opinion* (New York: Harcourt, Brace, 1922).

4. Charles Beard, *An Economic Interpretation of the Constitution of the United States* (New York: Macmillan, 1929).

5. Despite sharp divisions and questions surrounding the legitimacy of the Supreme Court decision, a winner was produced without undue conflict or violence.

6. Laurence Tribe and Thomas Rollins, "Deadlock: What Happens If Nobody Wins," *Atlantic Monthly* (October 1980), http://www.theatlantic.com/past/docs/issues/80oct/deadlock.htm (accessed May 23, 2013).

7. "END OF A CANDIDACY: Excerpts from Perot's News Conference on Decision Not to Enter Election," *New York Times*, July 17, 1992, http://www.nytimes.com/1992/07/17/news/end-candidacy-excerpts-

perot-s-conference-decision-not-enter-election.html (accessed on September 22, 2013).

8. Bruce Ackerman, *The Failure of the Founding Fathers: Jefferson, Marshall, and the Rise of Presidential Democracy* (Cambridge, MA: Belknap Press of Harvard University Press, 2005); Bruce Ackerman, *The Decline and Fall of the American Republic* (Cambridge, MA: Belknap Press of Harvard University Press, 2010).

9. Cited in Craig Borowiak, "Accountability Debates: The Federalists, The Anti-Federalists, and Democratic Deficits," *Journal of Politics* 69 (2007): 998–1014.

10. In a letter from Elbridge Gerry to James Warren, October 18, 1787, http://www.teachingamericanhistory.org/library/index.asp?document=1752 (accessed May 23, 2013).

11. Tom McCarthy, "America Loves Its Constitution—and Continues to Have No Idea What It Says," ABC News, March 24, 2011, http://abcnews.go.com/blogs/headlines/2011/03/america-loves-its-constitution-and-continues-to-have-no-idea-what-it-says/ (accessed May 23, 2013).

12. George Mason University Law professor Ilya Somin notes that most popular constitutional movements are rooted in misinformation and ignorance. The Tea Party, he concludes, is no exception to this rule, but its members are also no more misinformed than their liberal detractors. Ilya Somin, "Tea Party Movement and Popular Constitutionalism," *Northwestern University Law Review Colloquy* 105 (2011): 200.

13. George Orwell, "Politics and the English Language," published in *Horizon* (April 1946) and available online at http://www.orwell.ru/library/essays/politics/english/e_polit/.

14. Robert Bellah, "Civil Religion in America," *Journal of the American Academy of Arts and Sciences* 96 (1967): 1–21.

15. Manabu Saeki, "Direct Democracy Paradox: State Fiscal Policies in the United States and the Threat of Direct Initiatives," *Review of Policy Research* 23 (2006): 915–25; Donald Haider-Markel, Alana Querze, and Kara Lindaman, "Lose, Win, or Draw? A Reexamination of Direct Democracy and Minority Rights," *Political Research Quarterly* 60 (2007): 304–14; Daniel Lewis, "Direct Democracy and Minority Rights: Same-Sex Marriage Bans in the U.S. States," *Social Science Quarterly* 92 (2011): 364–83.

16. "The Perils of Extreme Democracy," *Economist* 398 (2011): 11.

17. Anthony King, *Running Scared: Why America's Politicians Campaign Too Much and Govern Too Little* (New York: Martin Kessler Books, 1997).

18. John Hibbing and Elizabeth Theiss-Morse, *Stealth Democracy: Americans' Beliefs About How Government Should Work* (Cambridge: Cambridge University Press, 2002); John Hibbing and Elizabeth Theiss-Morse, *Congress as Public Enemy: Public Attitudes Toward American Political Institutions* (Cambridge: Cambridge University Press, 1995).

19. Thomas Brunell, *Redistricting and Representation: Why Competitive Elections are Bad for America* (New York: Routledge, 2008).

20. Anthony King, "Running Scared," *The Atlantic Online*, January 1997, http://www.theatlantic.com/past/docs/issues/97jan/scared/scared.htm (accessed on September 22, 2013).

21. Bruce Ackerman, *The Failure of the Founding Fathers: Jefferson, Marshall, and the Rise of Presidential Democracy* (Cambridge, MA: Belknap Press of Harvard University Press, 2005); Bruce Ackerman, *The Decline and Fall of the American Republic* (Cambridge, MA: Belknap Press of Harvard University Press, 2010).

22. Jeffrey Tulis, *The Rhetorical Presidency* (Princeton, NJ: Princeton University Press, 1987).

23. Roderick Hart, *The Sound of Leadership: Presidential Communication in the Modern Age* (Chicago: University of Chicago Press, 1987).

24. Elvin Lim, *The Anti-Intellectual Presidency: The Decline of Presidential Rhetoric from George Washington to George W. Bush* (Oxford: Oxford University Press, 2008).

25. Joe McGinniss, *The Selling of the President, 1968* (New York: Trident Press, 1969).

26. Cited in Peter Newman, "The Lost McLuhan Tapes," *Maclean's*, July 22, 2013, http://www2.macleans.ca/2013/07/16/the-lost-mcluhan-tapes-2/ (accessed on September 22, 2013).

27. Lawrence Jacobs and Melanie Burns, "The Second Face of the Public Presidency: Presidential Polling and the Shift from Policy to Personality Polling," *Presidential Studies Quarterly* 34 (2004): 536–56.

28. Ruth Marcus, "Is Mitt Romney Likeable Enough to Win?" *Washington Post*, August 28, 2012, http://www.washingtonpost.com/opinions/ruth-marcus-is-mitt-romney-likable-enough-to-win/2012/08/28/5ae5d4f4-f144-11e1-892d-bc92fee603a7_story.html (accessed May 23, 2013).

29. Gregory Krieg, "Poll: Americans Pick President Obama Over Mitt Romney for Dinner Date," ABC News, September 11, 2012, http://abcnews.go.com/blogs/politics/2012/09/poll-americans-pick-president-obama-over-mitt-romney-for-dinner-date/.

30. This may give too much credit to McGovern-Fraser reforms for transforming the nature of American political campaigns. In 1936, Democrats ended the rule requiring a two-thirds majority to secure the nomination. Thanks to Oklahoma political scientist and ranconteur Keith Gaddie for the reminder.

31. Sidney Blumenthal, *The Permanent Campaign* (New York: Simon and Schuster, 1980).

32. "Obama on the 'Mistake of my First Term,'" *CNN*, July 12, 2012, http://politicalticker.blogs.cnn.com/2012/07/12/obama-on-the-mistake-of-my-first-term/ (accessed May 23, 2013).

33. Political scientists also share in the blame. Beginning in the 1950s, political scientists called for more responsible political parties as a mechanism for overcoming the institutional fragmentation inherent in American democracy. This call resulted in the party reforms that transformed electoral campaigns and made parliamentary-style parties possible. See *Toward a More Responsible Two-Party System* (New York: Rinehart, 1950).

34. Thomas Mann and Norman Ornstein, *It's Even Worse Than It Looks: How the American Constitutional System Collided with the New Politics of Extremism* (New York: Basic Books, 2012).

35. "White House Aiming for Bigness on Deficit Reduction Deal," Fox News, July 7, 2011, http://www.foxnews.com/politics/2011/07/07/white-house-pushing-for-bigness-in-deficit-reduction-deal/ (accessed May 28, 2013).

36. Christopher Hayes, *Twilight of the Elites: America After Meritocracy* (New York: Crown, 2012).

37. In the age of reality television, it is no longer a stretch to joke that we no longer elect a president but a reality television star. What show would you rather watch for the next four years—the Barack Obama show or the Mitt Romney show?

38. David Stasavage, "Polarization and Publicity: Rethinking the Benefits of Deliberative Democracy," *Journal of Politics* 69 (2007): 59–72.

2

POLITICAL PSYCHOLOGY AND DEMOCRATIC COMPETENCE

America is a mistake, admittedly a gigantic mistake, but a mistake nevertheless.
    —Sigmund Freud in a letter to his biographer, Ernest Jones[1]

America is the most grandiose experiment the world has seen, but, I am afraid, it is not going to be a success.
    —Sigmund Freud as quoted in Helen Walker Puner[2]

At the root of democratic governance is an individual capable of rational, self-interested decision-making, informed enough to understand the range of potential policy choices, and knowledgeable enough to make the best choices for herself and her community. So how do we square this assumption with what we know about public opinion, voting behavior, political knowledge, and individual psychology, in which, at best, citizens squeak by skimming Cliffs Notes from their civics texts and are woefully uninformed about current events, public policy, and political decision-making?

Decades of research reveals citizens as uninformed, inattentive, and unengaged. Add in research in cognitive psychology, political psychology, and behavioral economics demonstrating the cognitive limitations of human beings in making even the most mundane decisions (e.g., what soap to buy, where to eat) and questions about citizen competence begin to mount. What if citizens aren't just disinterested but the human mind has a limited capacity for civic engagement and political knowledge? What if individuals are incapable of managing the cognitive information that rains down upon them in the digital age? The most common response has been that citizens can make reasonably informed decisions with limited information, but this begs the following questions: Under what conditions—or institutional arrangements—are citizens more likely to make decisions consistent with the expectations and demands of democratic governance? Under what conditions do they fail? And is it possible to create institutional arrangements that lead to better choices?

Armed with a wealth of micro-data identifying individual characteristics and preferences as well as polling and focus group data tracking political trends, testing specific messages, and identifying the most persuasive words and phrases, elected officials and political consultants are better able to target communication, manipulate individual response, and gauge the effectiveness of campaign messages within very narrow contexts. In this type of environment, can individuals be manipulated into making "bad" decisions? If so, does our political system—as currently configured—reward candidates, political parties, consultants, and interest groups for distorting, manipulating, and obfuscating political information? Does it reward candidates for being honest and truthful? Or is effective manipulation rewarded with book contracts, high-priced speaking engagements, and network television commentaries?

POLITICAL PSYCHOLOGY AND ELITE DEMOCRATIC THEORY

We can begin with Sigmund Freud, the father of psychoanalysis, who observed that conscious thought was only the tip of the iceberg. Deep below reside unconscious desires and motivations guiding behaviors and decisions in ways that we scarcely understand. According to Freud's conceptualization, the most rational component of our individual psyches (the ego) served to rationalize our moralistic (the super ego) and instinctive (the id) behaviors. Driven by unconscious impulses, we know not what we do or why. Our explanations are not only post-hoc rationalizations but also frequently wrong.

Freud's theories have not been without their critics. Still, his articulation of the unconscious raises important substantive question about democratic governance. How can democracy function if individuals do not understand their own motivations? Or if their stated motivations are only psychological defense mechanisms covering more unsettling and darker primal urges? In one of the earliest explorations of these ideas, Graham Wallas in *Human Nature and Politics* discounted rational political behavior in favor of the subconscious and instinct.[3] "The political opinions of most men," Wallas wrote, "are the result, not of reasoning tested by experience, but of unconscious or half-conscious inference fixed by habit."

While rarely cast within the theoretical context of Freudian psychology,[4] there is a parallel in the contemporary literature on racial attitudes. No longer socially acceptable, explicit racial views find little accord in survey research, but evidence of implicit racial biases is relatively easy to uncover. Experiments, for example, routinely reveal very different responses with fairly subtle manipulations of skin color[5] or by racializing first names (e.g., Jamal versus James).[6] Jamal gets fewer interviews and job offers than James, and darker-skinned political candidates receive less favorable evaluations and fewer votes. Individuals may say that they believe in equality, but their choices and their biological responses betray deeper racial animosities and prejudices. Race matters even when we say it should not and does not.

Freudian psychology says little directly about its implications for democratic governance, but it clearly influenced Walter Lippmann's definitive and influential works on public opinion as well as the development of public relations by a nephew of Freud,

Edward Bernays.[7] "The impetus of Freud," Walter Lippmann wrote in his *Preface to Politics*,[8] "is perhaps the greatest advance ever made towards the understanding and control of human character. But for the complexities of politics it is not yet ready." In *The Century of the Self*, documentary filmmaker Adam Curtis contends that the tenets of Freudian psychoanalysis were used by political elites in post–World War II America to control the impulse drives underlying mass political behavior.[9] Nazi Germany was possible when political systems failed to control the public's most barbaric drives and base motivations.

Lippmann, for his part, emerged from his study of public opinion deeply cynical about the public's capacity for self-governance. Public opinion was defined not by objective information but by prejudice and apathy with "public opinion" oriented toward trivial "sideshows and three legged calves." The solution for Lippmann was a diversion from participatory democracy to a more elitist political system in which policy and decisions could be guided by experts and journalists who had a deeper understanding of the facts and who could act as trustees for a public too uninformed to guide policy in its own best interest.

It would be mischaracterization, however, to believe that Lippmann was "against" democracy[10]—only democracy in its most participatory forms. The public, Lippmann believed, should play a role during elections to make global decisions about the direction of the country and political control of governing institutions. True governance, however, should be left to experts who take into account not just what the public wants but also the public's best interests, like the mother who regulates a child's sugar intake. In characterizing the Lippmann-Dewey debates, media scholar Michael Schudson writes that "Lippmann never abandoned democracy, only utopian aspirations for the role of the public as a participant in democratic decision making on a daily basis."[11]

Edward Bernays, the father of modern public relations, similarly argued that public attitudes and preferences needed to be manipulated in order to preserve and support democracy. As Bernays wrote in the opening lines of *Propaganda*, "The conscious and intelligent manipulation of the organized habits and opinions of the masses is an important element in democratic society. Those who manipulate this unseen mechanism of society constitute an invisible government which is the true ruling power of our country. We are governed, our minds are molded, our tastes formed, our ideas suggested, largely by men we have never heard of. This is a logical result of the way in which our democratic society is organized. Vast numbers of human beings must cooperate in this manner if they are to live together as a smoothly functioning society."

Within a political context, this "engineering of consent" generated public support around policies and leaders that served the public interest. Within an economic context, it meant tapping underlying drives to create consumer needs. For current purposes, the importance is in the focus on individual psychology and its meaning for democratic theory. Individuals might be manipulated into supporting democratic norms, but this was not their natural inclination. Accordingly, elites played a special role in protecting democracy from a public driven by the sort of dark and primal instincts that made Nazi Germany possible.

Gustave Le Bon's crowd psychology fits well within this context:[12] If crowds are irrational, how do progressive forces control the crowds and keep the public from succumbing to its worst instincts? As an important aside, Gabriel Tarde connected crowds to modern communication (at least modern by 1898 standards).[13] Because crowds were less common in the streets and took shape via mass communication (i.e., newspapers), they were less threatening to democracy. One can speculate that the advent of social media turned this relationship on its head. Individuals with extreme viewpoints can find reinforcement in online settings that they could scarcely find in "public."

Collectively, understanding the individual psyche as driven by unconscious desires and instincts required a reconceptualization of democratic theory. The work of Joseph Schumpeter was particularly influential, advocating what David Ricci called a process theory of democracy, emphasizing democratic procedures (as op-

posed to citizen competence), competition among elites for political control, and the protection of individual rights.[14] Democracy,
under this view, should be guided by responsible leaders with the
public playing a limited but important role in "throwing the bums
out" when conditions deteriorated. Other scholars, such as Robert
Dahl, advocated an approach based on pluralism whereby individuals participated through interest groups, interest groups com-
peted for favorable policies, and negotiation and bargaining
yielded policies that generally reflected the public interest.[15]
While pluralism "solved" the problem of a generally disinterested
and poorly informed citizenry by advocating involvement through
organized groups, it remained inherently elitist. As famously observed by E. E. Schattschneider, "The flaw in the pluralist heaven
is that the heavenly chorus sings with strong upper-class accent."[16]

The Achilles' heel of elite democratic theory and pluralism was
the undue (and unfounded) confidence placed in political elites.
Even though elites might sometimes be guided by the best of
intentions, there was good reason to believe that structural incentives would ultimately undermine their ability to act in the public
interest. Sociologist Robert Michels's iron law of oligarchy proved
particularly instructive in this context.[17] According to Michels, organizational structures, even those that begin with democratic
aims and objectives, inevitably become oligarchies as a function of
organization, hierarchy, and specialization. Representative democracies similarly become elitist as elected leaders develop incentives to remain in power, control the flow of information to the
public, and accumulate control over policymaking, and as government bureaucracies became larger and more far reaching.

In *Twilight of the Elites*, author and journalist Christopher
Hayes points to failing, self-serving elites as evidence that the iron
law of oligarchy is in play in contemporary American politics.[18]
Not only are elites failing to improve economic conditions, but
they have also insulated themselves from economic downturns
while reaping the greatest benefits from the economic recovery.
The average citizen suffers as the rich grow richer.

There is something else amiss in Hayes's construction of America postmeritocracy: a growing social distance between economic and political elites and the collateral damage of their investment, business, and policymaking decisions. A generation ago, a CEO might have worked his way up from the mail room to board room. In the process, he would have learned what it meant to be an employee in the company he would eventually lead. Today, a CEO might not even have experience in the industry he is running but is instead part of a professional managerial class that roams from industry to industry. This social distance allows leaders to be inoculated from the negative repercussions of their decisions, such as layoffs or plant closures. Similarly, a president without military experience or family in active service is less directly connected to the consequence of decisions to send troops into hostilities. War becomes more possible when it is a decision that affects other people's lives.

This social distance is exacerbated by changes in where and how we live—in economically segregated and gated neighborhoods. Neighborhoods are increasingly segregated, not just by race, as they have always been, but also by income, beliefs, and lifestyle.[19] In their workplace and in their social lives, political and economic elites are surrounded by other elites, making it more difficult to empathize with the poor and working class, and making it easier to blame the poor for their misfortune. The homeowner who lost her home, they reason, should have never signed a loan with an adjustable mortgage rate. The factory worker who lost his job should have gone through job training and learned a new skill set. Failure of major financial institutions, in contrast, requires government intervention to avoid economic collapse.

Hayes's indictment of the elite class—written from a liberal perspective—fits well within the populist tones of contemporary conservative politics. Speaking at the Values Voter Summit in 2012, former presidential candidate and Pennsylvania senator Rick Santorum observed that Republicans "will never have the elite, smart people on our side, because they believe they should have the power to tell you what to do."[20]

It is a mistake, however, to believe that elite failure is something new or peculiar to the contemporary era. The landscape of American political history is littered with corrupt politicians and institutional failure, from the founding to the Gilded Age to Watergate to Iran-Contra to the Clinton impeachment to the Iraq War. Following the electoral practices of the time, George Washington bought votes with whiskey and beer.[21] During the Washington administration, Secretary of State Alexander Hamilton not only engaged in an affair with a married woman but also paid off her husband to keep the affair secret.

The Gilded Age, the most participatory and democratic period in American history, was also the most corrupt. Tammany Hall's "Boss" Tweed typified corrupt, party-machine politics built through political patronage in which political elites were enriched through kickbacks and bribery for government jobs and political favors. Indeed, it is hard to imagine that the game of contemporary politics could be more rigged than during the Credit Mobilier Scandal of 1872, in which congressmen received stock or cash for their support of First Transcontinental Railroad, or the Teapot Dome scandal, in which Navy petroleum reserves were leased to private oil companies without competitive bidding and in exchange for bribes to Secretary of the Interior Albert Fall.

Contemporary elite failure looks tame by comparison. Consider the Wall Street bailout in which major financial institutions failed and the federal government came to the rescue. One can fairly deplore the fact that our political system rewarded the failure of large banking institutions but did little to help struggling homeowners, but this was more a result of bad policy decisions than quid pro quo corruption.[22] The better questions are ones that ask why policies that disadvantaged homeowners relative to major financial institutions (i.e., banks) were adopted in the first place, and when and how our economic system became so dependent on a few large financial institutions that they became too big to fail.

The answer—as unsatisfactory as it is—is that democratic majorities endorsed policies that increased economic inequality while making the average worker more susceptible to economic downturns. Worse, the shortcomings are not easily overcome with more or better information or by a vigilant news media more committed to truth telling than "objectivity" because these shortcomings are deeply rooted in human psychology.

THE FAILURE OF THE DEMOCRATIC IDEAL

Faith in markets and democracy is rooted in the core belief that citizens act rationally. That is, they understand and act on an understanding of their best interests. Posssibly the most popular challenge to voter rationality is Thomas Frank's *What's the Matter with Kansas?*, in which he argues that rural citizens vote against their economic interests because of divisive cultural issues.[23] The result is policies that favor economic conservatism (e.g., low taxes) at the expense of more populist economic views. Perhaps stated differently, rural conservatives are lured away from their economic self-interest to vote in favor of pro-life, pro-gun, and pro-family Republican candidates. Or, in the words of President Barack Obama, "they cling to guns or religion or antipathy to people who aren't like them or anti-immigrant sentiment or anti-trade sentiment as a way to explain their frustrations." Frank's thesis has been challenged on a number of fronts, including his oversimplification of self-interest as exclusively economic in nature. However, for our purposes, it raises a key issue of voter psychology: Are citizens competent enough to vote rationally? Are they misled into voting against their self-interest?

The earliest evidence on this point was unequivocal. Voters fell far short of the democratic ideal. In *The People's Choice*, Paul Lazarsfeld, Bernard Berelson, and Hazel Gaudet reported that voting was primarily a function of social characteristics, while the effect of political campaigns was, surprisingly, minimal.[24] Voter choice could subsequently be predicted with a relatively small number of social characteristics (region, religion, and social class) and was reinforced by social networks and interpersonal discussions that confirmed rather than challenged existing predispositions. In a follow-up study of the 1948 campaign, Berelson, Lazarsfeld, and McPhee concluded in *Voting* that "the upshot of this is that the usual analogy between voting 'decision' and the more carefully calculated decisions of consumers or businessmen or courts, incidentally, may be quite incorrect. For many voters political preferences may be considered analogous to cultural tastes— in music, literature, recreational activities, dress, ethics, speech, social behavior."[25] Lazarsfeld et al. were wrong, but only in part: they greatly overstated the "carefully calculated" nature of consumer decisions. Consumer decisions, like political decisions, are easily influenced by the structure of choice, the broader context, and subtle, often barely discernible, cues.

Less than a decade after the publication of *Voting*, Angus Campbell, Philip Converse, Warren Miller, and Donald Stokes concluded in *The American Voter* that voting was largely a function of partisan loyalties, which were, in turn, rooted in early childhood socialization patterns.[26] Citizens became Democrats or Republicans for the same reasons that they rooted for the Tigers, Wildcats, or Bulldogs; they developed emotional attachments early in life based on family socialization. Once formed, these attachments were relatively stable and enduring. Partisan affiliation also served as an active filter on new information. Partisan voters paid attention to and remembered information that reinforced their existing views. They ignored or forgot the rest. As a result, political campaigns rarely swayed voters on the basis of evidence but instead served to reinforce existing predispositions. Equally troubling, when it came to policy-related issues, voters were woefully uninformed, lacking even basic knowledge about the political system. Later work by Philip Converse examined the degree of ideological thinking in the mass public in greater detail and found the public largely lacked consistent or stable belief structures.[27] Voters may gladly claim an ideological label (e.g., conservative) with little or no understanding of what the label actually means.

Writing at about the same time, Anthony Downs produced his own work, *An Economic Theory of Democracy*, not only questioning the competence of citizens but also challenging the rationality of democratic participation altogether.[28] Rational citizens, Downs concluded, realized the individual costs incurred by participation and the very small chance their participation mattered in determining the outcome of an election greatly outweighed any collective benefit they might secure from engaging in the political process. The same logic applies to political information. The time and costs incurred by learning about politics outweigh any benefit from being politically informed. Under Downs's formulation, a rational citizen would remain uninformed and disengaged.

Collectively, this early and definitive research raised troubling concerns for democratic theory. What should one make of democracy if votes are determined not by the content of the campaign but by predetermined social characteristics or deeply rooted political orientations? How can the assumption of an informed and engaged citizenry be reconciled with an uninformed and disinterested electorate? And how can a government "by the people" develop coherent policy if the people have incoherent and contradictory beliefs about what government ought to do?

RESCUING DEMOCRATIC THEORY AND PRACTICE

Faced with overwhelming evidence that citizens fail to live up to the highest democratic ideals, political science turned to developing an empirical understanding of how citizens actually make decisions. Admittedly, part of the problem was a flawed ideal of the democratic citizen, unrealistic and overly demanding for people living in a world where politics was not the single most abiding passion of their daily lives. V. O. Key Jr. was perhaps most forceful in pointing out this shortcoming, proclaiming that "voters are not fools."[29] In Key's analysis, the most rational voters were the 15 to 20 percent of the electorate who switched partisan loyalties based on the performance of the government in power, though, notably, Key also argued that voters who stood pat on their prior partisan commitments generally did so as a result of issue and value considerations. Loyal partisans were not irrational.

Key's theory of retrospective voting was critical in saving democratic theory from public ignorance, as it exacted a less demanding
tax on individual citizens. Citizens need not know the details of
policy proposals, party platforms, or position papers to understand
if their lives were better off than they were four years ago. As
Morris Fiorina explained in his explication of retrospective voting
at the individual level, "In order to ascertain whether the incumbents have performed poorly or well, citizens only need to calcu-
late the changes in their own welfare. If jobs have been lost in a
recession, something is wrong. If sons have died in foreign rice
paddies, something is wrong. If polluters foul food, water, or air,
something is wrong. And to the extent that citizens vote on the
basis of such judgments, elections do not signal the direction in
which society should move so much as they convey an evaluation
of where society has been."[30]

V. O. Key also stressed the importance of political elites in
creating and maintaining a functioning democracy. "The voice of
the people," Key concluded, "was but an echo," meaning that if
elites provided citizens with meaningful choices, citizens could
function relatively well. If the choices were meaningless, citizens
would choose badly. "If the people can choose only from among
rascals," Key cautioned, "they are certain to choose a rascal."[31]

Sociologist Robert Lane similarly challenged the view that
Americans lack coherent belief systems by exploring the political
beliefs of fifteen "common" men in Eastport in greater detail than
possible in a standardized survey questionnaire.[32] Rather than
imposing ideological structure, Lane explored how his subjects
constructed their understanding of the political world. While his
subjects lacked clearly identified belief systems as defined by a
liberal-conservative continuum, they expressed relatively stable
and coherent (albeit idiosyncratic) political beliefs. Subsequent
quantitative work has attempted to understand the structure of
political beliefs as multidimensional or in terms of connected sets
of beliefs organized around a central construct, or schema.[33]

Within the voting behavior and public opinion literature, Benjamin Page and Robert Shapiro rediscovered a rational public

through the "miracle of aggregation." Examining aggregate shifts in public opinion over a fifty-year time frame, Page and Shapiro found that opinion moved in expected directions in light of changes in the broader social, economic, and political environment.[34] Individual opinion might be incoherent and unstable, but the aggregation of opinion across individuals created a "rational public" capable of moving policy in expected, predictable directions. Public opinion, defined as an aggregate across individual opinions, could be meaningful even if individual opinion was poorly formed and woefully uninformed.

Recognizing that full information rationality was an impossible standard to meet—who had the time or mental capacity to carefully weigh all available options?—Herbert Simon articulated limited (or bounded) rationality as an alternative decision-making strategy within organizations.[35] Using limited information rationality, decision-makers would satisfice rather than optimize when choosing between options, meaning that they would select a satisfactory and workable solution meeting minimum standards rather than search for the "best" available option, a time-consuming and uncertain task. While Simon was initially writing about organizational behavior, the application to political decisions—and especially to vote choice—was a natural and easy extension.

Using cognitive heurists such as partisan affiliation, voters could make reasonably informed decisions with only skeletal information.[36] Knowing that a candidate was Republican, for example, allowed voters a fairly safe and reliable guide to the candidate's other issue positions. An uninformed public was similarly rescued by online processing models that downplayed the importance of factual recall. While citizens might forget the details of a campaign, this was a function of limited cognitive processing rather than a lack of attention or interest.[37] Instead of recalling the specifics, citizens keep a running tally of likes and dislikes of candidates and political parties. They forgot the details of why but remembered the general affective tally.

Democracy, according to this revisionist scholarship, was rescued not because individuals performed particularly well as citizens—they did not—but because they did just well enough for the system to muddle through and remain functioning and viable. Or perhaps stated differently, democracy was barely passing with a "C" grade, but at least it wasn't flunking out. Indeed, much of the research since V. O. Key's *The Responsible Electorate* begins with the assumption that democracy works and that the task of scholars is to understand why rather than impose preconceived notions about how citizens should think or act. The shortcomings of citizens are acknowledged but also downplayed or reinterpreted in light of the implicit but strong normative commitment to democratic governance.

While considerable insight has been gained from this approach, it raises important questions about the capacity of democracy to function in light of the limited cognitive capacity of the typical citizen. Should political institutions be arranged with an eye toward these cognitive shortcomings? Before we answer this question, however, we first need to consider why the application of cognitive psychology to political decision-making is inadequate to the task of saving democratic governance from its citizens.

THE LIMITS OF LIMITED INFORMATION RATIONALITY

If we take the tenets of democratic theory seriously, evidence should matter. Confronted with new disconfirming information, citizens should be persuaded to update and adjust their beliefs.

If only it were so.

Instead, citizens engage in what psychologists call "motivated reasoning," meaning they dig their heels into the ground and cling ever more tightly to their misguided and incorrect beliefs. This helps to explain why, after months of calling for the release of President Barack Obama's birth certificate, the so-called birthers refused to accept the birth certificate as valid.[38] And it helps to explain why many religious conservatives continue to believe that Barack Obama is a Muslim despite all evidence to the contrary.

Importantly, this is not simply a matter of being uninformed. Birthers paid (and continue to pay) close attention to this issue, and, in many ways, they are deeply knowledgeable about their peculiar and misguided obsession with the president's birthplace. They simply lack the motivation to change their beliefs. Their emotional attachment to the belief is stronger than any possible countervailing evidence.

Providing people with neutral, fair, and unbiased information on subjects they care deeply about is not enough. Biases to confirm supportive evidence and disconfirm incongruent evidence are too deeply ingrained. Psychologically, motivated reasoning occurs when people develop an affective attachment to a party, candidate, or policy position and subsequently interpret new information in a manner consistent with their existing preferences. Emotion comes first; reasoning—or, more accurately, rationalization—comes later. [39]

It gets even worse. In campaign settings, voters positively predisposed to a candidate may grow even more positive in light of negative information. [40] Not only can we not handle the truth, but we also hold on more tightly to our misguided beliefs in light of incongruent and contradictory information. Faced with evidence that President Obama is a Christian, we believe he is a Muslim even more strongly. Similarly, for the most strongly committed birthers, the release of President Obama's birth certificate only strengthened their conviction that he is not a natural-born U.S. citizen. In their view, the birth certificate must be a fraud.

Belief in the likelihood of certain outcomes also influences perceptions about procedural fairness. Or, to draw on a sports analogy, when the home team loses, the fans blame the officials and bad calls. [41] President Obama's 2008 victory was—not surprisingly—met with questions about his legitimacy as a candidate. If he was not a citizen and was ineligible to run, he could have never won the presidency. In this respect, motivated reasoning not only allows misinformation to persist but also leads to fundamental questions about the legitimacy of political outcomes.

The extension to science communication further illustrates the point. Despite a general consensus within the scientific community, climate change denial is relatively common, and it occurs among more—not less—scientifically knowledgeable conservatives.[42] While one might think that more educated and, presumably, more sophisticated citizens would be more open to evidence, this is decidedly not the case. Additional knowledge translates into stronger immunities to countervailing information and a greater arsenal of ammunition for resistance. Being more educated and more informed helps us to better defend staked-out positions, but it does not necessarily bring us closer to the truth. Or as Jonathan Haidt concludes, "Anyone who values truth should stop worshipping reason."[43]

One real-world consequence is that motivated reasoning leads to greater partisan polarization,[44] as each side clings to its own set of facts. Economic perceptions, for example, are less a function of actual economic conditions than partisan affiliation. Democrats in 2012 believed the economy was better than it actually was; Republicans believed it was far worse. There is likely a downward spiraling here. Motivated reasoning kicks in when individuals are motivated by directional goals (or argumentation) rather than accuracy (or truth seeking).[45] In a polarized political environment, directional goals are much more common, leading to greater polarization, which, in turn, leads to more motivated reasoning.

This is not to suggest that both sides are equally resistant to new information. Science journalist and blogger Chris Mooney argues that Republicans are more likely to engage in motivated reasoning.[46] A delicate balance of personality traits and environmental conditions, Mooney argues, and not directly ideology or partisanship, makes Republicans more resistant to change and more defensive of the status quo. Critics have pointed out that there is no shortage of motivated reasoning on the left, and that the real issue is when science issues become politicized and are redefined along ideological lines.[47] In politics, motivated reasoning is the rule rather than the exception. The bigger picture is this: better, more accessible information does not necessarily create better or more informed citizens. We can't educate ourselves to a better democracy.

To date, democracy's salvation has resided in cognitive short-cuts, or heuristics, that allow individuals to make reasonably informed decisions with minimal information. But what if the heuristics themselves are based on misinformation, ignorance, or both? What if they are subject to well-known cognitive biases and are misapplied or applied in the wrong context? And what if the heuristics point voters in the wrong direction? Vanderbilt University political scientist Larry Bartels cautions that the use of heuristics is not without consequence or error, meaning it is not random and does not necessarily cancel out in aggregate public opinion totals via the "miracle of aggregation."[48] Incumbent presidents, Bartels concludes, run approximately five points stronger and Democrats two points stronger thanks to uninformed voters. "Political ignorance matters," Bartels concludes, "not only for individual voters, but also for election outcomes."

Using a different methodology, political psychologists Richard Lau and David Redlawsk were "pleasantly surprised" to find that citizens vote correctly approximately 75 percent of the time in presidential elections, meaning they voted the same as they would have had they been fully informed.[49] Of course, if this is correct, it also means that citizens vote incorrectly 25 percent of the time in high-profile presidential elections in which information is readily available. How much higher is incorrect voting in state and local elections, nonpartisan elections, or referendum and initiative campaigns in which information is less readily available? With over half a million elected officials throughout the United States, there is likely to be a considerable amount of "incorrect" voting. More troubling, Lau and Redlawsk also find that incorrect voting is not randomly distributed, meaning that errors in voting have systematic causes and effects. Campaigns with more money, for example, are advantaged in luring voters into incorrectly voting for their candidate. So what other structural or institutional features are associated with "better," or more accurate, decision-making?

In a separate but related study, Lau and Redlawsk found that while heuristics may be used effectively by experts, they are used ineffectively (and incorrectly) by novices.[50] Perhaps the most damning critique of low information rationality comes from James Kuklinski and Paul Quirk, who contend that "contrary to the political heuristics and collective opinion perspectives, these findings make it unlikely that human cognition is well adapted to the tasks of citizens."[51] The use of heuristics is not, these authors contend, a rational calculation, but happens naturally and below the level of conscious thought. Citizens employing (or misemploying) heuristics often lack contextual knowledge to use cues effectively, may miss cues, or cues may be altogether absent from the broader information environment.

Nor are voters let off the hook by retrospective voting. Retrospective voting has intuitive appeal as it fits nicely with how we think about politics and reduces the information demands on the typical voter. If gas prices are going up, if friends and family are losing jobs, or if the stock market is underperforming, the easy decision is to vote against the incumbent party. While such calculations are simple, they are also likely to be wrong. Presidents have—at best—a limited ability to affect economic performance, particularly when confronted with divided government and a highly polarized political environment. Even if presidents could more effectively maneuver the levers of economic policy, their economic performance would be heavily colored by individual partisanship. Does President Barack Obama deserve credit for pulling the country back from the brink of a depression? Or does he deserve blame for an unemployment rate that has remained stubbornly above 8 percent? The answer to that largely depends on individual partisanship and not a fair and objective assessment of economic conditions.

In making economic evaluations, voters are remarkably short-sighted and uninformed. Rather than evaluate the past four years, they focus almost exclusively on short-term economic conditions (at most, the last six months). Ronald Reagan's famous question— "are you better off now than you were four years ago?"—is perhaps better stated as "what have you done for me lately?" Now add in that voters know very little about actual economic conditions[52] and instead use impressionistic assessments of economic performance based on cues from the news media and political elites. In 1992, for example, news coverage of the economy was worse than would have been predicted on the basis of economic conditions alone, a fact that played out in economic evaluations and vote choice in the 1992 campaign.[53] James Carville's well-known sign from the 1992 presidential campaign—"It's the economy, stupid"—could have served as a reminder to the campaign or as a message to uninformed voters. Media coverage in 1992 unintentionally assisted the Clinton campaign by focusing on negative economic news.

The consequences of low levels of economic literacy are not trivial. Economist Bryan Caplan argues that democracies make bad policies because of voter incompetence, particularly in the area of economic policy.[54] Comparing citizen understanding of economics to that of experts, he finds significant gaps in expert versus public understanding. "Despite their lack of knowledge," Caplan argues, "voters are not humble agnostics; instead, they confidently embrace a long list of misconceptions." These misconceptions include biases against market-based—as opposed to political—solutions, against international trade and in favor of protectionism, and toward pessimism and negative economic information. Bad economic news is punished more commonly than good economic performance is rewarded. As a result, economic policy is driven by poorly informed citizens voting on the basis of economic performance they scarcely understand. As Caplan concludes, "Most voters never take a single course in economics. If it is disturbing to imagine the bottom half of the class voting on economic policy, it is frightening to realize that the general population already does. The typical voter, to whose opinions politicians cater, is probably unable to earn a passing grade in basic economics."

In 2012, deficit reduction, government spending, and federal income taxes could have served as a useful heuristic for retrospective voting. Concern about government spending and growing deficits generated strong Republican turnout in the 2010 midterm elections and activated the Tea Party as an important player in electoral politics. On the other side of the partisan aisle, Republican Mitt Romney received negative publicity for not releasing his tax returns and for a comment—taped without his consent or knowledge—that he did not care about the 47 percent of Americans who do not pay federal income taxes. As Governor Romney observed,

> There are 47 percent of the people who will vote for the president no matter what. All right, there are 47 percent who are with him, who are dependent upon government, who believe that they are victims, who believe the government has a responsibility to care for them, who believe that they are entitled to health care, to food, to housing, to you-name-it. That that's an entitlement. And the government should give it to them. And they will vote for this president no matter what. . . . These are people who pay no income tax.[55]

Interestingly, while Romney was not far off the percent of people who paid no federal income tax (it is actually 46 percent), 80 percent of Americans believed they paid federal income taxes.[56] Clearly, the numbers do not add up. If citizens incorrectly believe they are paying federal income taxes when they are not, how can they possibly vote on tax issues? Along these lines, it is perhaps surprising to learn that the tax burden facing the average household went down, rather than up, during President Obama's first term. Concern about tax increases, one might contend, is prospective and rooted in concerns about Obamacare rather than retrospective and based on the actual tax burden.[57] In "Homer Gets a Tax Cut," Larry Bartels similarly notes the oddity that Americans who benefited very little (if at all) from the Bush tax cuts still supported the cuts. For Bartels, the result is not reflective of a tolerance for inequality but rather a failure on behalf of the American public to connect inequality to policy. "Much of the public," he writes, "is simply unclear about basic facts in the realm of tax policy."[58] No wonder that the repeal of the estate tax, which primarily benefited wealthy Americans, could be retooled as a populist message to repeal the "death" tax.

Overall, while cognitive heuristics help to explain the daily functioning of democratic governance, their value in "rational" decision-making may be greatly overstated as they are also subject to well-known biases that affect individual decision-making. Within the field of behavioral economics, Dan Ariely has argued that consumers are "predictably irrational," meaning that while decision-making fails to follow the dictates of rationality, the biases that affect decision-making are predictable.[59] Given three choices, for example, consumers have a natural tendency to pick the middle option. Similarly, social norms can be more powerful as a motivator than price. The important takeaway from behavioral economics is that institutional structures matter. Or perhaps stated differently, how we present choices affects the quality of decision-making.

Political psychologists Milton Lodge and Charles Taber find that an automatic decision-making process (as opposed to evidence-based reasoning) is more likely when citizens (1) feel strongly about an issue, candidate, or event and when those feelings are readily accessible; (2) are under time pressures to make a decision; (3) are distracted by other issues or events; (4) notice their setting but are unaware that it might affect their decision-making; and (5) are not likely to consider why they feel or act in a certain way. Lodge and Taber conclude that these factors "characterize the world of politics for many of us more of the time."[60]

MAKING POLITICAL CHOICE DIFFICULT

The American political system does a poor job of structuring choice. First, we ask too much from the average citizen. Our unending presidential election cycle requires far too much time and emotional investment. By the end of the process, most voters simply want the election over, no matter who wins. As a result, we are often dissatisfied with our candidates and our choices by the end of the campaign. The fault, however, lies less with President Barack Obama, Mitt Romney, and their respective campaigns and more with a campaign cycle that ensures that we are weary of the candidates and the campaigns long before Election Day. Thomas Patterson's seminal work, *Out of Order*, advocated a simple reform of electoral process: shorten it.[61] Doing so would decrease citizen frustration with the never-ending campaign cycle and, arguably, increase citizen engagement and information levels by shifting politics from a permanent campaign into seasonal activity. The long ballot, widely employed in American elections, similarly requires that citizens have adequate information on who to vote for school board, coroner, district judge, and a plethora of statewide and local officials as well as a host of state constitutional amendments and/or local ballot initiatives. Citizens have difficulty with a single choice at the top of the ballot, so how do they meaningfully vote for coroner? As if this were not enough, we hold far too many elections (in presidential election years, midterms, local elections, primary elections, etc.). If we begin with the assumption that citizens have a limited capacity for political information, the political system we have created via historical circumstance is the exact opposite of what one would rationally design.

Second, campaigns are now armed with better data on individual decision-making and a more deeply rooted understanding of cognitive psychology. In 1928 when Edward Bernays wrote *Propaganda*, his concern with "engineering consent" was to promote democratic norms to avoid democracy's worst pathologies. His good intentions are unquestionably overstated: Bernays earned his reputation using advertising to break down social norms against women smoking in public so that they would buy Lucky Strike cigarettes. Yet, even if overstated, concerns about the long-term health of democratic governance are now generally only asked at the end of a political career or a long (and usually unsuccessful) political campaign. Retiring senators and representatives, for example, lament the decline in civility and the increased polarization and long for the days when politics was a means of solving problems.

The question confronting today's candidates and consultants is not how to help citizens overcome these cognitive biases and make better decisions but how to manipulate these biases to craft winning political campaigns. The truth in reframing political messages is less important than effectiveness. The most common pathology is the oversimplification of complex issues. Tax cuts, for example, magically reduce deficits and spur economic growth regardless of the broader economic context. A close second is the politicization of facts to score political points. If politicizing a scandal or decrying media bias forces partisans to reconsider a politically damaging news story, then so be it.

On this point, I might concur with Christopher Hayes that elites are failing, but I would dissent on this important point: they are failing because they have learned to appeal more effectively to a public that is too easily mislead, that wants to believe the worst in the other side, and that is willing to disregard evidence if it contradicts preexisting beliefs. The failure of contemporary American politics is a distinctly democratic failure.

Finally, the rise of digital media affords citizens more choice in information. Were the tenets of liberal democratic theory actually true, more choice would translate into exposure to a wider range of political views. Being able to immediately do a Google Search for candidate issue positions on an iPhone, for example, should translate into a more informed citizenry with a deeper and richer understanding of political difference. The reality is much more sobering.[62] Politics is a small part of Internet activity, as the choice afforded by digital media allows citizens to avoid politics altogether or to seek out like-minded partisans who confirm rather than challenge individual viewpoints. Digital democracy turns Elizabeth Noelle-Neumann's *Spiral of Silence* on its head. Instead of minority viewpoints being silenced by the pressures of conformity, almost every view can find a supporting ear and confirming voice in cyberspace. On the Internet, cognitive biases do not simply exist as they did before—they find room and constant reinforcement to flourish and grow. No longer filtered by the gatekeepers that once controlled the mainstream news media, political elites fertilize public misinformation and nurture cognitive biases by appealing directly to supporters via online social networks. If the public engages in motivated reasoning, the job of partisan political consultants is to ensure that their supporters never run out of ammunition.

The consequence is that the public buys policies they believe they want but don't really need. They opt for tax cuts when what they need is more responsible government and deficit reduction. They grow frustrated with partisan gridlock but then elect ideological bomb throwers rather than compromisers and problem solvers. The result is increasing frustration with a political system that doesn't seem to be working very well, but little or no recognition that the undoing of American government can be found in the voice of the people. Loud and incoherent, it speaks in garbled tones but with great authority.

Ironically, the result is policies—endorsed by democratic majorities—that have contributed to growing inequality and a shrinking middle class and that further threaten the future of democratic governance.

NOTES

1. Quoted in B. R. Hergenhahn, *An Introduction to the History of Psychology* (Belmont, CA: Wadsworth, 2008), 530.

2. Helen Walker Puner, *Sigmund Freud: His Life and Mind* (New Brunswick, NJ: Transaction, 1992), 119.

3. Graham Wallas, *Human Nature in Politics* (New York: Knopf, 1908), 103.

4. Charles Lawrence, "The Id, the Ego, and Equal Protection: Reckoning with Unconscious Racism," *Stanford Law Review* 39 (1987): 317–88.

5. Nayda Terkildsen, "When White Voters Evaluate Black Candidates: The Processing Implications of Candidate Skin Color, Prejudice,

and Self-Monitoring," *American Journal of Political Science* 37 (1993): 1032–53.

6. Roland G. Fryer and Steven D. Levitt, "The Causes and Consequences of Distinctively Black Names," *Quarterly Journal of Economics* 119 (2004): 767–805.

7. Walter Lippmann, *Public Opinion* (New York: Harcourt, Brace, 1922); Walter Lippmann, *The Phantom Public* (New York: Macmillan, 1925); Edward Bernays, *Crystallizing Public Opinion* (New York: Liveright, 1923); Edward Bernays, *Propaganda* (New York: Liveright, 1928).

8. Walter Lippmann, *Preface to Politics* (New York: Mitchell Kennerley, 1913).

9. Adam Curtis, *The Century of the Self, Part II, The Engineering of Consent* (March 2002).

10. Michael Schudson, "The 'Lippmann-Dewey Debate' and the Invention of Walter Lippmann as an Anti-Democrat 1986–1996," *International Journal of Communication* 2 (2008): 1031–42.

11. Schudson, "The 'Lippmann-Dewey Debate,'" 1035.

12. Gustave Le Bon, *The Crowd: A Study of the Popular Mind* (Macmillan, 1896).

13. Gabriel Tarde, *On Communication and Social Influence* (Chicago: University of Chicago Press, 1898).

14. David Ricci, "Democracy Attenuated: Schumpeter, the Process Theory, and American Democratic Thought," *Journal of Politics* 32 (1970): 239–67; Joseph Schumpeter, *Capitalism, Socialism, and Democracy* (New York: Harper, 1942).

15. Robert Dahl, *A Preface to Democratic Theory* (Chicago: University of Chicago Press, 1956).

16. E. E. Schattschneider, *The Semisovereign People* (New York: Holt, Rinehart, and Winston, 1960).

17. Robert Michels, *Political Parties: A Sociological Study of the Oligarchical Tendencies of Modern Democracy* (New York: Hearst International, 1915).

18. Christopher Hayes, *Twilight of the Elites: America After Meritocracy* (New York: Crown, 2012).

19. Richard Fry and Paul Taylor, *The Rise of Residential Segregation by Income* (Washington, DC: Pew Research Center, 2012), http://www.pewsocialtrends.org/2012/08/01/the-rise-of-residential-segregation-by-income/ (accessed May 23, 2013); Bill Bishop, *The Big Sort: Why the*

Clustering of Like-Minded America is Tearing Us Apart (New York: Houghton Mifflin, 2008).

20. Connor Simpson, "Rick Santorum Doesn't Have 'Smart People' on His Side," *The Atlantic Wire*, http://www.theatlanticwire.com/national/2012/09/rick-santorum-doesnt-have-smart-people-his-side/56895/.

21. Dennis Pogue, *Founding Spirits: George Washington and the Beginnings of the American Whiskey Industry* (Buena Vista, VA: Harbour Books, 2011).

22. One might fairly argue that it reflects institutionalized corruption legitimized by the American system of campaign finance.

23. Thomas Frank, *What's the Matter with Kansas? How Conservatives Won the Heart of America* (New York: Metropolitan Books, 2004).

24. Paul Lazarsfeld, Bernard Berelson, and Hazel Gaudet, *The People's Choice: How the Voter Makes Up His Mind in a Presidential Campaign* (New York: Duell, Sloan and Pearce, 1944).

25. Bernard Berelson, Paul Lazarsfeld, and William McPhee, *Voting: A Study of Opinion Formation in a Presidential Campaign* (Chicago: University of Chicago Press, 1954).

26. Angus Campbell, Philip Converse, Warren Miller, and Donald Stokes, *The American Voter* (New York: Wiley, 1960).

27. Philip Converse, "The Nature of Belief Systems in the Mass Public," in *Ideology and Discontent*, edited by David Apter (New York: Wiley, 1964).

28. Anthony Downs, *An Economic Theory of Democracy* (New York: Harper & Row, 1957).

29. V. O. Key Jr., *The Responsible Electorate: Rationality in Presidential Voting, 1936–1960* (Cambridge, MA: Harvard University Press, 1966).

30. Morris Fiorina, *Retrospective Voting in American National Elections* (New Haven, CT: Yale University Press, 1981), 181.

31. V. O. Key Jr., *The Responsible Electorate*, 2–3.

32. Robert Lane, *Political Ideology: Why the American Common Man Believes What He Does* (New York: Free Press, 1962).

33. George Marcus, David Tabb, and John Sullivan, "The Application of Individual Differences Scaling to the Measurement of Political Ideologies," *American Journal of Political Science* 18 (1974): 405–20; Pamela Johnston Conover and Stanley Feldman, "How People Organize Their

Political World: A Schematic Model," *American Journal of Political Science* 28 (1984): 95–126; Shawn Treier and D. Sunshine Hillygus, "The Nature of Political Ideology in the Contemporary Electorate," *Public Opinion Quarterly* 73 (2009): 679–703.

34. Benjamin Page and Robert Shapiro, *The Rational Public: Fifty Years of Trends in Americans' Policy Preferences* (Chicago: University of Chicago Press, 1992).

35. Herbert Simon, *Administrative Behavior* (New York: Macmillan, 1947).

36. Samuel Popkin, *The Reasoning Voter: Communication and Persuasion in Presidential Campaigns* (Chicago: University of Chicago Press, 1991); Arthur Lupia and Mathew McCubbins, *The Democratic Dilemma: Can Citizens Learn What They Need to Know?* (Cambridge: Cambridge University Press, 1998); Paul Sniderman, Richard Brody, and Philip Tetlock, *Reasoning and Choice: Explorations in Political Psychology* (Cambridge: Cambridge University Press, 1991).

37. Milton Lodge, Kathleen McGraw, and Patrick Stroh, "An Impression Driven Model of Candidate Evaluation," *American Political Science Review* 83 (1989): 299–419.

38. David Redlawsk, "A Matter of Motivated Reasoning," *New York Times*, April 22, 2011, http://www.nytimes.com/roomfordebate/2011/04/21/barack-obama-and-the-psychology-of-the-birther-myth/a-matter-of-motivated-reasoning.

39. Jonathan Haidt, *The Righteous Mind: Why Good People Are Divided by Politics and Religion* (New York: Pantheon Books, 2012), and Milton Lodge and Charles Taber, *The Rationalizing Voter* (New York: Cambridge University Press, 2013).

40. David Redlawsk, "The Affective Tipping Point: Do Motivated Reasoners Ever Get It?" *Political Psychology* 31 (2010): 563–93.

41. Thomas Brunell argues that because citizens are happy when their team "wins," congressional districts should be drawn to achieve lopsided partisan imbalances. See Thomas Brunell, *Redistricting and Representation: Why Competitive Elections Are Bad for America* (New York: Routledge, 2008).

42. Chris Mooney, "The Science of Why We Don't Believe Science," *Mother Jones*, May/June 2011, http://www.motherjones.com/print/106166.

43. Jonathan Haidt, *The Righteous Mind*, 89.

44. Milton Lodge and Charles Taber, *The Rationalizing Voter* (New York: Cambridge University Press, 2013).

45. Hugo Mercier and Dan Sperber, "Why Do Humans Reason? Arguments for an Argumentative Theory," *Behavioral and Brain Sciences* 34 (2011): 57–111.

46. Chris Mooney, *The Republican Brain: The Science of Why They Deny Science—and Reality* (Hoboken, NJ: Wiley, 2012).

47. Dan Kahan, "What Do I Think of Mooney's 'Republican Brain,'" Cultural Cognition Project at Yale Law School, http://www.culturalcognition.net/blog/2012/7/27/what-do-i-think-of-mooneys-republican-brain.html (accessed May 23, 2013).

48. Larry Bartels, "Uninformed Votes: Information Effects in Presidential Elections," *American Journal of Political Science* 40 (1996): 194–230; Larry Bartels, "The Irrational Electorate," *Wilson Quarterly* (2008), http://www.wilsonquarterly.com/article.cfm?aid=1250 (accessed May 23, 2013).

49. Richard Lau and David Redlawsk, "Voting Correctly," *American Political Science Review* 91 (1997): 585–98.

50. Richard Lau and David Redlawsk, "Advantages and Disadvantages of Cognitive Heuristics in Political Decision Making," *American Journal of Political Science* 45 (2001): 951–71.

51. James H. Kuklinski and Paul J. Quirk, "Reconsidering the Rational Public: Cognition, Heuristics, and Mass Opinion," in *The Elements of Reason: Cognition, Choice, and the Bounds of Rationality*, edited by Arthur Lupia, Mathew D. McCubbins, and Samuel L. Popkin (Cambridge: Cambridge University Press, 2000).

52. Thomas Holbrook and James Garand, "Homo Economus? Economic Information and Economic Voting," *Political Research Quarterly* 49 (1996): 351–75.

53. Marc Hetherington, "The Media's Role in Forming Voters' National Economic Evaluations in 1992," *American Journal of Political Science* 40 (1992): 372–95; Kirby Goidel and Ronald Langley, "Media Coverage of the Economy and Aggregate Economic Evaluations: Uncovering Evidence of Indirect Media Effects," *Political Research Quarterly* 48 (1995): 313–28.

54. Bryan Caplan, *The Myth of the Rational Voter: Why Democracies Choose Bad Policies* (Princeton, NJ: Princeton University Press, 2007).

55. David Corn, "Secret Video: Romney Tells Millionaire Donors What He REALLY Thinks of Obama Voters," *Mother Jones*, September 17, 2012, http://www.motherjones.com/politics/2012/09/secret-video-romney-private-fundraiser.

56. Steve Kornacki, "Study: '47 Percent' Not Hurting Mitt," *Salon*, September 20, 2012, http://www.salon.com/2012/09/20/study_47_percent_isnt_hurting_mitt_where_it_counts/.

57. Politifact, "For 'the average middle-class family, your taxes today are lower than when I took office,'" evaluation of President Barack Obama rated as "true" based on data from the Urban Institute-Brookings Institution Tax Policy Center, http://www.politifact.com/truth-o-meter/statements/2011/dec/01/barack-obama/obama-says-taxes-lower-middle-class/.

58. Larry Bartels, "Homer Gets a Tax Cut: Inequality and Public Policy in the American Mind," *Perspectives on Politics* 3 (2005): 15–31.

59. Dan Ariely, *Predictably Irrational: The Hidden Forces that Shape Our Decisions* (New York: Harper, 2008).

60. Lodge and Taber, *The Rationalizing Voter*, 25.

61. Thomas Patterson, *Out of Order* (New York: Knopf, 1994).

62. Matthew Hindman, *The Myth of Digital Democracy* (Princeton, NJ: Princeton University Press, 2009); Markus Prior, *Post-Broadcast Democracy: How Media Choice Increases Inequality in Political Involvement and Polarizes Elections* (Cambridge: Cambridge University Press, 2007).

3

WHY WE VOTE FOR ECONOMIC INEQUALITY

Along with horse racing, bourbon, and basketball, Kentucky is defined by its rolling hills of bluegrass. Growing up in the state, you never fully realize how truly different the grass is, how it defines place, identity, and culture. It is just there, a permanent part of the backdrop.

The American political culture is similarly defined by trace elements that we never fully consider because they have always been, because they fill the backdrop of our collective experience and our shared identity. The American commitment to individualism is one of these elements, so deeply rooted in the political ethos that it is rarely thought of or questioned. It simply is. People make it because of their hard work, ingenuity, and drive. If they fail, it is because they lack these qualities.

When it comes to our material well-being, we get what we deserve.

That this is a myth makes it no less powerful.

Its validity is rarely, if ever, questioned, and it influences our thinking in subtle, pervasive, and profound ways. Inequality has long been a staple of American politics, tolerated because of a collective belief that inequalities create incentives for personal betterment and reflect a society defined by economic possibilities.

But what if inequality in the United States is increasingly disconnected from economic mobility? What if the gap between the
haves and have-nots results not in greater striving on the lower
rungs but in a shrinking middle class? And what if, despite these
changes, campaign rhetoric continues to portray a society defined
not by rising inequality but by the fairness of economic markets?
Or worse, that the frustrations of those squeezed in the middle
and lower rungs of American society are the fault, not of an economic system that provides undue rewards to economic winners,
but of government regulations and social safety nets designed to
help protect the public and address social inequalities?

YOU DIDN'T BUILD THAT

The reaction to President Barack Obama's misstep in a speech
given in July 2012 illustrates the depth of commitment to individualism and the pushback for even the faintest suggestion that individuals do not pull themselves up by their own bootstraps:

> Look, if you've been successful, you didn't get there on your
> own. You didn't get there on your own. I'm always struck by
> people who think, well, it must be because I was just so smart.
> There are a lot of smart people out there. It must be because I
> worked harder than everybody else. Let me tell you some-
> thing—there are a whole bunch of hardworking people out
> there.
>
> If you were successful, somebody along the line gave you
> some help. There was a great teacher somewhere in your life.
> Somebody helped to create this unbelievable American system
> that we have that allowed you to thrive. Somebody invested in
> roads and bridges.
>
> *If you've got a business—you didn't build that.* Somebody
> else made that happen. The Internet didn't get invented on its
> own. Government research created the Internet so that all the
> companies could make money off the Internet. The point is, is
> that when we succeed, we succeed because of our individual

initiative, but also because we do things together. There are
some things, just like fighting fires, we don't do on our own.[1]
[emphasis added]

The quote speaks to the importance of infrastructure and community in creating the conditions that allow individual businesses
to succeed and grow, but it was the phrase "you didn't build that"
that struck a responsive and reactionary chord. It set off a fire-
storm on the right as an indicator of Barack Obama's "true feelings" about free enterprise and capitalism and served as the refrain for the 2012 Republican National Convention. Government,
and not individual initiative, mattered in the creation, development, and success of business. The irony that many of the most
patriotic "love it or leave it" Americans believe that America—as a
community, country, and government—has little to do with their
personal success is striking. President Obama, for his part, walked
back from the comment, acknowledging that "of course Americans
build their own businesses" and protesting that the quote was
taken out of context.

It was not.

Regardless, the depth of the reaction is revealing of our cultural commitment to individualism. The roots of this commitment
were observed first and in greatest detail by Alexis de Tocqueville,
who traced the origins of the American political culture to the
"conservative" nature of the American Revolution, the absence of
a landed aristocracy, the widespread commitment to egalitarian
ideas among the Founders, and the material well-being of the
colonists.[2] In the United States, economic mobility could be found
in the availability of land and a westward expansion that encouraged and celebrated a rugged individualism.

Despite its advanced capitalist economic system, the United
States proved more hostile to socialist political parties than other
industrial democracies.[3] Political culture in the United States—
the deep backdrop of American politics, inconspicuous but rigidly
adhered to—limited the range of ideological debate to the narrow
territorial boundaries of classic liberal political thought. When

George Wallace proclaimed, "There's not a dime's worth of difference between the two major parties," he was right, but not for the
reasons he imagined.[4]

Even in contemporary politics, the "socialist" label immediately
conveys prima facie evidence that an idea is unacceptable and not
worth considering. President Obama's Patient Protection and Af-
fordable Care Act (Obamacare) may have been modeled on the
Massachusetts program crafted by Governor Mitt Romney and on
ideas originated at the conservative Heritage Foundation, but
once labeled "socialized medicine" it could no longer be accepted
on the right.[5]

Similarly, Obama administration efforts to roll back Bush administration tax cuts have been labeled "class warfare." As Republican vice presidential nominee Paul Ryan explained, "We should
take this head on, which is, the president is preying on the emotions of fear, envy and resentment, and he's speaking to people in
America as if they're fixed in some class. That's the European
model. That's the model our ancestors left to come create an opportunity society, equality of opportunity, equal protection of the
law—not equality of outcome. Government's role is not to equal-
ize the results of our lives. And we should take that on in a moral
way and defend the system of upward mobility."[6]

Myths may be socially constructed, but they are often rooted in
some truth or partial truth. The rags-to-riches Horatio Alger stories were always oversold but connected with the economic mobility myth deeply ingrained in American culture. They were just
true enough historically to persist. Alexis de Tocqueville and Karl
Marx both commented on the fluidity of social class and income in
the United States, and Louis Hartz defined the liberal consensus
that defined *American exceptionalism* in terms of the absence of
identifiable social classes. The ideal that attracted (and continues
to attract) immigrants from throughout the world was that, in
America, success was determined not by birthright but by hard
work and individual enterprise.

Paul Ryan's comment fairly captures this belief, but not the
contemporary economic reality. Within the United States, studies

reveal, there is less economic mobility than in other industrial democracies.[7] The statistics are staggering: nearly two-thirds of Americans born in the upper class stay there, while approximately two-thirds of those born into poverty remain poor.[8] While most Americans do earn more than their parents, family wealth is one of the single best predictors of future economic success. It is much harder to climb up or fall down the American economic ladder than most of us imagine.

Even so, the stickiness of the American political system is mostly found on the bottom rungs. Individuals who grow up in poverty are much more likely to be mired in poverty than under the "European model," with its stronger social safety net and greater unionization of the working class. After reviewing income data over time, Northwestern economics professor Joseph Ferrie concluded that the conditions that once defined America as "exceptional" (i.e., westward exception and geographic mobility) are no longer in place.[9]

Politically, economic mobility has been sold as a tradeoff that comes with greater economic inequality, but what happens when economic mobility stalls and inequality rises? The answer is a declining middle class and a threat to the stability of the American political system. Figure 3.1 illustrates the gains in income for the

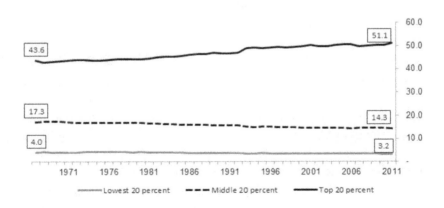

Figure 3.1. Share of Income (as a percent), 1967–2011

upper 20 percent of earners even as the share of national income is declining for lowest 20 and middle 20 percent. Only the upper 20 percent has seen their share of national income grow from 1967 to 2011. Or perhaps stated more simply, economic inequality is on the rise.

Looking at the top 20 percent, however, only scratches the surface. The share of national income for the top 1 percent of earners (displayed in figure 3.2) has increased even more dramatically—from 8.4 percent in 1967 to 17.4 percent in 2010—while the share of income for the top 0.1 percent has increased from 2.16 percent to 7.5.[10] In real 2010 dollars, average income for the top 1 percent has grown from $330,706 in 1967 to $857,477. Average income for everyone else increased from $39,251 in 1967 to $49,235 in 2010. In its annual report, *The State of Working America*, the Economic Policy Institute describes the last decade (2001–2010) as a "lost decade" in terms of income and wage growth.[11] To place these numbers in historical perspective, consider this: income inequality is now what it was at the time that F. Scott Fitzgerald was writing *The Great Gatsby* in the Roaring Twenties, just before the beginning of the Great Depression. The Great Recession failed to level the income distribution, as upper income earners recovered quickly from the economic downturn while everyone else continued to struggle.

Greater economic inequality, however, says little or nothing about worker productivity. Maybe growing inequality reflects differences in effort or ingenuity? The data suggest otherwise. Since 1979, productivity has increased by 80 percent, while incomes have remained flat or stagnant.[12] This stands in sharp contrast to the period after World War II, when productivity gains grew in conjunction with income and wages.[13] It is not the case that greater productivity automatically yields income growth in the middle or lower rungs of the income distribution. In the current period, increased economic productivity is associated with growing economic inequality. Alan Krueger, chairman of the Council of Economic Advisers in the Obama administration, has dubbed the combination of declining economic mobility and increased eco-

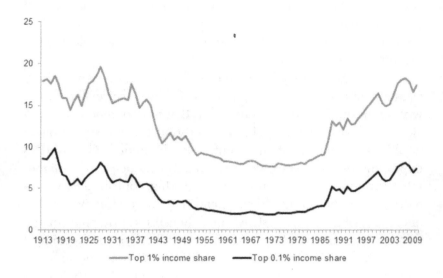

Figure 3.2.   Income Share for the Top 1 Percent and the Top 0.1 Percent, 1913–2010

nomic inequality the "Great Gatsby Curve."[14] Indeed, looking across countries, the relationship is fairly clear: greater economic inequality translates into less—not more—economic mobility.

What is most curious about this combination of economic trends is that it is not just the result of inevitable economic cycles or the invisible hand of the labor market, but instead reflects intentional policy decisions. For many observers, including economist Joseph Stiglitz, this reflects a political failure rather than market failure.[15] "Real democracy," Stiglitz argues, "is more than the right to vote once every two or four years. The choices have to be meaningful. The politicians have to listen to the citizens. But increasingly, and especially in the United States, it seems the political system is more akin to 'one dollar one vote' than 'one person one vote.'"

Rather than respond to the needs of the many, the political system is increasingly responding to the needs of the few and the powerful. Political scientists Larry Bartels and Martin Gilens have convincingly and independently demonstrated that Senate roll call votes and policy decisions are highly responsive to the collective opinions of wealthier citizens, occasionally responsive to middle income citizens, and unresponsive to the poor.[16]

There is great irony here. One of the fears long expressed by classic political philosophers, and which found expression in the writings of the Founding Fathers, was that pure democracy would yield to a participatory politics advocating the redistribution of wealth. That fear, as it turns out, was unfounded. Given equal opportunities to participate, the wealthy participate at higher rates, through a larger array of venues (voting, contributing, volunteering, and contacting officials), and they more effectively influence the political power structure.[17] Recall the principles of the iron law of oligarchy (discussed in chapter 2): democratic political organizations and movements inevitably trend toward oligarchy as they become more organized and as movement and party leaders develop incentives to remain in power. The same is true of democratic political systems. Even if we began with perfect "one person, one vote" equality, the system quickly yields to differences in political power and influence. *The more democratic the political system, the more transparent and open the political processes, the more opportunities for public input and involvement, the greater the participatory biases, and the greater the influence of higher income, better educated citizens.*

Digital democracy may have similarly opened the door to greater participation, but it is not peasants with pitchforks who are storming a virtual Bastille. Instead, the participatory biases that have long defined conventional politics also define online political expression. The "digital haves" look remarkably similar to the haves in the broadcast era, with one notable exception: they have even more opportunities to express their political views and, potentially, to influence policy and political discourse.

A note of a caution is in order here: This is not an argument that wealthier voters subvert democratic processes and that what looks like democracy is really a carefully disguised oligarchy controlled by political, business, and military elites, or what sociologist

C. Wright Mills called the power elite.[18] There is no grand conspiracy to keep the poor in place or to oppress the working class. There need not be. The ecosystem of contemporary politics allows this to occur under the rules of procedural fairness, transparency, and greater democracy. Or perhaps stated differently, wealthier interests win fairly and squarely under our current institutional structure because they are better able to translate their resources into political influence. What is different from previous eras is the lack of effective representation of working-class economic interests. Labor unions, for example, proved powerful enough to force a recall election against Wisconsin governor Scott Walker in June 2012 when he stripped them of their collective bargaining rights, but they were vastly outgunned by corporate money and easily defeated in the recall election. The failed recall effort proved a poor barometer of the state's electoral mood, as President Barack Obama easily won Wisconsin's ten Electoral College votes, thus illustrating the disconnect between the electoral appeal of labor unions and the Democratic Party.

Marxists observers of American politics have often noted a false consciousness, an inability to identify the true nature of social relations and class oppression because of the dominance of a central ideology.[19] One need not be a Marxist to recognize that the organizational infrastructure of American politics increasingly tilts to the right, and with good reason: conservatives have consciously and aggressively created an ideological infrastructure to promote their ideological goals and policy positions.

In *Winner-Take-All Politics*, Jacob Hacker and Paul Pierson describe how the right gained—and maintained—an organizational edge in American politics that has translated into policies that favor wealthier interests.[20] Not only has the right built organizational capacity, but labor unions—historically the voice of the working class—have declined and faded from political prominence.[21] Figure 3.3 illustrates the decline of labor union membership from just under a quarter of all wage and salary earners in 1973 to 12 percent in 2011. The decline is even more precipitous if we exclude public service wage and salary earners where unions

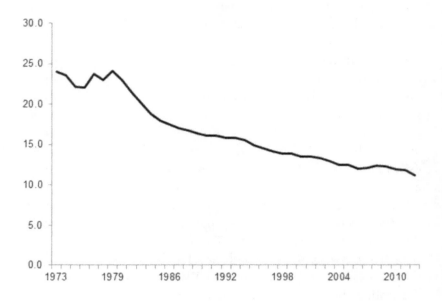

Figure 3.3.   Union Membership among All Wage and Salary Earners, 1973–2012

remain strong but are increasingly under attack (as in Wisconsin). But it is not just about the decline of labor union membership— labor union influence in campaigns (measured by campaign spending) has declined as well. Since 1992, labor contributions have grown from $41 million to $141 million in 2012. Typically, Democrats receive 90 percent (or more) of all labor contributions. To place the numbers in context, however, the financial industry contributed $61 million in 1992 and $653 million in 2012. If the winners and losers in American politics are defined by organizational presence, the working class is increasingly at a loss relative to business interests and professional associations.[22]

Concurrently, issues of race and religion have divided the working class. On the issue of race, Richard Nixon's southern strategy was a conscious effort to pull working-class white voters away from the Democratic Party and into the Republican Party. The trends in partisan affiliation are undisputable: the percent of white working-class voters who identify with the Democratic Party has declined from 38.9 percent in 1972 to 25.6 percent in 2008.[23]

One of the more remarkable changes in American public opinion has been the gradual erosion of support for overtly racist sentiments or preferences. Implicit racial appeals, however, can be quite effective and appear quite frequently in contemporary politics. Think Willie Horton in 1988.[24] Or the Jesse Helm "hands ad" in which a pair of white hands rips up a rejection letter as the voiceover declares, "You needed that job, and you were the best qualified, but they had to give it to a minority because of a racial quota. Is that fair? Harvey Gantt says it is." The strategy has continued for a simple reason: it has proved effective. In 2012, a Mitt Romney ad accused President Obama, inaccurately, of ending the work requirements for welfare reform. The accuracy matters less than the association of President Obama with welfare. Or as Lyndon Johnson reportedly said after trying to get an untrue accusation out that an opponent slept with barnyard animals, "I just want to hear him deny it."

Curiously (and perhaps surprisingly), recent evidence suggests that implicit racial appeals are less effective on less educated, working-class white voters and are more effective on those college-educated white voters who pick up on and respond to the not-so-subtle racial cues. Working-class whites have already moved solidly in the Republican direction, while college-educated whites remain persuadable and potentially responsive to racial cues. President Barack Obama has been celebrated as the first "post-racial" president, but the evidence suggests that his historic 2008 campaign and his first term in office activated—rather than diminished—racial attitudes as a driver of political evaluations.[25] During the Clinton administration, for example, health care reform was not an issue that divided Americans along racial lines. Today, support for health care reform is increasingly defined as a racial issue, as President Barack Obama, by his mere presence, invokes racial considerations.[26]

Religion, too, pits voters who might support greater economic equality against liberals who are perceived as destroyers of traditional social norms. Economic issues get lost in issues of gay marriage, abortion, and abstinence. This is the thesis of Thomas Frank's influential *What's the Matter with Kansas?* Jacob Hacker and Paul Pierson take it an additional step, noting that as "evangelicals have been organized into politics on nonmaterial grounds. Most voters of moderate means, however, have been organized out of politics, left adrift as the foundations of middle-class democracy have washed away."[27]

Evangelicals, who are mostly of modest economic means, have a curious and symbiotic relationship with Republican economic conservatives. Campaigns, especially Republican primary campaigns, are run and generally won on social issues. Governing, however, is often directed by powerful and highly effective business interests. In the 2012 election, Mitt Romney spent much of the primary season convincing social conservatives he was conservative enough. During the general election, he increasingly moved to the middle. Romney political advisor Eric Fehrnstrom acknowledged as much when he said, "I think you hit a reset button for the fall campaign. Everything changes. It's almost like an Etch-A-Sketch. You can kind of shake it up and restart all of over again."[28]

Overall, organizational politics in the United States tilts increasingly to the right even as shifts in American public opinion about the appropriate size, scope, and role of the federal government have remained relatively stable. This is a remarkable achievement. In the 1960s (and earlier), it might have been fair to describe partisan politics as a battle between Democratic organizational muscle (defined largely as union muscle) versus Republican money. Increasingly, Republicans have gained organizational influence by investing in party organization, while Democrats, beginning most prominently with Democratic Congressional Campaign Committee chairman Tony Coelho in the 1980s, have chased corporate financial backing.

President Barack Obama, often deplored as a socialist on the right, was heavily financed by banking and financial interests in his 2008 campaign. It might be surprising, for example, to learn that President Obama raised more money from the financial sector in

2008 than Republican John McCain. Similarly, Bill Clinton, who was criticized for selling access to the Lincoln Bedroom for campaign contributions, focused on keeping inflation low rather than on unemployment and job creation. Both President Obama and President Clinton adapted to the new reality of American politics, a politics driven by campaign contributions and organizational money. Neither fundamentally changed this reality.

Organizationally, Democrats have been unable to match the development of the conservative ideological infrastructure, including think tanks (like the Heritage Foundation), Fox News, talk radio, and investments in political party organizations at the state and local levels. Not that they haven't had notable successes: MoveOn.Org stands as an important contrast, and for a brief period Democrats had the advantage in 527s and other soft-money political organizations. In the online world, Democrats compete well in the blogosphere and Twitterverse, and President Barack Obama has aggressively developed the Democratic ground game via text messaging and social media. When Democrats are chasing corporate backing within a larger backdrop of labor union decline, however, they may be winning a battle but losing a war. Increasingly, the game is played on the side of the field sponsored by corporate interests.

In addition to organization presence, wealthier interests may simply be better at selling their message and leveraging democratic processes and procedures for favorable policies. "There is another way for moneyed interests to get what they want out government," economist Joseph Stiglitz writes: "convince the 99 percent that they have shared interests."[29] In an electoral system driven by money and in which every message is carefully tested for effectiveness, persuasion often occurs through emotional appeals and short, simple, field-tested messages.[30]

Nuance and complexity fail in an age in which presidential debates are won not by reasoned arguments but by short zingers and personal image, and when policy speeches are summarized as five-second soundbites and treated as a strategic calculation rather than sincere belief. Republicans have adapted more effectively to this new reality than Democrats, Jonathan Haidt argues, because they understand that morality is rooted more in intuition and group identification than rationality or reasoning.[31] When Democrats do win, it is on the basis of equally simplistic messages— "Hope and Change" or "It's the economy, stupid"—and compelling personal narratives.

Within this context, it is worth recalling the principles of motivated reasoning: citizens begin the reasoning process with their conclusions already in hand. The search is not for truth but for supportive evidence. An organizational infrastructure that reinforces preexisting beliefs; that makes the search for supportive evidence easier, quicker, and more convenient; and that understands that intuition, emotion, and belief are more powerful than careful systematic reasoning is necessarily advantaged. Even when both sides understand this, the political game falls short of the democratic ideal. Campaigns aren't about issues or ideas; they are about emotional response.

WHY POLITICAL IGNORANCE MATTERS MORE IN CONTEMPORARY POLITICS

Imagine that democratic governance worked as intended. An engaged and enlightened citizenry would stand as a floodwall against participatory distortions, and democratic government would have to respond to the collective needs of the citizenry. Absent an engaged and informed citizenry, politics becomes a sport of organizational combat.[32] While American politics have become increasingly democratic (see chapter 1), the reality of American politics is that it remains pluralistic at its core. Politics takes place through organizations, and the organizational impetus is driven by money, organizational skill, infrastructure, and message. It is inherently elitists and growing more so, as corporate economic interests become more skilled in setting the policy agenda and winning policy debates.

But if citizens have always been less than fully engaged, what is the big deal? Why can't our political system continue to muddle through as it has for over two hundred years?

The answer is quite simple: armed with an understanding of cognitive psychology and with increasingly sophisticated tools of political influence, contemporary political campaigns more effectively brandish political ignorance as a campaign weapon. "The 1 percent," Joseph Stiglitz argues, "now have more knowledge about how to shape the preferences and beliefs in ways that enable the wealthy to advance their cause."[33] Americans recognize the reality of economic inequality, for example, but they greatly underestimate how wide the gaps are between the haves and the have-nots, the consequences of this inequality, and the ability of government to effectively address the problem.[34]

Elite manipulation occurs because mass political beliefs are ill defined and malleable and because the tools of persuasion have grown increasingly effective. Because of two-party political competition, we never fully realize the potential of what elite manipulation might look like in a one-party system (as is the case in China). Political elites battle over the nature of reality (is the economy in recovery or is it lagging?), as well as the appropriate policy-related remedies for "fixing" economic stagnation (tax cuts or economic stimulus). However, due to the decline of the Democratic Party as a labor party and a voice of the working class, not to mention the importance of corporate fundraising to electoral politics, the system is tilted heavily and increasingly toward corporate economic interests.

The total amount of money spent on federal elections in 2012 was $6.3 billion, up from $5.3 billion in 2008, $4.1 billion in 2004, and $3.1 billion in 2000. Yet most Americans give little or nothing to a candidate or political party. According to the American National Election Studies, 13 percent of Americans gave money to a political campaign in 2008. Most of these contributions are relatively small in size and not particularly consequential. In 2012, for example, if President Barack Obama spent $730 million, how much influence could a $100 contribution possibly buy? But what if the people who give to political campaigns have distinct political preferences from those who do not? Is it possible that they push policy in a particular direction? How responsive are politicians to donors relative to voters?

According to OpenSecrets.Org, only 0.3 percent of Americans gave $200 or more to political candidates in 2012. President Barack Obama and Republican Mitt Romney spent over $1 billion in their pursuit of the White House. Notably, defenders of the status quo used to argue that this pales in comparison to the advertising budgets of major corporations, but this is less true with each passing election cycle, particularly when one includes the "independent" spending of so-called super PACs.

One might also argue—as has been argued in the past—that increased spending yields a stronger and more vibrant democracy. Research in political science reveals relationships between campaign spending and political competition (more spending equals more competitive elections), campaign spending and voter turnout (more spending equals greater participation), and campaign spending and political knowledge (more spending equals greater knowledge). Other, related research has demonstrated that campaign advertising yields more knowledge gains for individual voters than news exposure (though this says more about the quality of political news than the informative power of political advertising). If we apply this research to 2012 elections, the predictions of political scientists should be straightforward and simple: we should see the most engaged, knowledgeable, and involved electorate in the history of American politics.

This was decidedly not the case. Long before the first ballot was cast, most Americans were sick of the political process and ready for the election to be over. Money may be necessary for communication, but there is no reason to believe that the communication will be helpful (or even truthful) for learning about campaigns and candidates. Indeed, the willful distortion of information and the selective interpretation of breaking news, events, and statistics is an important, even critical, part of contemporary campaigns. This occurs not only in the context of political advertising but also in the context of spinning news coverage. Former president Bill Clinton, despite numerous scandals, proved masterful at spinning the news in favorable directions and avoiding the consequences of scandals.[35] Former president George W. Bush was equally adept at presenting favorable versions of the "truth" by spinning the story lines around major policy initiatives.[36]

Declining trust in the media, institutional incentives for sensationalized coverage, and focus on the strategic game of politics have made the news media ineffective as arbitrators of the truth. As Harvard political scientist Thomas Patterson observed in his classic work *Out of Order*, this is not a role the news media should be playing. Indeed, the more the news media insert themselves as players into the political process, via selective fact-checking and interpretative journalism, the less credible they appear.[37]

Information is only informative if the source is seen as credible, the information is actually true (and not just selectively true), and citizens are open to reevaluating their existing beliefs, preferences, and choices. None of these conditions appear to be true in contemporary politics. Information is distrusted (being presented selectively by candidates and parties and interpreted narrowly by the news media), and citizens are more akin to cognitive misers than Bayesian statisticians. More troubling is the fact that the money that is used to communicate messages also influences the content of these messages. It is not the case that money is a neutral conveyer of knowledge or disinterested medium. The Supreme Court once equated money in political campaigns to the gasoline that fuels a car. What good is the right to drive a car if you can't purchase the fuel necessary to drive it? In contemporary politics, the analogy is deeply flawed. Money is not only the gas that makes the car go—it is also the car and driver.

One needn't dig deeply into the campaign finance reports to realize a startling truth: the differences in funding sources for President Barack Obama and Mitt Romney are not as different as you might imagine.[38] President Obama, for example, gets more money from lawyers and lobbyists ($18.9 million), but lawyers and lobbyists are also an important source of funding for Mitt Romney

($10 million). Mitt Romney, with deep ties in the financial industry, received $40 million in contributions from the finance, insurance, and real estate sector, but President Obama has received more than $14 million from this sector. Indeed, one of the notable stories from this election cycle is the shift from 2008, when President Obama received $15 million from the finance, insurance, and real estate sector compared to only $9 million for John McCain. Many of the biggest players in Washington politics give to both Democratic and Republican candidates, as they are less concerned with who occupies the White House than with their access and influence over the policymaking process.

A critic might point out that these sector totals blur important differences across candidates. Fair enough, but when only 0.3 percent of the population is giving $200 or more and total election expenditures exceed $5.8 billion, one can fairly question the value of money in the political process relative to votes. An additional criticism might be levied that the influence of money over policy decisions is overstated. It is not just that special interests give in to the expectation of policy favors, but also that representatives and senators ask for contributions and industries cannot afford to say no. For our purposes, the direction of the influence is less important than the consequence. The search for campaign dollars tilts electoral politics away from the lower and middle classes and toward citizens and organizations who can contribute to political campaigns.

Election scholars have long noted that campaign money is necessary but not a sufficient condition for winning election. If this is indeed the case, how can candidates not be aware of the interests of their financial supporters? How is it possible that those interests do not influence, if not outright determine, the positions of elected officials, particularly on issues that are not particularly visible or salient to their constituents? "In today's Washington," journalist Robert Kaiser writes, "money builds bulwarks that defend the status quo, even when political power changes hands because of election results." One can fairly ask whether the bailout of the banking industry would have been fundamentally different had John McCain won in 2008. Would the financial winners and losers have been any different after four years of a President McCain? As money has become more important in politics, Kaiser argues, "The quality of governance has palpably declined."[39]

Unfortunately, there is more to the story than ineffective governance. After showing that policy decisions reflect the policy preferences of wealthier Americans but not voters in the lower or middle classes, Martin Gilens concludes, "As money becomes more critical to winning elections, pleasing the people who supply the money naturally becomes more important to office seekers and officeholders."[40] The reason is simple: the people who give have distinct political preferences. Wealthy Democrats, for example, may appear distinct from wealthy Republicans, but they also differ in important ways from middle- and working-class Democrats. First, there are simply more Republicans among the "super rich." And second, super rich Democrats tend to be more moderate when it comes to economic policy.[41] The contemporary Democratic Party differs from the Republican Party in notable and important ways, but it, too, is inherently elitist and disconnected from the concerns of the working and middle class. As Francis Fukuyama explains,

> The main trends in left-wing thought in the last two generations have been, frankly, disastrous as either conceptual frameworks or tools for mobilization. Marxism died many years ago, and the few old believers still around are ready for nursing homes. The academic left replaced it with postmodernism, multiculturalism, feminism, critical theory, and a host of other fragmented intellectual trends that are more cultural than economic in focus. Postmodernism begins with a denial of the possibility of any master narrative of history or society, undercutting its own authority as a voice for the majority of citizens who feel betrayed by their elites. Multiculturalism validates the victimhood of virtually every out-group. It is impossible to generate a mass progressive movement on the basis of such a motley coalition: most of the working- and lower-middle-class citizens victimized by the system are culturally conservative and

would be embarrassed to be seen in the presence of allies like this.[42]

A Democratic Party disconnected from its working-class base, for example, could more easily support NAFTA, free trade, and other measures of globalization. Larry Bartels notes that, historically, income growth has occurred when Democrats are in power, while economic inequality has grown with Republicans at the helm. The incomes of middle-class families, he observes, have grown twice as fast under Democratic rule, while the incomes of the working poor have grown six times as fast. Yet voters are remarkably myopic, unaware of these trends and overly responsive to short-term economic trends and, oddly, income growth among top wage earners. If we are looking for a culprit for greater economic inequality and income stagnation, the scene of the crime is covered with the fingerprints of working- and middle-class wage earners.

"One of the most puzzling features of the world in the aftermath of the financial crisis is that so far," Francis Fukuyama writes, "populism has taken primarily a right-wing form, not a left-wing one."[43] Occupy Wall Street is an exception, but it pales in comparison to the larger, more vibrant, and more impactful Tea Party. One might fairly note that the Tea Party is not truly a grassroots movement and that it has been supported by Fox News and with Koch brothers' financial backing, but this only proves the point that conservatives have been more successful in building their ideological infrastructure and appealing to working- and middle-class voters. What is curious is that the angst that drives Tea Party supporters is not fundamentally different from the underlying motivations of the Occupy Wall Street movement. Both are rooted in perceptions that the playing field is no longer level and a deep discontent with a political system that is inadequate to the task of representing their interests and concerns.

One of the ironies of the Tea Party is that its demands—tax cuts, spending cuts, and smaller government—are incongruent with addressing middle-class decline caused by technological innovation and globalization. These inconsistencies are perhaps best captured by the signs demanding "Government, Keep Your Hands of My Medicare."[44] More importantly, they lead to a fairly pessimistic assessment of the future. As Francis Fukuyama concludes, "Indeed, there are a lot of reasons to think that inequality will continue to worsen. The current concentration of wealth in the United States has already become self-reinforcing: as the economist Simon Johnson has argued, the financial sector has used its lobbying clout to avoid more onerous forms of regulation. Schools for the well-off are better than ever; those for everyone else continue to deteriorate. Elites in all societies use their superior access to the political system to protect their interests, absent a countervailing democratic mobilization to rectify the situation. American elites are no exception to the rule."

Absent some fundamental change, middle-class decline is likely to continue, with profound implications for democratic governance.

WHY A VIBRANT MIDDLE CLASS IS CRITICAL TO DEMOCRACY

The link between a middle class and democracy was noted first by Aristotle, who observed that the middle class "is least likely to shrink from rule, or to be over-ambitious for it." The wealthier classes, Aristotle argued, would be too unwilling to submit to authority, while the poorer classes would be too obedient. As Aristotle concludes,

> Thus it is manifest that the best political community is formed by citizens of the middle class, and that those states are likely to be well-administered in which the middle class is large, and stronger if possible than both the other classes, or at any rate than either singly; for the addition of the middle class turns the scale, and prevents either of the extremes from being dominant. Great then is the good fortune of a state in which the

citizens have a moderate and sufficient property; for where some possess much, and the others nothing, there may arise an extreme democracy, or a pure oligarchy; or a tyranny may grow out of either extreme—either out of the most rampant democracy, or out of an oligarchy; but it is not so likely to arise out of the middle constitutions and those akin to them. [45]

As with political culture, the strong middle class in the United States has served to forestall the growth and development of communist parties and created the conditions necessary for democratic governance and growth. [46] Whereas the lower classes might succumb to authoritarian leaders and the upper classes might tend toward oligarchy, the middle class serves as a moderating and stabilizing influence by penalizing extremist political parties and viewpoints. Seen in this light, the decline of the middle class is not simply puzzling from an economic perspective—it also presents a fundamental challenge to democratic governance. As Supreme Court justice Louis Brandeis once observed, "We may live in a democracy, or we may have wealth concentrated in the hands of a few, but we can't have both."

In *Critical Elections and the Mainsprings of American Politics*, political scientist Walter Dean Burnham articulated a theory of realignment that serves as an apt description of the current political and economic context. [47] A political system built around the idea of incremental change, Burnham argued, cannot keep pace with broader social and economic shifts. The result is normal politics in which policy changes are small and incremental, occasionally punctuated by critical periods, marked by crisis and disruption, in which the political system realigns and catches up with socioeconomic shifts.

The contemporary American political system continues to function as if the economic system were not increasingly strained by technological change, globalization, deindustrialization, and rising inequality. The Great Recession failed to fundamentally realign the political structure. Indeed, the recovery did more to confirm rather than challenge existing patterns of income inequality, as the wealthy recovered while the middle and working classes continue to struggle. As a result, we continue to trend slowly and inevitably toward crisis.

What is perhaps most distressing is that the crisis is almost entirely of our own making.

NOTES

1. "'You Didn't Build That': A Theme Out of Context," *CNN*, September 1, 2012, http://www.cnn.com/2012/08/31/politics/fact-check-built-this/index.html (accessed May 23, 2013).

2. Alexis de Tocqueville, *Democracy in America* (Saunders and Otley, 1835).

3. Louis Hartz, *The Liberal Tradition in America* (New York: Harcourt, Brace & World, 1955).

4. Quoted in Martin P. Wattenberg, *The Decline of American Political Parties, 1952–1996* (Cambridge, MA: Harvard University Press, 1996), 51.

5. James Taranto, "Heritage Rewrites History," *Wall Street Journal*, February 8, 2012.

6. Jason Cherkis, "Paul Ryan: 'We Should Not Shy Away From Class Warfare,'" *Huffington Post*, October 5, 2012, http://www.huffingtonpost.com/2012/10/05/paul-ryan-class-warfare_n_1942639.html (accessed May 23, 2013).

7. Jason DeParle, "Harder for Americans to Rise From Lower Rungs," *New York Times*, January 4, 2012, http://www.nytimes.com/2012/01/05/us/harder-for-americans-to-rise-from-lower-rungs.html?_r=0.

8. "Pursuing the American Dream: Economic Mobility Across Generations," *Economic Mobility Project—Pew Center for the States,* July 2012, http://www.pewstates.org/projects/economic-mobility-project-328061.

9. Joseph Ferrie, "The End of American Exceptionalism? Mobility in the U.S. since 1850," unpublished manuscript, 2005, http://faculty.wcas.northwestern.edu/~fe2r/papers/Exceptionalism.pdf.

10. Data are taken from Facundo Alvaredo, Anthony B. Atkinson, Thomas Piketty, and Emmanuel Saez, *The World Top Incomes Data-*

base, http://g-mond.parisschoolofeconomics.eu/topincomes (accessed October 16, 2012).

11. Economic Policy Institute, *The State of Working America*, http://stateofworkingamerica.org (accessed May 24, 2013).

12. Alan Dunn, "Average America v. the One Percent," *Forbes*, March 21, 2012, http://www.forbes.com/sites/moneywisewomen/2012/03/21/average-america-vs-the-one-percent/ (accessed May 23, 2013).

13. Economic Policy Institute, *The State of Working America*, http://stateofworkingamerica.org (accessed May 23, 2013).

14. As discussed in Paul Krugman, "How Fares the Dream," *New York Times*, January 15, 2012, http://www.nytimes.com/2012/01/16/opinion/krugman-how-fares-the-dream.html?_r=0 (accessed May 23, 2013).

15. Joseph Stiglitz, *The Price of Inequality: How Today's Divided Society Endangers Our Future* (New York: W. W. Norton, 2012), xix.

16. Larry Bartels, *Unequal Democracy: The Political Economy of the New Gilded Age* (Princeton, NJ: Princeton University Press, 2008); Martin Gilens, *Affluence and Influence: Economic Inequality and Political Power in America* (Princeton, NJ: Princeton University Press, 2012).

17. Kay Lehman Schlozman, Sidney Verba, and Henry Brady, *The Unheavenly Chorus: Unequal Political Voice and the Broken Promise of American Democracy* (Princeton, NJ: Princeton University Press, 2012).

18. C. Wright Mills, *The Power Elite* (New York: Oxford University Press, 1956).

19. Georg Lukacs, *History and Class Consciousness* (London: Merlin Press, 1967), originally written in 1920.

20. Jacob Hacker and Paul Pierson, *Winner-Take-All Politics* (New York: Simon & Schuster, 2010).

21. It would, of course, be a mistake to say that labor unions have lost all influence. They remain an important and influential player in contemporary politics, but historically their relative importance has unquestionably declined.

22. In fairness, one may argue that unions do not fairly or accurately represent working-class interests. But this proves the point, for if unions aren't representing these interests, who is?

23. Based on data from the American National Election Study. Including partisan leaners, the decline is from 56 percent in 1952 to 49

percent in 1972 to 43 percent in 2008. See http://www.electionstudies. org/studypages/cdf/cdf.htm (accessed May 24, 2013).

24. Tali Mendelberg, *The Race Card: Campaign Strategy, Implicit Messages, and the Norm of Equality* (Princeton, NJ: Princeton University Press, 2001).

25. Donald Kinder and Allison Dale-Riddle, *The End of Race? Obama, 2008, and Racial Politics in America* (New Haven, CT: Yale University Press, 2012).

26. Michael Tesler, "The Spillover of Racialization into Health Care: How President Obama Polarized Public Opinion by Racial Attitudes and Race," unpublished paper, http://mst.michaeltesler.com/uploads/ ajps11full.pdf (accessed May 23, 2013).

27. Hacker and Pierson, *Winner-Take-All Politics*, 149.

28. Tim Cohen, "Romney's Big Day Marred by Etch a Sketch Remark," *CNN Politics*, March 21, 2012, http://articles.cnn.com/2012-03-21/politics/politics_campaign-wrap_1_mitt-romney-eric-fehrnstrom-general-election?_s=PM:POLITICS (accessed May 23, 2013).

29. Joseph Stiglitz, *The Price of Inequality*, 146.

30. The tendency toward authoritarianism within the working class identified by Seymour Martin Lipset in 1959 recognized the preference for simple solutions to complex political problems. See Seymour Martin Lipset, *Political Man: The Social Bases of Politics* (Garden City, NY: Doubleday, 1960).

31. Jonathan Haidt, *The Righteous Mind*.

32. Jacob Hacker and Paul Pierson use this phrase in *Winner-Take-All Politics*.

33. Joseph Stiglitz, *The Price of Inequality*, 148.

34. Ibid.

35. Howard Kurtz, *Spin Cycle: Inside the Clinton Propaganda Machine* (New York: Free Press, 1998).

36. Ben Fritz, Bryan Keefer, and Brendan Nyhan, *All the President's Spin: George W. Bush, the Media, and the Truth* (New York: Touchstone, 2004).

37. As I argue in the next chapter, a partisan press is not necessarily a bad thing, but much of the "fact-checking" operates under the guise of objectivity.

38. Thomas Edsall, "Political Dividends," *New York Times*, March 26, 2012, http://campaignstops.blogs.nytimes.com/2012/05/26/political-dividends/ (accessed May 23, 2013).

39. Robert Kaiser, *So Damn Much Money: The Triumph of Lobbying and the Corrosion of American Government* (New York: Vintage Books, 2009), 23.

40. Martin Gilens, *Affluence and Influence*, 197.

41. Andrew Gelman, "The Small But Important Group of Super-Rich Funders of the Democratic Party," *The Monkey Cage*, May 26, 2012, http://themonkeycage.org/blog/2012/05/26/the-small-but-important-group-of-super-rich-funders-of-the-democratic-party/.

42. Francis Fukuyama, "The Future of History: Can Liberal Democracy Survive the Decline of the Middle Class?" *Foreign Affairs* (January/February 2012), http://www.foreignaffairs.com/articles/136782/francis-fukuyama/the-future-of-history (accessed May 24, 2013).

43. Ibid.

44. In the most comprehensive assessment to date, political scientists Theda Skocpol and Vanessa Williams find that Tea Party activists are generally supportive of social security and Medicare but opposed to "big government" spending for "underserving" populations. Theda Skocpol and Vanessa Williams, *The Tea Party and the Remaking of Republican Conservatism* (New York: Oxford University Press, 2012).

45. Aristotle, *Politics*, XI, http://www.fordham.edu/Halsall/ancient/aristotle-politics.txt.

46. Seymour Lipset, *Political Man*.

47. Walter Dean Burnham, *Critical Elections and the Mainsprings of American Politics* (New York: W. W. Norton, 1970).

4

THE NEWS MEDIA, NEW MEDIA, AND DEMOCRACY

In the HBO series *The Newsroom*, Jeff Daniels plays television news anchor William McAvoy: a man born in the spirit of Edward R. Murrow, committed to overcoming the commercial pressures of audience ratings to produce a high-quality news product. He is journalism's fictional Saint Paul, resurrected on the road to corporate ratings and a conventional but uninteresting nightly news program.

Created by Aaron Sorkin, the creator of *The West Wing*, the show returns to a familiar theme. In *The West Wing*, President Josiah Bartlett rediscovered his inner progressive to battle against special interests, conservative and entrenched politicians, and politics as usual. In *The Newsroom*, the hero is the television news anchor, reinvigorated with the courage to speak truth to power; call out politicians who oversimplify, mislead, and manipulate the public; and consequently create a stronger and healthier democracy. The underlying assumption is that better news can create a better (read: more progressive) polity, as if the only thing separating the United States from Sweden is a better educated and more informed public.

One need only consider the success of Fox News to understand why *The Newsroom* is fiction. Consumers want news that conforms to their values and that places information in the context of what they already believe.[1] Conservatives find soft comfort in the "fair and balanced" coverage of Fox News, while liberals increasingly turn to MSNBC and Rachel Maddow, the left wing's answer to Sean Hannity, or even to Jon Stewart and Stephen Colbert on Comedy Central. Selective exposure may lead to confirmatory news, but new grazers, those viewers who watch the news with the remote in hand, learn less about politics and are more likely to stop grazing when sensational news stories are aired.[2]

The problems inherent in this narrative of the journalist as democracy's savior, however, run much deeper than an increasingly partisan news media, reflecting a model of the news media that is no longer congruent with the contemporary information environment and is based on a serious misreading of human psychology.

Journalism cannot save democracy. It should not even try.

THE NEWS MEDIA IN JOURNALISM SCHOOLS

For the past ten years, I have worked as a political scientist in a journalism school. Disciplinary differences are mostly small but are often pronounced when it comes to the role of journalism in a democratic society. Journalism faculty and administrators, a collective of former news reporters and editors, generally subscribe to a "social responsibility model" of the press in which democracy is equated with information, which, in turn, is equated with the news. Seen from the lens of the aging demographic of print news reporters, the decline of newspapers is not a story of how technology and economics create new models for delivering information; it is a tragic tale of civic and cultural decay.[3]

For the journalist, journalism is the cornerstone of democratic governance. Thomas Jefferson's well-worn quote is representative of the underlying faith in the power of newspapers to serve as the knowledge base of democratic governance: "Were it left to me to decide whether we should have a government without newspapers or newspapers without a government, I should not hesitate a moment to prefer the latter." Almost entirely ignored or forgotten are other Jefferson quotes, including this statement made during the election of 1800: "The man who reads nothing at all is better educated than the man who reads nothing but newspapers." In a letter written in 1794, Jefferson similarly observed that "I do not take a single newspaper, nor read one a month, and I feel myself infinitely the happier for it." Jefferson may have understood the value of newspapers to democratic governance, but he was also well aware of the shortcomings of news that distorted the truth or propagated rumors and misinformation.

There is a historical misconception at play as well. Jefferson did not live in a time of objective journalism but in an age of a partisan press. Newspapers were inherently elitists, marketed to a relatively small but literate population.[4] It was not until the 1830s that the penny press democratized the news and expanded literacy rates, thus connecting newspapers to democratic governance in important, even revolutionary, ways. Expanded literacy rates and relatively easy access to news made an informed citizenry more than a theoretical possibility. While we often celebrate the "free" press, this radical transformation of the news media was made possible by government subsidies via reduced postage rates, tax breaks, and the publication of public notices.[5] The news, however, never matched the democratic ideal of being informative and enlightening. Indeed, the newspapers went from being substantive and partisan to highly sensational, built to attract the largest possible audience for the smallest possible costs. Informing the public took a back seat (as it always has and always will) to the commercial pressures of selling the news.

The *New York Times* and the experiment with objectivity did not begin until 1896, but that was also a market-based strategy aimed at differentiating the *New York Times* from other, more sensational news sources.[6] Approximately a century later, Fox News found its niche as the "fair and balanced" conservative alternative to the mainstream media, not out of ideological conviction, but as a marketing strategy designed to capture an identifiable and disaffected segment of the news audience.

Despite fundamental transformations in how the news is produced and distributed, journalists (and journalism professors) continue to see the news media as playing a central role in democratic governance by creating an informed and engaged citizenry. How else, absent the diligent and objective reporting of journalists, would citizens learn about what is really going on in their government? Watergate, according to this view, is the crowning achievement, the moment when truth won out over the powerful, when the dark crevices of American politics were exposed by democracy's heroes, journalists Bob Woodward and Carl Bernstein. The Watergate investigation stood on the shoulders of earlier progressive muckraking efforts (Lincoln Steffens, Ida Tarbell, Upton Sinclair) at exposing government incompetence and corruption. The journalist, according to this narrative, wasn't simply part of the front line assembling the news as product, but had a higher calling of service to community, nation, and democracy.

Pre-Watergate, the definitive moment was Edward R. Murrow standing up to and calling out Senator Joseph McCarthy for his misuse of power during the Red Scare of the 1950s. Murrow's unique space in American political history defines the myth: if only more journalists would follow the Murrow tradition and aggressively call out politicians when they lie, mislead, or equivocate, democracy would function much more effectively.[7] The fictional Will McAvoy is the latest embodiment of this idealized, but flawed, progressive view of the news. Journalists can be objective observers of the world writing the first draft of history or they can be combatants calling out the powerful, but they cannot be both.

Collectively, the events in the late 1960s and 1970s fundamentally changed the relationship of the news media and government. Prior to Watergate and Vietnam, the news media and presidents shared a relationship of trust. For example, it is well known that the news media knew of, but did not report on, President Kennedy's numerous sexual liaisons. After Watergate, coverage became increasingly negative and interpretive, as journalists strived to be the next Woodward and Bernstein. Journalism changed as a profession as well. The stereotypical journalist, typing in a dark room, drinking whiskey, and fighting for the common man, was replaced by the professional journalist, the upper-middle-class professional journalism school graduate. The result is a journalistic detachment from the interests of the working class. As journalism historian John Nerone observes, "The news industry orphaned the working-class market while it was still profitable. It began by shifting content, eliminating the 'labor beat' and relegating labor reporting to the business page, and avoiding any editorial support of working-class movements. It substituted other forms of 'populist' content, especially crime news, sports, and celebrity gossip, the standard fare of tabloid journalism."[8]

In a separate analysis, Nerone observes that professionalism never quite worked as intended: "Rather than speaking truth to power, professional journalism usually reproduces the voices of the powerful."[9] The result has been a declining trust in both government and the news media. "To the average citizen," former University of California–Berkeley Journalism School dean Neil Henry writes, "a Journalist is the television talker who is paid a considerable retainer to regularly make noise on cable news programs, arguing any question of the day regardless of whether he or she knows anything about the topic or not."[10]

Declining trust in the media is not simply reflective of the loss of journalistic innocence (or perhaps more accurately, government-press collusion) in the post-Watergate era. Georgetown University political scientist Jonathan Ladd points instead to an increasingly polarized political environment and to technological change.[11] A polarized political environment means more partisan criticism of the press as candidates and parties attempt to "work the referees" for favorable news coverage. Technological change likewise increases competition and choice, and subsequently results in more sensational tabloid-style news coverage as news outlets compete for audiences, which, in turn, negatively affects confidence in the news media.

Even if the contemporary political environment were open to a modern-day Edward R. Murrow, it is unlikely that he could have a similar effect. First, the audience for any given news program is considerably smaller. In the 1970s, with limited programming options, approximately half of Americans watched the nightly news. Four decades later that number has declined from 50 percent to 20 percent, with the news audience shrinking and graying every year. Second, news is increasingly seen through a partisan lens. Consistent and systematic partisan bias is more difficult to detect than is commonly believed or acknowledged. Most credible studies of media bias in the mainstream media indicate that identifiable structural biases are rooted more in institutional characteristics than in partisan preferences. As a result, bias is reflected in patterns of coverage that reflect breaking news events, negativity, conflict, and novelty. Big, slow-moving stories like globalization generate less news coverage than breaking events like Superstorm Sandy, even though globalization has more lasting political, social, and economic impacts. One reason citizens are myopic is the constant focus on breaking news and episodic (as opposed to thematic) framing.[12] Political conflict similarly attracts more attention than political compromise. Third, trust in media organizations is not only very low but also declining. In 1976, 72 percent of Americans reported that they had a great deal or fair amount of trust and confidence in the mass media. By 2012, only 40 percent reported a great deal or a fair amount of trust.[13]

If Edward R. Murrow were reborn and dropped into a nightly news program, he would be seen not as an agent of truth but as a partisan, and his efforts to speak truth to power would be heard by a smaller and more polarized audience. At least half his audience would view any pronouncement as driven by partisan bias and not by an unwavering commitment to truth. In short, it is not the absence of journalists willing to speak out that plagues the news industry—it is much larger changes in the information environment. If we think of the information environment as an ecosystem, it is not the marine life that is different; rather, the entire sea has changed.

THE NEWS MEDIA IN A POLITICAL CONTEXT

The news media are one of a number of important political institutions, no more (or less) important as a provider of information than political parties, political candidates, interest groups, or any other source of news and information. Institutional characteristics (e.g., competitive elections and political parties) matter as well.

The news as a product is the result of a careful negotiation between political actors (e.g., the president and opposition party leaders) and reporters.[14] Political actors control access to information, while the news media play an institutional role in governance, serving as an informational conduit allowing political actors and institutions to communicate with each other and as a platform for announcing governing decisions. If President Obama announces a shift in administrative policy, for example, the news media are not simply reporting on the decision; the actual decision is occurring via the press conference or the breaking news story. The news media as a political institution are an intractable part of governing. The late Timothy Cook termed this the "negotiation of newsworthiness," which describes a subtle (or not-so-subtle) dance played out by reporters and politicians to set the political agenda on favorable topics and issues and to define the frames around which news stories are told. The quaint but naïve idea that the public officials would act and journalists would write the news story explaining the who, what, when, where, and why never reflected the reality of how news was actually produced.

Journalists do not write news stories in a political vacuum. Nor are they, as is commonly believed, free of political control. First, government subsidizes the production of news by providing easy access to information, prepackaged news content (press releases and video news releases), and established routines that make the news easier and cheaper to cover.[15] Second, reliance on official sources constrains the content of news stories in important ways. Washington University political scientist Lance Bennett observes that, largely due to news-gathering norms and routines, news stories are indexed to the range of governmental debate.[16] In the prelude to the Iraq War, the absence of Democratic opposition meant that news coverage largely adopted the justifications, evidence, and spin provided by the Bush administration.[17] Reporters who raised questions were stripped of their access to high-ranking officials and were accused of being biased and unpatriotic by talk radio and Fox News commentators.

Journalistic norms and values also constrain the content of news stories. Journalist Chris Mooney and science communication scholar Matthew Nisbet have written independently and in tandem about the "false balancing" journalists engage in when covering science-related news stories. First, the decision to cover science-related news as controversy affects how audiences interpret the meaning of the news.[18] Read a news story on climate change, embryonic stem cell research, or evolution, for example, and you might believe the scientific evidence is in dispute surrounding any (or all) of these issues. In reality, there is an overwhelming scientific consensus that climate change is occurring, that embryonic stem cell research holds greater medical potential than adult stem cell research, and that evolution is not only occurring but also the single best explanation for the origin of the human species. Traditional journalistic norms of fairness, however, constrain reporters from pointing out that one side of the "controversy" is supported by the balance of scientific evidence, while the other side is not. When reporters stray outside of norms for "balanced" coverage, they are often accused of bias in their reporting.

The extension from science to policy news is quite straightforward. As University of Pennsylvania Wharton School economist Justin Wolfers, writing for the Freakonomics blog, explains, "If you follow the economic policy debate in the popular press, you would be excused for missing one of our best-kept secrets: There's remarkable agreement among economists on most policy questions. Unfortunately, this consensus remains obscured by the two laws of punditry: First, for any issue, there's always at least one idiot willing to claim the spotlight to argue for it; and second, that idiot may sound more respectable if he calls himself an economist."[19]

The effects of controversial economic policies, like the Obama administration economic stimulus plan and the bank bailout, are not particularly controversial among economists. They largely succeeded in reducing unemployment and averting a larger economic collapse. Reading economic news coverage, however, one might mistakenly believe there is a real debate over the economic consequence of the stimulus package or the bailout. "The disjuncture between the political debate about economics and the consensus of economists," Wolfers believes, is larger today than ever before.

When policy is in dispute, journalists treat the two opposing sides as though they were equal even when the evidence is not in dispute. Smart politicians (and most are far smarter than we give them credit for) use this journalistic norm to dispute the fairness of coverage or to present distorted and/or politicized evidence. More generally, they incorporate journalism's norms and routines into their press strategies to spin the news in favorable directions. Public perceptions of news media bias, for example, are less connected to any actual change in news content than to an increase in elite claims of bias.[20]

In the negotiation of newsworthiness, technological change has empowered political actors (as well as other sources) relative to the news media. The widespread adoption and use of social media allows for instantaneous dissemination of messages without editorial gatekeepers or journalistic filters. The news media remain important but are less so when a politician or interest group can communicate directly with supporters and followers and, in so doing, directly control the agenda and framing of the message. In Louisiana, Governor Bobby Jindal's 2011 campaign followed what is becoming the Republican playbook: strictly limit access to the campaign, exert tight control over messaging, and allow reporters only in heavily managed campaign events. Journalists recoil, but, hungry for access, they generally play by the rules set down by the administration.

Tom Jensen of Public Policy Polling (PPP) places the issue in a slightly different perspective: "Perhaps 10 or 20 years ago it would have been a real problem for PPP if our numbers didn't get run in the Washington Post but the fact of the matter is people who want to know what the polls are saying are finding out just fine. Every time we've put out a Virginia primary poll we've had three or four days worth of explosion in traffic to both our blog and our main website."[21]

From the perspective of the political actor, the question is fairly simple: Why let the journalist tell your story when you can tell it yourself? Why let a gatekeeper filter the news when the gates are wide open and no filter is required? Journalists may long for the "authentic" politician, but political consultants realized long ago that the risk of an unscripted politician committing a gaffe is far greater than any potential benefit of a positive relationship with the press corps. John McCain, for example, learned the hard way that the goodwill he built by being a maverick Republican on the "straight talk express" in 2000 dissipated when he became the Republican nominee in 2008. The news media may love an outsider willing to criticize and challenge his own party, but that love fades quickly when the maverick becomes the candidate. He re-learned the lesson when he nominated Sarah Palin in 2008, who often went rogue, meaning she went off-script, exposing her vulnerability as a candidate with limited foreign policy expertise or knowledge.

Political actors are further empowered by a partisan news environment that allows more choice in granting access to favored media organizations and reporters. If you are a conservative Republican, why go on MSNBC if you have the option to go on Fox? If you worry that mainstream news organizations will ask tough questions, go on "soft" news programs like *The View* or *The Daily Show*. This occasionally backfires (e.g., see the Katie Couric interview of Sarah Palin), but it is generally an effective strategy for affecting the tone and frame of news coverage and for appealing to less attentive voters.[22] News organizations with an ideological bent can become even more so as politicians strategically opt into (or out of) news stories.

The transformation of the broader information environment and the empowerment of political sources relative to journalists are troubling signs for journalists and editors wedded to a dated "public representative" model of the news. Journalists less wedded to a 1970s model have discovered freedom from news organizations, while independent bloggers who can attract an audience have found media organizations are more than willing to trade journalistic norms for audience. Perhaps the biggest winner of the 2012 elections—other than President Barack Obama—was Nate Silver, a sports statistician turned political statistician turned blogger turned celebrity. Estimates are that Silver's Five-Thirty-Eight blog generated 20 percent of the total traffic to the *New York Times* during the days immediately preceding the 2012 election.[23] Silver's appeal on the *New York Times* is perhaps a bit ironic, as he offered something too often missing from contemporary journalism, including the *New York Times*: analysis based not on insider knowledge and punditry, but on data and evidence. Or perhaps, stated differently, a truly objective evaluation of where the campaign stood at any given moment, free of insider knowledge and spin.

New media organizations—like *Politico*, *Salon*, *Real Clear Politics*, and the *Huffington Post*—have similarly found ways to use online platforms to create informative and profitable news organizations. There may not be a textbook business model for running a successful online news organization, but nimble news organizations are adapting and evolving. The *Drudge Report* similarly and infamously scooped *Newsweek* in first reporting on the Clinton-Lewinsky affair in January 1998, making Matt Drudge a household name and raising ethical issues about the ability and willingness of news organizations to double check their sources in an age of digital journalism.[24] Ethical questions notwithstanding, the Internet made it possible for Matt Drudge to become a leading source of political news and gossip, even if his news stories were routinely off the mark. While political insiders and journalists are often critical of the *Drudge Report*, they routinely check the site. Less controversial and more informative sites, like Taegan Goddard's *Political Wire* or Mike Allen's *Politico Playbook*, have developed as well by filling a niche in the online market space.

Broadly speaking, the crisis confronting journalism is not a crisis of information. Information is plentiful and can travel as quickly as news stories can be written, far more quickly and more efficiently than a newspaper can be delivered or a television newscast can be produced. By the time the folded newspaper hits the front step, the headline is old news. No, the real crisis is an economic crisis rooted in a business model that is unsustainable in a digital age. How do you pay for the creation of content? For those who believe journalism can save democracy, this serves as an important reminder that news organizations exist not to inform the public but to sell the news. The crisis confronting journalism is likewise only secondarily and indirectly a crisis of democratic governance. It is first and foremost a crisis of economics, defined in terms of declining audience and dwindling audience share for traditional news organizations. Information is the currency of democracy, and the news media are only one potential provider in an increasingly competitive marketplace.

THE FUTURE OF NEWS (OR LEARNING TO LOVE THE PARTISAN PRESS)

The past decade has witnessed a radical transformation of not only the news industry but also the broader media environment. The growth of digital media exponentially expanded the availability and choice of content, creating a more polarized news environment. This politicization of the news media, created first by talk radio in the 1990s and then by the ascendance of Fox News, undermined a central pillar of the objective journalism pioneered by the *New York Times* and Adolph Ochs in 1896, which has defined core journalistic values for nearly a century. Today, "fair and balanced" is little more than a marketing slogan aimed at conservative voters who perceive bias in the mainstream media. Occupying the "fair and balanced" niche allows Fox News to be neither while claiming to balance out mainstream news channels and CNN. But make no mistake, both "fair and balanced" and "all the news that's fit to print" were first and foremost market-based decisions. Objectivity was valued for its potential to attract larger audiences and greater advertising revenues. Any sort of democratic implications finished a distant second.[25] Objectivity has been abandoned for the same reason. It no longer fills the needs of a marketplace driven by developing and sustaining niche markets.

Decisions by *Time* magazine and other print media to move to an online-only or limited print schedule are similarly rooted in market-based considerations—declining circulations and advertising revenues—as consumers find cheaper and more timely information online. Why read the local paper when a quick Google search can provide information more efficiently and on topics that are more personally relevant? Why scan the classified ads when Craigslist is available and provides a more user-friendly search function and real-time updating?

The ascendance of digital media over print has also fundamentally altered what it means to report the news. Information is instantaneous and overflowing. Filtering and making sense of the information deluge is the challenge. Comedians like Jon Stewart and Stephen Colbert become politically poignant in this environment because citizens do not need more or better information; they need perspective, interpretation, and guidance. The mainstream media has struggled with the balance between core but outdated values and a digital media environment in which information can be more cheaply and effectively communicated via Twitter and blogs than on the printed page delivered on neighborhood doorsteps or through news stories. In confronting the challenge, most news organizations followed exactly the wrong economic model, opting for generic wire service content, increasing prices in response to declining demand, and focusing on national politics instead of providing consumers with unique local voices and perspectives. Most daily newspapers are filled with content that can be easily found elsewhere.

News organizations may not have been entirely to blame. Economist James Hamilton argues that profit-driven news media have little incentive to produce quality news. "Those making efforts to improve media markets need to recognize that news emerges not from individuals seeking to improve the functioning of democracy but from readers seeking diversion, reporters forging careers, and owners searching for profits."[26] A low-quality news product, Hamilton contends, is a predictable result of profit-driven news media. Louisiana State University political scientist Johanna Dunaway similarly reports that corporate ownership of newspapers and local market pressures lead to less issue coverage and, subsequently, a lower-quality news product.[27] News organizations, however, are culpable for failing to recognize and adapt to the end of an era defined by news products sold to mass audiences. Marketer, author, and entrepreneur Seth Godin describes the end of the mass market this way: "The defining idea of the twentieth century, more than any other, was mass. Mass gave us efficiency and productivity, making us (some people) rich. Mass gave us huge nations, giving us (some people) power. Mass allowed powerful people to influence millions, giving us (some people) control. And now mass is dying."[28]

For Godin, the end of mass marketing is liberating, as it frees companies to stop focusing on the average and to become truly exceptional. There is a direct parallel to news organizations. During the broadcast era, the news media focused on a mass audience, while political campaigns zeroed in on the median voter. The objective content of the news, driven by well-established professional values, was written so as not to offend or mobilize or persuade. In today's media market, this is a failed—and failing—strategy, as the mass market has been replaced by the niche market.

Princeton University political science professor Markus Prior has provided the most exhaustive and sophisticated examination to date of what the transformations in media choice mean for democratic governance.[29] He concludes that greater choice in content leads to greater inequality in political involvement and to greater political polarization. Citizens who used to watch the nightly news because they had limited options now watch entertainment programming. Neil Postman's *Amusing Ourselves to Death*, written for a broadcast age, proves even more prescient in a digital age in which entertainment options are virtually unlimited.[30] In the "brave new world" of digital media, democracy is not taken from us by force but is given away so that we can watch episodes of *American Idol* and *Toddlers & Tiaras* on Netflix. We are the frog, unaware but slowly coming to a boil in a large pot of cool water.

Before Postman, Marshall McLuhan famously declared "the medium is the message," a recognition that television fundamentally changed the way we perceived the world. Linear rational thought is best captured and reflected in the printed word rather than in the cascading images brought to life through more visual media.[31] It was print that made the Enlightenment, faith in reason, free markets, and democracy possible. For McLuhan, the world of images created by television would bring us closer together, connecting us in a global village. His insights into the future proved less reliable than his recognition of the importance of the medium relative to content. It is not just the news and information we consume but also the way we consume it that matters. Reading a newspaper is different from watching the same story on a television screen, which likewise differs from viewing the content online. Across each medium, we process information differently with different consequences for what we retain and how we are affected.

For Postman, television amused but did not inform. The nightly news became entertainment, scoring low on information and high on the dramatic and the sensational. Vice President Al Gore, that rarest of political species—the popular vote winner, yet Electoral College loser—concurred in *The Assault on Reason*, calling television "a distracting and absorbing medium that seems determined to entertain and sell more than it informs and educates."[32] Gore's hope was that the Internet, open to direct communication and the pursuit of truth, could reinvigorate democratic governance by re-creating a "well-connected citizenry." His mistake was to believe that the citizenry was ever "well-connected." The period of the American founding was deeply substantive, but highly elitist. The golden age of political parties was highly participatory, but crass and corrupt. The highly engaged citizen was mobilized not to engage in democracy for democracy's sake, but rather to partake of the partisan spoils. The Progressive reforms were aimed at eliminating these abuses, but in the process they effectively limited mass participation.

The Internet did, indeed, change everything, though like many technological revolutions, the transformations did not occur over night. Text-based information might have been readily available in the early 1990s thanks to new technologies like Gopher, but it was not until html browsers became easier to use and share visual information that the web became heavily populated. With information instantly available and the ability to interact directly with the media and politicians, many observers envisioned a reinvigorated participatory democracy.

Information alone, however, was never enough. The rapid growth of the Internet occurred only after users learned to exploit the technologies for commercial purposes. Perhaps more troubling from the standpoint of democratic theory, greater opportunities to participate expanded the involvement of those already engaged, while greater entertainment options distracted the less informed and less engaged. As Markus Prior astutely observed, the politically involved found a wealth of information, while the politically disengaged surfed for the Web for entertainment and distraction.

Media scholars have subsequently rediscovered Postman and McLuhan, whose insights seem even more applicable to the digital age than the television age in which they wrote. Does the nature in which we consume information in the digital age affect the way we think, separate and independent from the content we consume? Nicolas Carr, author of *The Shallows: What the Internet Is Doing to Our Brains*, argues that digital information has shortened our attention span and reduced our ability to think with real depth and reflection.[33] Google, Carr famously declared, is making us stupid. If the printing press made our thinking linear and rational, if television focused our attention on visual imagery and distracted us from democratic governance, the Internet has given us a collective case of attention deficit disorder.

Carr's critics note correctly that the impact of the Internet on intelligence is not so easily discernible, nor does the balance of evidence clearly line up on the negative side of the intelligence ledger. The Internet may hurt memory even while it improves our analytical skills, for we may be able to more quickly evaluate information despite our memory becoming increasingly fragile. Carr himself has backed off the "stupid" claim, but he maintains that the nature of the medium changes the way we think about the world. Instead of a deep and reflective intelligence, we are increasingly utilitarian in our search for information and increasingly impatient when information is not immediately at our fingertips. When download times slow, we move on quickly to the next website. Regardless, there can be little doubt that technology has transformed us, affecting us in ways we are not yet ready to fully understand or appreciate.

Here, Markus Prior's work on the content of online communications is particularly important. In allowing greater choice, the Internet encourages confirmation biases, the focus on news and information we already agree with, and reasoning for argumentation rather than truth seeking. Virtually any misguided belief can be confirmed on a website or blog. The result of these choices made over time is an increasingly partisan and polarized information environment, as liberals gravitate to liberal news sources and conservatives to conservative news sources. It also furthers the inherent biases of pluralistic democracy. By opening up more channels for political influence, it increases the influence of the active and the engaged, while the voices of the apathetic, the ambivalent, and the moderate are reduced to a low murmur barely audible in a noisy information environment.

Whether such changes are intrinsically good or bad for the political system is an empirical question. Why, for example, should "objective" information from the *New York Times* be preferred to a partisan statement from the Republican National Committee? On the basis of democratic theory, one might argue that objective news allows citizens to carefully weigh and evaluate new information, thus updating their beliefs with "real-world" data. Yet we already know this is not how people process information. They are not Bayesian statisticians. An identifiably partisan statement, in contrast, contains important cues that can help the reader or viewer decode the meaning of the news and place it within the context of their existing beliefs and values. From the standpoint of cognitive psychology, the partisan statement contains more useful information and can be processed more efficiently and effectively.[34] Recent research has found that the value of "neutral" political news may be overstated, as "biased" stories may, in fact, provide more substantive content.[35]

At the aggregate level, a partisan press may do more to engage and mobilize voters even if it misinforms. Studies of Fox News viewers, for example, find that they are more likely to believe Saddam Hussein was directly involved in the 9/11 terrorist attacks and are less likely to believe in the science documenting evidence of climate change or to correctly identify the provisions of the Obama administration's health care reform.[36] On important issues of the day, they are more likely to be misinformed in ways that are predictable, given the content of Fox News programming. Exposure to like-minded news sources, however, increases participation in campaign activities.[37] For better or worse, misinformation is not a deterrent to political involvement.

University of Pennsylvania political scientist Diana Mutz describes this as a central paradox of democratic governance: we can have participatory democracy or deliberative democracy, but not both.[38] Which is to say, the path to mobilizing, exciting, and engaging larger numbers of citizens to participate politically diverges significantly and incompatibly from a path toward a high-minded and deliberative discussion of policies and ideas. In advancing his thesis that Americans in the television age were "amusing themselves to death," Neil Postman pointed appreciatively to the richness of the Lincoln-Douglas debates, three-hour long contests in which the candidates spoke at sixty- or ninety-minute intervals about the great issue of the day: slavery. Subsequent research has done much to debunk the mythology surrounding these debates. The audience was mobilized into attendance by party machines, paid little attention to speakers they could not hear, and attended more for the spectacle than for the substance.[39] The high-minded and substantive rhetoric of Lincoln and Douglas also included personal attacks, demagoguery, and grandstanding. The debates were more than mere political theater, but it is a mistake to believe that theatrics were missing or that a mass audience was there simply to listen to the great oratory.[40]

The larger picture is this: First, no media system is ideal. Indeed, the way that news is produced and disseminated contains inherent tradeoffs. News media created to engage an audience looks very different from news media created to inform. Second, media systems are not static but constantly evolving and changing as media organizations search for audience and revenue using the best available tools. Greater choice means more media outlets are competing for the attention of dwindling audiences. The clearest implication, seen in the development of Fox News and its careful cultivation of the conservative news audience, is that the era of the mass news audience is over (at least in the short term). Attracting a loyal but segmented news audience is more effective in the current environment than creating objective content for the average news consumer. A related implication is that other hard news sources will be increasingly specialized and targeted to elite news audiences.

WHY THE PRESS FAILS

This returns us to our opening theme: journalism cannot save democracy. This is not the fault of journalists working to inform the public, but rather of a public that opts to be uninformed (and misinformed) about candidates, policy, and politics. Journalism's failure results from hubris, a misguided belief that journalists should play an important role as arbiters of the truth rather than as producers of information for defined markets. As noted earlier, during the Iraq War, many on the left criticized the news media for not being aggressive enough in uncovering the truth behind

the Bush administration's motives to go to war. This failure, however, was not the fault of the news media alone, but also of the
Democratic Party, which neglected to offer a compelling counter-
narrative.

Writing at the dawn of the digital age, Harvard political scientist Thomas Patterson captured much of the malaise of contemporary media-centered politics before it fully set in. Our political
system, he argued, relies too much on the news media to structure
political campaigns. It is a task they are ill suited for and, subsequently, perform poorly.[41] Presidential nominating contests, for
example, are a historical accident, wrought upon us by the unintended consequences of the 1968 Democratic Convention and
perpetuated—despite obvious and persistent flaws—because of
the economic benefits they accrue to a limited number of states
and localities. While journalists and pundits often laud the serious-
ness of Iowa and New Hampshire voters, there is no logical reason
these states should have "first in the nation" status. Perhaps stated
even more bluntly, no rational human being would have designed
the system we have for selecting major party presidential nominees.

Nor is there any reason for spending more than two years to
elect a president. The absurdity of the process was well illustrated
in 2012 when Minnesota governor Timothy Pawlenty, thought to
be an early contender, dropped out of the Republican primary
contests after a straw poll and before the first delegate was selected or the first real vote was cast. Herman Cain, by contrast,
was almost entirely built up and then destroyed by news coverage
that first lauded him for his novelty, earnestness, and difference,
and, having built him up, subsequently subjected him to the type
of serious scrutiny that undermines the presidential campaigns of
politically inexperienced candidates.

Louisiana governor Bobby Jindal, who has pinned his national
ambitions clearly and visibly on his sleeve, offered a Republican
postmortem to *Politico* less than a week after the 2012 election in
which he said Republicans needed to end "dumbed down conservatism" to become, once again, the party of ideas.[42] Like other

2016 contenders, he is beginning the process of positioning himself for a 2016 presidential run. The news media began its speculation on 2016 contenders within twenty-four hours of the final vote.

According to Patterson, the length of the campaign season means issues are old news to the news media before most of the public is even paying attention. Subsequently, campaign coverage tends to focus on campaign strategy and the horse race as the campaign season extends into its later months.[43] Coverage is also increasingly negative in tone. According to a content analysis conducted by the Pew Research Center's Project for Excellence in Journalism, mainstream news coverage in 2012 for both Barack Obama and Mitt Romney was mostly negative. While President Obama had a relative advantage in terms of receiving less negative coverage, that advantage was rooted in horse race–related coverage and disappeared after Mitt Romney's victory during the first debate.[44] Indeed, if there is any pronounced and systematic bias in news coverage, it is based less on partisanship than on what Patterson terms the "strategic game" narrative, in which every action is interpreted in the context of campaign strategy and negativity. As Patterson notes, the news media occupies an untenable position in American politics: they are asked to remain neutral and objective in their coverage, while also being called upon to interject themselves Edward R. Murrow–style into the campaign as arbiters of truth and fact. They cannot help but fail.

Reactions to the 2012 presidential debates illustrate the dilemma for news organizations and journalists. When President Barack Obama lost decisively in the first debate, many liberals criticized Jim Lehrer for letting the debate spin out of control and for letting Mitt Romney's factual statements go unchecked. Mitt Romney was able to move decisively to the center during the first debate without anyone effectively calling him out for shifting positions. In the second debate, CNN moderator Candy Crowley played a more aggressive role in moderating, earning the ire of conservatives for siding with President Obama on whether he called the embassy attacks in Benghazi "an act of terror." Technically, President Obama was correct, but the larger question of adequate preparation and effective response ended up lost in the shuffle. This is the Catch-22 of the contemporary news media: aggressively interject as the intermediary between competing political parties or allow candidates and parties to debate, thus potentially allowing misrepresentations.

This question only matters if we believe that journalists play a special role in democratic governance as opposed to producing news as a product that is sold in the information marketplace. Far too many journalists, academics, and liberals believe that if the press would only be more aggressive in asserting "truth," the political process would work more effectively. This is the logic behind fact-checking sites like Politifact and the *Washington Post* Fact Checker. But what if the truth is indeterminate? Can we say definitely that health care reform will not add to the deficit based on Congressional Budget Office projections? How much should we allow for the possibility that such projections might be wrong? Is this not a fair subject for debate, as opposed to "pants on fire" or "Four Pinocchio" declarations from fact-checkers who pretend objectivity? The easiest facts to check are generally uninteresting, while the most important facts are almost always subject to dispute and clouded in uncertainty. More to the point, this raises the Thomas Patterson critique: the news media are ill suited to structuring elections, or, extending this only slightly, to refereeing between competing candidates and parties.

It is also based on a flawed understanding of individual psychology (as noted in chapter 2). Confronted with evidence that they are wrong, individuals do not simply accept the truth and revise their existing beliefs. If the beliefs are important, they reconstruct or rationalize the new information to fit into their existing beliefs or simply discredit the evidence. The irony is that fact-checkers may harden, rather than soften, the beliefs of the most informed and involved segments of the electorate. The 2012 presidential election provides a high-profile case-in-point.

Weighing the empirical evidence across states, statistician and *New York Times* Five-Thirty-Eight blogger Nate Silver concluded President Obama had a better than 80 percent chance of winning reelection. The reaction on the right was to question both the motive of Silver (who works for the *New York Times*) and the evidence: the polls were obviously overrepresenting Democratic partisans. Conservative Dean Chambers even created a website, Unskewed Polls, dedicating to reweighting the poll results to "more accurately" reflect the voting population and to show Mitt Romney easily winning the 2012 election. In some accounts, this reflected a vast left-wing conspiracy of pollsters to create the illusion of an inevitable second term. It was, of course, possible that the numbers were wrong. Pollsters have struggled with declining response rates and increasingly hard-to-reach cell-only and cell-mostly populations. The possibility of bias looms larger with each passing election cycle. Alternatively, the unlikely outcome in Nate Silver's simulations might have become the actual, if improbable, result. Mitt Romney might have drawn the equivalent of an inside straight and won despite the odds. The idea of systematic bias, however, was more than merely far-fetched—it was wrong. Nate Silver and the pollsters outperformed the pundits, as the polls (and random sampling) proved to be robust in the face of declining response rates.

The pundits, in contrast, were about as accurate as a coin toss.[45] Conservative pundits who went with their gut or with unskewed polling averages and against the balance of evidence were even less accurate. So why does the punditry class dominate the airwaves? Because they give voice to a particular perspective (usually partisan), because they are entertaining, and because they express their views in a language of simplicity and confidence, but mostly because talking head programming is cheaper to produce than real news. Unlike pundits, statisticians express events as probabilities and with caution, well aware of the uncertainty inherent in the numbers. The more important point is this: even experts, well versed in politics and with a wealth of experience, refuse to accept the truth when it runs contrary to what they believe or want to be true.

Intelligence and information, political scientist Brendan Nyhan observes, is no safeguard against conspiratorial thinking. Indeed, intelligence may increase resistance to new information that runs counter to what we already know. As an example, Nyhan points to Jack Welch, who smelled a rat in the release of lower-than-expected unemployment numbers in September 2012. More generally, politically knowledgeable Republicans who heard the claim were more likely to express doubt about the reported unemployment rate and to believe the number had been manipulated for political gain.[46]

The transformation of the information environment from passive consumers with limited choice to on-demand content and infinite choices fundamentally alters how individuals construct their world. During the broadcast era, Elizabeth Noelle-Neumann could construct "the spiral of silence," a theory that pressures toward conformity silence minority viewpoints. In the digital age, however, virtually every perspective can be found, supported, and reconfirmed. If you want to disregard the polling that indicates President Obama is winning the election, you can quickly and easily find reasons to do so: the polls must overrepresent Democratic partisans. When Fox News projected Ohio for President Barack Obama and consequently named him the winner of the 2012 presidential election, Karl Rove questioned whether the decision had been made too quickly. The question led to an interesting and awkward exchange with Michael Barone, the conservative editor of *The Almanac of American Politics*, in which Barone explained that while not all the numbers were in, Ohio was indeed lost because of the pattern of returns.

More easily accessible information does not lead to a more informed voter if much of the information is noise. Nearly one in three Republicans believed President Obama was a Muslim in an August 2010 Pew Center survey.[47] Two years later, in June 2012, 44 percent of Americans said they did not know what religion President Obama practiced, while 11 percent said he was Muslim and 8 percent said he did not have a religion.[48] In a digital age, information is more readily available, but so, too, is misinformation.

Social media, like Facebook and Twitter, allow the dissemination of misinformation through trusted "friends." Alexis Madrigal of *The Atlantic* observes that during Hurricane Sandy fake photos quickly went viral through social media.[49] More troubling, fake photographs, like pictures of sharks in New Jersey, outpaced the real photographs in terms of viral dissemination. How does democracy survive if the information environment is filled with noise? One might optimistically hope that citizens can reason their way to truth, but we are well aware of the cognitive limitations and biases inherent in the reasoning process. Confronted with evidence that their beliefs are incorrect does not lead people to correct their misguided beliefs; instead, citizens often "double down" on their incorrect assumptions and beliefs.

In 2005, comedian Stephen Colbert coined the term "truthiness" to capture and parody George W. Bush's gut-level decision-making. In so doing, he added a term to the lexicon that captures emotional or instinctive responses that disregard evidence, facts, or logic.[50] Colbert's term fairly captures the nature of human psychology: we respond emotionally first and rationally second.

Spreading misinformation about an opponent has long been a dirty campaign trick. During the 2000 presidential primary in South Carolina, for example, push polls were used to spread rumors that John McCain had fathered an African American child out of wedlock, that his wife was a drug addict, that he was a Manchurian candidate, and that he was gay. The Bush campaign team denied involvement. Perhaps ironically, by pointing out the misinformation, the news media may help to perpetuate rumors, lies, and innuendo. Ten years later in Massachusetts, a "Twitter bomb" was unleashed on Democratic Senate candidate Martha Coakley.[51] The bomb worked through the identification of interested users, the creation of fake Twitter accounts, and replying to these identified users to get them to spread the misinformation. Because the information comes via Twitter, it is difficult to connect to a specific source or to check the veracity of the information (in this case, it was the conservative American Future Fund). The spreading of misinformation is easier and more efficient, as links, photographs, and blog posts are shared across and within networks.

The mistake is to believe that socially responsible news organizations can fix these problems by supplying more and better information. The news media do not create or sustain democratic governance. This is the job of an informed and engaged citizenry. If the citizenry is willfully misinformed or intentionally ignorant, if they refuse to adjust beliefs in light of new evidence, democracy will fail on its own accord. Digital media are, perhaps ironically, a greater threat to democratic governance because they are inherently democratic. They provide greater choice in content. They allow citizens a simple and straightforward vote on a recurring basis—live up to your democratic responsibilities or become distracted by YouTube videos, Netflix, and porn.

Many citizens—the most politically engaged and informed—take full advantage of these opportunities (though even for the most informed the search is for confirmation of preexisting beliefs), but the net result is greater political polarization as they dig deeply into their ideological trenches. Other citizens avoid politics altogether, opting instead for entertainment and distraction. These patterns are no different (though perhaps they are more pronounced) from the knowledge gap created by the advent of television and the movement away from daily newspapers to the nightly news. Seen in this light, the real threat to democracy is not rooted in technology or in the supply of information via for-profit media organizations—these are mere symptoms. The real threat is the cognitive limitations of the typical citizen and the demands created by democratic governance in the information age. Put bluntly, the average citizen is simply ill equipped for the challenges of democratic governance in a digital age.

Journalism cannot change this, and its efforts to address the democratic malaise have, arguably, only aggravated the illness. Nor is technology to blame, except in a very rudimentary way: by increasing the speed by which information (and misinformation) travels, the digital age accelerates the threat of democratic governance identified first by Plato and echoed in the writings of James Madison:

"Tyranny naturally arises out of democracy." —Plato

"Democracies have ever been spectacles of turbulence and contention; have ever been found incompatible with personal security or the rights of property; and have in general been as short in their lives as they have been violent in their deaths." —James Madison

By more directly connecting the citizenry to policy in real time, digital media at once makes the system more democratic and places it at greater risk. In the American context, tyranny seems less likely than paralysis and gridlock. The result is ineffective governance that fails to address long-standing problems, and that slides slowly but surely toward crisis. Whether this crisis takes the form of the fiscal cliff or conflict in the Middle East or the social security crisis or health care or economic depression, its root cause will most certainly be a failure of democratic governance. The solution will not be found in a more vigilant news media or calls for greater democratic participation and input.

So what can journalism do? Ditch the objectivity norm (which Fox News, MSNBC, and others have already done) and tell stories with powerful narratives, depth, and complexity. Provide audiences with developed, intellectually honest perspective, not raw information. Seek the truth based on the best available evidence and expert judgment rather than focusing on the narrow "gotcha" journalism of fact-checking. Acknowledge uncertainty and error as part of a process of discovery and learning. These stories may not reach a mass audience, but they might reach an audience that actually matters.

NOTES

1. Natalie Stroud, *Niche News: The Politics of News Choice* (Oxford: Oxford University Press, 2011).

2. Jonathan Morris and Richard Forgette, "News Grazers, Television News, Political Knowledge, and Engagement," *International Journal of Press/Politics* 12 (2007): 91–107.

3. John S. Carroll on "Why Newspapers Matter," http://www. niemanwatchdog.org/index.cfm?fuseaction=ask_this.view&askthisid= 203, from a speech made to the American Society of Newspaper Editors, April 26, 2006.

4. Charles E. Clark, "The Press the Founders Knew," in *Freeing the Presses: The First Amendment in Action*, edited by Timothy E. Cook (Baton Rouge: Louisiana State University Press, 2005).

5. Paul Starr, *The Creation of the Mass Media: Political Origins of Modern Communications* (New York: Basic Books, 2004); Timothy E. Cook, *Governing with the News: The News Media as a Political Institution* (Chicago: University of Chicago Press, 1998).

6. James Hamilton, *All the News That's Fit to Sell: How the Market Transforms Information into News* (Princeton, NJ: Princeton University Press, 2004).

7. The research of Iowa State journalism professor Raluca Cozma shows that the golden age of journalism is likely overstated. Cozma concludes that NPR coverage of the Iraq was, in fact, qualitatively better than CBS coverage of foreign affairs from 1940 to 1942. See Raluca Cozma, "From Murrow to Mediocrity," *Journalism Studies* 11 (2010): 667–82.

8. John Nerone, "The Death (and Rebirth?) of Working-Class Journalism," *Journalism* 10 (2009): 353–55.

9. John Nerone, "To Rescue Journalism from the Media," *Cultural Studies* 23 (2009): 243–58.

10. Neil Henry, *American Carnival* (Berkeley and Los Angeles: University of California Press, 2007), 55.

11. Jonathan Ladd, *Why Americans Hate the Media and How It Matters* (Princeton, NJ: Princeton University Press, 2012).

12. Shanto Iyengar and Donald Kinder, *News That Matters* (Chicago: University of Chicago Press, 1987).

13. Media Use and Evaluation, *Gallup*, November 14, 2012, http://www.gallup.com/poll/1663/media-use-evaluation.aspx. Specific question wording is as follows: "In general, how much trust and confidence do you have in the mass media—such as newspapers, TV, and radio—when it comes to reporting the news fully, accurately, and fairly—a great deal, a fair amount, not very much, or none at all?"

14. Timothy E. Cook, *Governing with the News: The News Media as a Political Institution* (Chicago: University of Chicago Press, 1998).

15. Edward S. Herman and Noam Chomsky, *Manufacturing Consent: The Political Economy of the Mass Media* (New York: Pantheon, 1988).

16. W. Lance Bennett, "Toward a Theory of Press-State Relations in the United States," *Journal of Communication* 40 (1990): 103–27.

17. W. Lance Bennett, Regina Lawrence, and Steven Livingston, *When the Press Fails: Political Power and the News Media from Iraq to Katrina* (Chicago: University of Chicago Press, 2007).

18. Chris Mooney and Matthew Nisbet, "Undoing Darwin," *Columbia Journalism Review* (September/October 2005): 30–39; Chris Mooney, *The Republican War on Science* (New York: Basic Books, 2005).

19. Justin Wolfers, "The Secret Consensus among Economists," Freakonomics.com, July 25, 2012, http://www.freakonomics.com/2012/07/25/the-secret-consensus-among-economists/ (accessed May 24, 2013); Betsey Stevenson and Justin Wolfers, "The U.S. Economic Policy Debate is a Sham," *Bloomberg*, July 23, 2012.

20. Mark Watts, David Domke, Dhavan Shah, and David Fan, "Elite Cues and Media Bias in Presidential Campaigns: Explaining Public Perceptions of a Liberal Press," *Communication Research* 26 (1999): 144–75.

21. Quoted in Mark Blumenthal, "Can I Trust This Poll?" in Kirby Goidel, ed. *Political Polling in a Digital Age: The Challenge of Measuring and Understanding Public Opinion* (Baton Rouge: Louisiana State University Press, 2011), 64.

22. Matthew Baum, "Talking the Vote: Why Presidential Candidates Hit the Talk Show Circuit," *American Journal of Political Science* 49 (2005): 213–34.

23. Marc Tracy, "Nate Silver is a One-Man Traffic Machine for the Times," *The New Republic*, November 6, 2012, http://www.tnr.com/blog/plank/109714/nate-silver-the-times%E2%80%99-biggest-brand# (accessed May 24, 2013).

24. "Clinton-Lewinsky Allegations Fuel Debate about Journalism and the Internet," *CNN Politics*, January 30, 1998, http://articles.cnn.com/1998-01-30/politics/pandora.web_1_matt-drudge-web-site-lewinsky-story?_s=PM:ALLPOLITICS (accessed on May 24, 2013).

25. James Hamilton, *All the News That's Fit to Sell: How the Market Transforms Information into News* (Princeton, NJ: Princeton University Press, 2004).

26. James Hamilton, *All the News That's Fit to Sell*, 65.

27. Johanna Dunaway, "Markets, Ownership, and the Quality of Campaign News Coverage," *Journal of Politics* 70 (2008): 1193–1202.

28. Seth Godin, *We Are All Weird* (The Domino Project, 2011).

29. Markus Prior, *Post-Broadcast Democracy: How Media Choice Increases Inequality in Political Involvement and Polarizes Elections* (Cambridge: Cambridge University Press, 2007).

30. Neil Postman, *Amusing Ourselves to Death: Public Discourse in the Age of Show Business* (New York: Penguin Group, 1985).

31. Marshall McLuhan, *Understanding Media: The Extensions of Man* (New York: McGraw Hill, 1964).

32. Al Gore, *The Assault on Reason* (New York: Penguin, 2007).

33. Nicholas Carr, *The Shallows: What the Internet Is Doing to Our Brains* (New York: W. W. Norton, 2010).

34. Natalie Stroud, *Niche News: The Politics of News Choice* (Oxford: Oxford University Press, 2011).

35. Johanna Dunaway, Jeremy Padgett, and Rosanne Scholl, "Substance v. Bias: Are Neutral Campaign News Stories Less Informative?" paper presented at the annual meeting of the 2013 Midwestern Political Science Association, Chicago, Illinois, April 11–14, 2013.

36. Chris Mooney, "The Fox News 'Effect': A Few References," Desmogblog.com, May 19, 2011, http://www.desmogblog.com/fox-news-effect-few-references (accessed May 24, 2013).

37. Susanna Dilliplane, "All the News You Want to Hear: The Impact of Partisan News Exposure on Political Participation," *Public Opinion Quarterly* 75 (2011): 287–316.

38. Diana Mutz, *Hearing the Other Side: Deliberative Versus Participatory Democracy* (Cambridge: Cambridge University Press, 2006).

39. The most recent historical account emphasizes that while the debates were political theater, they were also substantively important; see

Allen Guelzo, *Lincoln and Douglas: The Debates that Defined America* (New York: Simon & Schuster, 2008).

40. Garry Wills, "Do the Lincoln-Douglas Debates Really Matter?" *Argumentation & Advocacy* 46 (2010): 150–58.

41. Thomas Patterson, *Out of Order* (New York: Knopf, 1994).

42. Jonathan Martin, "Jindal: End 'Dumbed Down Conservatism,'" *Politico*, November 13, 2012, http://www.politico.com/news/stories/1112/83743.html (accessed May 24, 2013).

43. Thomas Patterson, *Out of Order*.

44. "Winning the Media Campaign 2012," Pew Research Center's Project for Excellence in Journalism, November 2, 2012, http://www.journalism.org/analysis_report/winning_media_campaign_2012 (accessed May 24, 2013).

45. Nate Silver, *The Signal and the Noise: Why So Many Predictions Fail—But Some Don't* (New York: Penguin, 2012).

46. Brendan Nyhan, "Political Knowledge Does Not Guard Against Belief in Conspiracy Theories," *YouGov*, November 5, 2012, http://today.yougov.com/news/2012/11/05/political-knowledge-does-not-guard-against-belief-/ (accessed May 24, 2013).

47. "Growing Number of Americans Say Obama is a Muslim," Pew Research Center, August 9, 2012, http://www.people-press.org/2010/08/19/growing-number-of-americans-say-obama-is-a-muslim/ (accessed May 24, 2013).

48. Frank Newport, "Many Americans Can't Name Obama's Religion," *Gallup Politics*, June 22, 2012, http://www.gallup.com/poll/155315/many-americans-cant-name-obamas-religion.aspx (accessed May 24, 2013).

49. Alexis Madrigal, "If You Can't Beat 'em, Subvert 'em: Countering Misinformation on the Viral Web," *The Atlantic Politics*, October 31, 2012, http://www.theatlantic.com/technology/archive/2012/10/if-you-cant-beat-em-subvert-em-countering-misinformation-on-the-viral-web/264366/# (accessed May 24, 2013).

50. "Scientists Discover the Truth Behind Colbert's 'Truthiness,'" *Science Daily*, August 8, 2012, http://www.sciencedaily.com/releases/2012/08/120808081334.htm (accessed May 24, 2013).

51. Eni Mustafaraj and Panagiotis Metaxas, "From Obscurity to Prominence in Minutes: Political Speech and Real-Time Search," Proceedings WebSci10: Extending the Frontiers of Society On-Line, Ra-

leigh, North Carolina, April 26–27, 2010, http://journal.webscience.org/
317/ (accessed May 24, 2013).

5

GRIDLOCK AND AMERICAN POLITICAL INSTITUTIONS

At approximately 9:18 p.m. (EST) on November 6, 2012, Fox News conceded that President Barack Obama had an insurmountable lead in Ohio. The significance was immediate and profound. With Ohio in hand, President Barack Obama vaulted past 270 Electoral College votes and into a second term. Democrats breathed a collective sigh of relief. The stagnant and ailing U.S. economy had never fully recovered from the Great Recession and President Obama's approval rating hovered persistently and fragilely at just under 50 percent.

Republicans reacted with disbelief and anger. Prior to the election, many prominent Republicans expressed doubt about swing state election polls that showed President Obama with small but consistent leads across the battleground states. They were certain the polls underestimated Republican support and reasoned that late-breaking undecided voters would move toward Mitt Romney in the closing days of the campaign. Instead, the polls consistently underestimated President Barack Obama's support by failing to capture the strength of the Obama campaign's ground game.

The 2012 election was never as close as it appeared.

Believing the election would end with Mitt Romney as a Republican Al Gore, losing the Electoral College while winning the popular vote, Donald Trump called for revolution via Twitter. The Electoral College, Trump said, was a "travesty" and "a disaster for democracy."[1] As it turned out, Trump's call for revolution was premature. President Obama ended the night with a majority of the popular vote, muting the Electoral College criticism but doing little to quell the anger and disbelief on the political right.

Motor city madman, rocker, and survivalist Ted Nugent, whose hits included "Cat Scratch Fever" and "Wango Tango," was livid. He tweeted, "Pimps whores & welfare brats & their soulless supporters hav [sic] a president to destroy America."[2] Victoria Jackson of *Saturday Night Live* fame similarly declared the election "the day America died." She was not alone in her fears. Hyperbolic reactions from the right were well rooted in misperceptions that the election was closer than it really was and in pre-election propaganda that a second Obama administration would destroy "American" values. Symptomatic was conservative author Dinesh D'Souza's film *2016: Obama's America*, which portrays the United States at the end of President Obama's second term—in decay, torn by war and economic collapse. For many conservatives, the Obama victory was yet another sign of America's moral, social, and economic decline.

Conservatives are not alone in overreacting to election defeats. Liberal Democrats threatened to move to Canada following George W. Bush's reelection in 2004—as they have in every contemporary election won by a Republican. Less than a week after George W. Bush won reelection, *Slate* magazine published a guide for disaffected Democrats considering taking refuge in the Great White North as inquiries into emigration skyrocketed.[3] Following the 2012 election, disaffected Republicans opted for a different route, filing petitions with the White House to secede from the union. The petition for Texas to secede received over one hundred thousand signatures, though it is not clear that all the signatures were from Texas. The irony of self-proclaimed patriots threatening to the leave the union after an open, fair, and democratic election that turned out unfavorably for their side should not be lost. These are the type of people who place Confederate flags next to their "America: Love It or Leave It" bumper stickers without recognizing the contradiction, and who hear Bruce Springsteen's "Born in the U.S.A." as a Ronald Reagan–inspired affirmation of American values instead of tale of loss and disaffection. The reaction reinforces a central theme: we really only like democracy when our side wins.

Extremist views are certainly not confined to a political ideology or political party, but they tend to find greater prominence and acceptance among relatively "mainstream" conservatives. Fox News personality Bill O'Reilly offered this assessment in the aftermath of the election: "It's not a traditional America anymore. And there are fifty per cent of the voting public who want stuff. They want things. And who is going to give them things? President Obama. He knows it and he ran on it. Whereby twenty years ago President Obama would have been roundly defeated by an establishment candidate like Mitt Romney. The white establishment is now the minority." Rush Limbaugh similarly declared, "I went to bed last night thinking we are outnumbered. I went to bed last night thinking we've lost the country. I don't know how else you look at this."[4]

Such hyperbolic reactions are, at least in part, a reflection of a changing media environment. Increased competition for an increasingly fragmented audience across an array of channels and platforms raises the premium on capturing attention and cultivating a loyal following. Shrill and outrageous statements cause the equivalent of highway rubbernecking, while partisan attacks attract a loyal niche market. Anne Coulter, whose fame is almost entirely based on her willingness to say the outrageous, went so far as to accuse Democrats of treason during the Bush administration and to defend the Red Scare tactics of Senator Joseph McCarthy.[5] Such rhetoric would be harmless if people did not believe it, but unfortunately too many citizens do and they are being led toward less tolerance, less support of individual rights, and less support for democratic norms and procedures. A Fairleigh Dickinson University Public Mind Poll conducted in May 2013 found that 29 percent of all respondents and 44 percent of Republicans believed that armed revolution might be necessary to protect liberties in the next several years.[6]

The post-election wailing and gnashing of teeth amid a deeper backdrop of partisan rancor and polarization raises disturbing issues about the legitimacy of our political system. Legitimacy is a term used by political scientists to convey acceptance of the rules of the game and, by extension, even outcomes one happens to disagree with. Democrats who refused to accept the Supreme Court decision in *Bush v. Gore*, for example, were questioning not just the outcome (Bush wins!) but also the legitimacy of a decision made by the nine unelected justices who comprise the Supreme Court. Republican reactions to President Obama's victory indicate a similar and disconcerting disregard for the legitimacy of the system (i.e., that the process is fair and that the outcomes, while perhaps not preferred, reflect the end result of a set of rules we have all agreed upon). Had Mitt Romney won the election, the Democratic reaction would have been no less muted, as the loss would have stemmed not from a poorly run campaign, the failure of Democratic ideas to win over independent voters, or the failure of Obama administration policies to resuscitate a moribund economy, but rather from the suppression of Democratic voters through voter identification requirements or negative and untruthful campaigning by Republican super PACs.

Perhaps even more troubling, Republican doomsday scenarios outlining the catastrophes awaiting the end of President Obama's second term are almost entirely separated from the reality of American government, a system designed not only to limit executive power but also to make coordinated control of government nearly impossible. First, Republicans still control the U.S. House of Representatives. Second, absent Tea Party insurgencies against mainstream Republicans like Indiana's Richard Lugar in 2012 or Delaware's Mike Castle in 2010, Republicans would almost certainly have control of the U.S. Senate. Indeed, Republican lamentations over the 2012 elections should focus not on President Barack Obama's victory but on how Republicans effectively shot off their collective left foot by deposing electable but moderate

Republican incumbents in favor of unelectable ideologues. Third, even without control of the Senate, Republican Senate Minority Leader Mitch McConnell has proved adept at using the filibuster to block policies and nominations.[7]

Republican fears over what the next four years may bring are rooted in a fundamental misunderstanding of presidential power and the realities of constitutional governance. The irony that this reality escapes the Tea Party's constitutional purists should not be lost. Our collective fear should not be what President Obama might do in a second term but rather the partisan gridlock that will result from divided government and an increasingly polarized political environment. While one can hope for better outcomes, the most realistic result of the 2012 elections is that our political system will once again prove inept at addressing our most pressing and persistent problems.

There is, of course, one caveat worth offering. Should Republican obstructionist tactics throw the political system into a major fiscal crisis (i.e., should we march lemming-like over the fiscal cliff), they will effectively make their worst-case scenario a reality. As has been true throughout American history, President Obama would likely be strengthened by crisis, as he would be armed with public expectations that he act decisively even if it meant stepping outside existing constitutional boundaries.

President Obama's reelection does little or nothing to change the polarized political environment that defines contemporary American politics, nor does it alter the motivation or ability of Republicans to block legislative action. Indeed, he entered his second term with considerable less political capital than when he began his first term and enjoyed unified partisan control of the House of Representatives and the Senate. To be successful, he will likely have to learn how to play the "small ball" politics perfected by Bill Clinton during his second term. Absent a major crisis, there will be no radical policy transformations, and our political system will continue to be mired in partisan paralysis and gridlock.

THE LIMITS OF PRESIDENTIAL POWER

As Americans, we celebrate power in the executive branch. Our greatest presidents, Abraham Lincoln and Franklin Delano Roosevelt, expanded the power of the presidency during times of crisis, reaching far beyond the constitutional limits imposed by the Founding Fathers. Writing in 1956, political scientist Clinton Rossiter described the president as "a kind of magnificent lion who can roam widely and do great deeds so long as he does not break from his broad reservation."[8] The American presidency is likewise often described as the most powerful office in the world. While such descriptions may fairly capture American economic and military might, they fail to convey the very limited formal powers of the executive branch.

The executive office created by the Founding Fathers was considerably smaller and more limited in scope and power than the presidency that exists today. It has grown over time as a result of a combination of public expectations and historical precedent, but the formal powers of governance reside mostly in the U.S. Congress. The power to declare war and regulate interstate commerce and the power of the purse all reside in the legislative branch.

Executives, at least as envisioned by the Founders, were mostly administrators whose primary responsibilities involved implementing laws passed by Congress. The historic transformation of the executive branch from a position of limited power to the most powerful office in the world occurred, first, because of America's shifting position in the world and, second, because Congress has either failed to act or been unwilling to act during times of crisis. Take, for example, the expectation that the president submit a budget to Congress. It wasn't until the passage of the Budget and Accounting Act in 1921 that presidents were required to submit a budget, increasing the expectation that presidents would play a larger role in the budget-making process. Presidents were given the power by an unwieldy legislature that found it difficult to act. Writing about regulatory powers, legal scholar David Frohnmayer described the erosion of legislative power and the accumulation power in the executive branch this way: "As with chastity, congressional power is never lost, rarely taken by force, and almost always given away."[9]

Even so, the formal powers of the presidency remain limited, though not inconsequential. Writing in 1960, presidential scholar Richard Neustadt observed that "presidential power is the power to persuade," an explicit acknowledgment that most presidential power is rooted not in the formal powers created by the U.S. Constitution but rather in the informal powers of the presidency. In arriving at his dictum, Neustadt recounted President Harry Truman's concern for General Dwight Eisenhower's ability to operate within America's divided and fragmented constitutional structure: "He'll sit here, and he'll say, 'Do this! Do that!' And nothing will happen. Poor Ike—it won't be a bit like the Army. He'll find it very frustrating."[10]

Limited formal power has hardly limited public expectations that presidents can act effectively and decisively to solve long-standing problems. Nor has it stopped presidents from acting.[11] Hence, the dire portrayal of *2016: Obama's America* and the fundamental challenge of contemporary democratic governance: a public unwilling to reconcile contradictory expectations, overly confident that better leaders could solve all our problems if only they had common sense, and leadership that faces very real and growing constraints in its ability to act. In most areas of public life, presidents must have buy-in from other institutions (primarily Congress) to successfully act.

In a highly polarized era, buy-in is more difficult to achieve. Indeed, there is good reason to believe the challenge of presidential leadership is greater today than it was a decade ago during the Bush administration, during the Clinton administration in the 1990s, during the Reagan administration during the 1980s, or during the Eisenhower administration during the 1950s. First, the growth in presidential power was partly rooted in the ability of presidents to speak directly to and for the nation. Franklin Delano Roosevelt was able to reach into the living room via the fireside chat thanks to the widespread adoption of radio. John F. Kennedy and Ronald Reagan used television imagery to connect directly and personally with mass audiences. During an era of mass communication, presidents could "go public" as a strategy for moving policy in Washington when negotiation failed.[12]

The digital age has increased the speed by which information travels but has also fragmented the audience, making it more difficult for presidents to speak directly to the nation, defined as a mass audience of American citizens. It has also empowered political opponents to speak directly to their supporters, hardening the lines of political division among the most partisan and engaged citizens. Notably, this trend preceded the development of Internet and the fragmentation created by digital media. Writing in 1999, political scientists Matthew Baum and Samuel Kernell connected the declining audience for presidential addresses to the increased programming choices made available by the widespread adoption of cable television systems. "If modern presidents lose their prime-time audience," these authors cautioned, "they will surrender a political asset that will be difficult to replace by other means."[13] Giving the public the ability to change the channel during a presidential address not only made it more difficult to reach large audiences but also forced network television stations to consider whether a presidential address was a significant news event and worth a potential loss in audience to Comedy Central, ESPN, or the Lifetime Network. Baum and Kernell concluded their study with this important question: "How will presidents promote themselves and their policies to a citizenry that depends almost entirely on television for its news and information yet is increasingly unwilling to allow them into their home?"

The trend toward decreasing audiences for presidential addresses and news events has continued through the Bush and Obama administrations.[14] Perhaps more troubling, declining audiences mean presidents are less likely to reach those citizens they most need to persuade—independents and opposition partisans—and are instead "preaching to the choir."[15] If the broadcast era was ideal for reaching large audiences, digital media are ideal for speaking, more narrowly, to fellow partisans.[16] Instead of trying to reach to the middle, political communication is increasingly a call to arms targeted toward like-minded political activists. An already polarized political environment, subsequently, becomes even more polarized.

Second, it is more difficult to lead in a polarized political environment. Partisanship has always been an important screen for filtering and interpreting political information. What is unique about the contemporary political environment is how far partisanship has reached beyond obvious partisan considerations (e.g., how President Obama is performing as president) and into matters of fact. Even scientific research, because it has significant policy implications, has become highly politicized. The absence of a shared understanding of reality makes partisan compromise and agreement more difficult to reach and political debate less meaningful and useful for resolving political differences. Indeed, the connotations for the word "compromise" are increasingly negative, reflecting a lack of resolve as opposed to a willingness find a place of mutual agreement. Yet compromise is essential for a system of government designed around the principles of checks and balances and separation of powers.

Political scientists Amy Guttmann and Dennis Thompson trace the root of the problem to the inherent contradictions of a political system built on political campaigns that reward uncompromising position-taking versus actual governing, which demands compromise. "The relentless pressures of campaigning," they argue, "are overtaking the demands of governing. Because legislating in the public interest is all but impossible without compromise, the domination of campaigning over governing has become a critical problem for American democracy."[17]

The increased polarization of elected officials also provides less room to find compromise. If we think of partisan ideology as a Venn diagram, there is simply less shared space across the two political parties. The evidence on this point is unequivocal. Using congressional roll call votes, political scientists Nolan McCarty, Keith Poole, and Howard Rosenthal show that ideological polarization in the U.S. House of Representatives is greater than at any time since 1879 (which serves as the beginning of their trend line).[18] Polarization in the U.S. Senate is similarly greater than at any time other than the Gilded Age in the 1880s.

The trends in polarization correspond with declining competition in U.S. House races. Since the 1950s, the number of safe House districts has increased while the number of marginal (or competitive) districts has declined. This leads to an inescapable but inconvenient conclusion: while Congress is failing as a political institution, individual members are largely successful in representing their constituents. They are, as Guttmann and Thompson note, elected to be principled and uncompromising in a way that ensures actual governing will be more difficult or perhaps impossible.

This is, at least partly, rooted in the sophistication of contemporary redistricting software, which allows the careful construction of districts designed to elect favored politicians. In the topsy-turvy world of modern politics, representatives are too often able to select their voters (as opposed to voters selecting their representatives). The task has become easier because of the tendency of Americans to sort into like-minded communities on the basis of beliefs and lifestyle.[19] The result has been more partisan Republicans in safer, more Republican districts; more partisan Democrats in safer, more Democratic districts; and a small number of competitive seats (roughly fifty to sixty) where the balance of the House of Representatives is most often determined.

As the increased polarization in the intentionally malapportioned U.S. Senate reveals, however, redistricting is, at best, only a partial explanation. The broader cultural shift toward greater polarization is more clearly linked to the ideological realignment of the political parties.[20] Over the last several decades, Republicans have won U.S. Senate and House seats once controlled by conservative Democrats.[21] Blue Dog Democrats, those moderate to conservative Democrats who once formed an important swing voting block and played a critical role in negotiating compromise with the Republican Party, are now an endangered species. Democrats, for their part, have increasingly won in the Northeast, picking up seats once controlled by Rockefeller Republicans, a term that signifies fiscally conservative but socially liberal Republicans and that has lost almost all real-world significance. In more recent election cycles, Democrats have been assisted by Tea Party conservatives who have challenged and defeated RINOs (liberal or moderate Republicans in Name Only) in Republican primaries only to ensure a Democratic victory in the general election. As a consequence of these shifts, the political parties are now more ideologically and geographically distinct than perhaps at any other time in U.S. political history. [22]

The result has been an increasingly dysfunctional political system. Indeed, long-time congressional observers Thomas Mann and Norman Ornstein of the Brookings Institute argue that the dysfunction of American politics is worse today than at any time in recent history. [23] The culpability for this dysfunction, they argue, resides mostly with the Republican Party, which increasingly operates as a parliamentary-style political party in a constitutional system. Partisan blame aside, there is a mismatch between the institutional characteristics and the broader political environment that makes governing nearly impossible.

Historically, political parties in the United States were formed as loose coalitions, organized to win elections. Ideology took a back seat to winning. The result was considerable ideological overlap across the two parties. Conservative Democrats, mostly from the South, were an important voting block within the Democratic Party, while liberal Republicans, mostly from the Northeast, were an important constituency within the Republican Party. Individual representatives and senators frequently defected from their party in legislative roll votes. Indeed, they were encouraged to do so by party leaders to guarantee their electoral safety. Given the choice between a liberal Republican and a Democrat, Republicans gladly chose the former. The Democratic Party did the same, tolerating conservative defectors in order to maintain partisan control of the chamber.

Beginning with Newt Gingrich's ascent as a minority leader and, ultimately, speaker of the House, the Republican Party increasingly adopted the tactics and organizational structures of a parliamentary-style political party. Hierarchically organized and ideologically driven, the Republican Party targeted and defeated southern conservative Democrats to gain control of the House of Representatives in 1994 for the first time in over forty years. The rightward drift of the Republican Party helped Democrats win seats from more liberal Republicans in the Northeast. The net result of these shifts was that the political parties are more polarized than at any time in the past eight decades. As noted earlier, to find equivalent levels of polarization one would need to travel back to the late 1800s, when America was going through a period of rapid industrialization.

The mismatch between public expectations and presidential power creates a major obstacle for democratic governance. Public opinion neither appreciates nor understands the obstacles to effective governance or the public's own role in making the system even more dysfunctional. Representatives and senators are elected not on the basis of institutional performance (i.e., has Congress effectively dealt with long-standing and persistent issues?) but rather on the position-taking of individual representatives and senators. The result is an executive branch with limited authority but saddled with expectations that it will act to address the nation's problems and a legislative branch in which individual members can succeed even as the institution fails to address the nation's problems.

To understand this disconnect, ask yourself a simple question: Could long-standing and persistent problems, like the federal deficit, be more easily resolved if we could remove politics from decision-making? Could a group of unelected experts, in the form of a special committee or commission, solve problems that our elected officials cannot? If you answered yes, ask yourself the obvious follow-up: Why? In *The Deadlock of Democracy*, written in 1963, political scientist James MacGregor Burns provided an answer that continues to have relevance today: "The cure for democracy, people used to say, is more democracy. A half century of hard experience has shown this cliché to be a dangerous half-truth. The cure for democracy is leadership—responsible, committed, effective, and exuberant leadership."[24] For Burns, deadlock was rooted in ineffective, loosely organized political parties that proved unable to overcome the institutional and structural barriers created by the U.S. constitutional system. Half a century later, we can definitively conclude that stronger, more tightly organized political parties have not solved the problem of gridlock. So what's the problem?

Washington Post columnist Robert Samuelson referenced *The Deadlock of Democracy* in a column written just prior to the 2004 election to offer this assessment:

> Many pressing problems are known and something often can be done, even if the remedies may be disagreeable and incomplete. These remedies, though, cannot be deployed unless they're sanctioned by public opinion . . .
>
> If the public won't abide honest discussion of clear problems—and our leaders can't lead opinion—then the problems simply fester. In this campaign, neither Bush nor Kerry has risen above that dilemma.
>
> That suggests that many of our largest social problems will progressively worsen until they get so bad that we're forced to deal with them. Or they deal harshly with us. This is the true deadlock, and it may be incurable.[25]

We can blame our leaders, but the reality is that "we the people" cannot handle the truth, nor we will make the sacrifices necessary to solve the problems we say we care about. The result is special commissions, like the National Commission on Fiscal Responsibility and Reform (Simpson-Bowles), intended to solve the problems that our democratic government cannot adequately address. When commissions can offer solutions that democratic institutions cannot, the nature of the problem becomes abundantly clear: it is not because these problems cannot be solved, but because "we the people" cannot tolerate the solutions.

THE BROKEN BRANCH

Before assuming his current position as the director of the Center on Congress, Lee Hamilton served in the U.S. House of Representatives for thirty-four years. A smart, policy-oriented centrist Democrat from rural and conservative southern Indiana, Representative Hamilton developed a reputation for being substantively grounded and results oriented. While he could be partisan, he was willing to call out his own party when he thought it necessary and he routinely defended the U.S. House of Representatives as an institution. In his current role, he works to educate the public on what the U.S. Congress does and why it matters. It is an uphill battle, as he is fighting not only against public ignorance and misconceptions but also against a legislature that is so increasingly dysfunctional it defies explanation or defense.

Once upon a time, the U.S. Congress was a relatively collegial place. Institutionally, power was centered in committees and the all-important committee chairs, who were selected primarily on the basis of seniority. Automatic decision rules (like seniority) limited the politics in selecting leaders and placed a premium on legislative knowledge and experience. Individual representatives and senators were recognized for their hard work, tenure in office, and substantive knowledge. Congressional scholars often noted the differences between legislators they categorized as show horses and work horses. Real power was vested not in the spotlight-seeking show horses but in the work horses, who understood both the substance of policy and congressional rules and procedures. West Virginia senator Robert Byrd, for example, could accumulate significant power—independent from any position of formal leadership—because of his deep and rich understanding of the rules and procedures that governed the U.S. Senate.

Beginning in the 1990s, retiring members would lament that serving in Congress wasn't as much fun, and that the environment was increasingly partisan and poisonous. Where they used to be friends with members who sat across the aisle, an increasingly politicized environment made legislative politics more personal and less congenial for friendships that reached across party lines. Where congressional leaders once worked closely together, communication was increasingly limited or absent.

When talking politics, it is always a mistake to oversell the "good old days," as those days were always better for some than others. The decentralization of legislative power into committees and subcommittees allowed members to develop substantive expertise, but it also meant that policy was often controlled by a relatively small group of members. Agricultural policy, for example, was often set by members from rural farming districts. As the focus of politics narrowed, partisanship mattered less than serving local constituents. It isn't clear if the public interest, broadly defined, was better served in this earlier era.

The U.S. House of Representatives was often likened to a feudal system in which committee chairs played the role of feudal barons, making coordinated policy difficult to achieve. Because 90 percent of legislation died in committee, committee chairs exercised a powerful veto over the policy-making process. Before President Lyndon Johnson could pass the landmark Civil Rights Act of 1964 and the Voting Rights Act of 1965, he first needed to move the legislation through the southern conservative Democrats who controlled the congressional committees. To do so, he needed the support of more liberal Republicans. If the Civil Rights Act and Voting Rights Act were being considered by the contemporary U.S. Congress, final passage (or failure) would likely be on a party-line vote.

Once considered the world's greatest deliberative assembly, the U.S. Senate is similarly immersed in partisan rancor and dysfunction.[26] Unlike the House of Representatives, which is organized around strong partisan leadership and majority control, norms in the U.S. Senate have long valued individualism and independence, making partisan leadership less powerful and influential. Recall that the U.S. Senate was originally designed to serve as an aristocratic check on the more plebian and populist House of Representatives. Increasingly, however, the Senate functions as a partisan chamber that no longer values deliberation, reflection, or political independence, and instead operates mostly along party lines. Debates over the filibuster and proposals to reform Senate rules are symptomatic of an increasingly polarized chamber. Figure 5.1, for example, illustrates the dramatic increase in cloture motions from 1917 to 2012. Cloture motions are used to end filibusters and require sixty votes to pass, and can be fairly read as an indication that the process is not working.

The root cause of Senate dysfunction, however, is not institutional rules but an increasingly polarized political environment. Or, to borrow a phrase from the gun control lobby, the filibuster doesn't kill Senate legislation—senators kill Senate legislation. Republican Minority Leader Mitch McConnell summarized this cultural shift with a statement made on November 4, 2010: "The single most important thing we want to achieve is for President Obama to be a one-term president."

The U.S. Congress, created by the Founding Fathers to represent but also temper public opinion, is now so embroiled in partisan politics that it no longer functions very well in the absence of

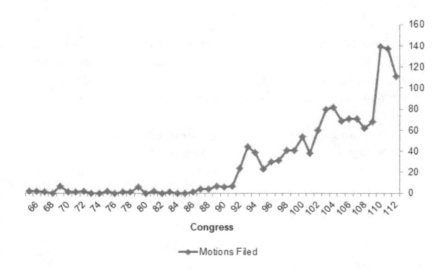

Figure 5.1. Number of Cloture Motions Filed in the U.S. Senate from the 65th Congress to the 112th Congress, 1917–2012

overwhelming one-party control. Even then, it is expected that the minority party will do everything within its power to obstruct and derail the majority. Perhaps this seems obvious in the contemporary context, but it is certainly not how the American political system has historically functioned. Three short decades ago, President Ronald Reagan constructed an effective congressional majority out of his fellow Republicans and southern conservative Democrats. It would be a mistake to attribute this coalition solely to Reagan's political skills rather than to a political environment that made such coalition building possible.

Brookings scholars Thomas Mann and Norman Ornstein observe that the advent of strong majority leadership did not reinvigorate Congress as an institution—as scholars like James MacGregor Burns had hoped—but instead made Congress more subservient to presidential leadership. Where members of the U.S. House of Representatives and U.S. Senate once shared strong institutional identities, contemporary members think of themselves first and foremost as partisans oriented toward achieving partisan political goals.

The tipping point was the Republican Revolution in 1994 and the ascendance of Newt Gingrich as speaker of the House of Representatives. Prior to Gingrich, the norm in the House of Representatives was that the minority party had an obligation to work with the majority to solve the nation's long-standing problems. Minority leader Robert Michel (R-IL) typified this approach to legislative leadership. Consider, for example, this statement made in the aftermath of Ronald Reagan's victory in 1980:

> Our strategy will be one of beginning with negotiation not only at the top, but right down to the sub-committee level where I intend to the strengthen the lines of communication in the House, with our counterparts in the Senate and with the White House.
>
> With or without negotiations we will be continually probing across the aisle and I'd like to count upon your volunteering to

help strategize and execute commando raids for votes from the
other side on specific pieces of legislation.[27]

Two years later, after Republicans lost twenty-six seats in the 1982
midterm elections, Michel addressed concerns that he was too
conciliatory: "Sometimes I've been criticized for being too much
of a pragmatist, too ready to get things done, to work things out.
Let me tell you something: Political principles without effective
action are mere dreams."

Newt Gingrich offered a very different style of leadership.
Throughout his career, Gingrich ignored institutional norms for
focusing on committee work and for first paying one's dues and
instead aggressively sought out the political spotlight. A 1989 pro-
file in *Vanity Fair*, for example, described his legislative record as
"negligible" while praising his ability to speak glibly on a wide
range of substantive matters.[28] Using the "new" technology of
C-SPAN, Gingrich gave speeches to an often empty chamber
challenging the patriotism of Democratic members and earning a
sharp rebuke from Democratic Speaker Tip O'Neill. Once Gingrich assumed the position of minority whip, he used his leadership position as a megaphone for denouncing Democrats, including charges about an unethical book deal that ultimately forced
Democratic Speaker Jim Wright to resign. A PBS *Frontline* series
on Newt Gingrich's political career noted the Wright investigation
as the turning point, the critical moment when Gingrich went
from being a quotable curiosity to a serious player in national
politics. Conservative activist Paul Weyrich described its importance this way: "Because he took on Wright and won, he became a
serious political figure, at that point. Up to that point, he was
regarded as an interesting political figure, somebody that was very
good for a quote, but not somebody who was perhaps going to be
in the power structure. When he took on Jim Wright and he won,
he was regarded very seriously from that moment on."[29]

Gingrich's ability to use the media to score political points
while not being particularly effective as a legislator signaled a new
style of political leadership focused not on legislative achievement

but on one's ability to attract and maintain media attention for political and personal gain. Gingrich's approach, confrontational rather than conciliatory and aimed at conflict rather than compromise, was not just a difference in personal style but also one that fundamentally altered the House of Representatives. In legislative parlance, the show horses had increasing political value as the work horses toiled in obscurity and oblivion.

When Gingrich successfully led the Republican Revolution in 1994, the die was cast. The norms that defined the political culture within the U.S. House of Representatives were fundamentally and forever altered; partisan goals played an increasingly important role in the functioning of the chamber. Only, as Mann and Ornstein correctly observe, strong partisan leadership did not make the legislative process more efficient, nor did it facilitate legislative accomplishment. Indeed, strong partisan leadership and greater partisan unity made the legislative process even less functional. In 2006, Mann and Ornstein declared the Congress the "broken branch" of government.[30] Four years later, they would observe that the dysfunction was "even worse than it looks."[31]

Conservatives and libertarians might argue there is an upside to congressional dysfunction—at least bad laws are not getting made. Political scientist Morris Fiorina, alternatively, offered a justification rooted in public opinion and democratic governance. Citizens vote intentionally for divided government, Fiorina argued, to balance power and limit government action.[32] Evidence on this point is not entirely convincing. Barry Burden and David Kimball, for example, find that ticket splitting occurs not because voters are seeking a partisan balance, but as a result of incumbency, campaign finance, and lopsided congressional campaigns.[33] Michael Lewis-Beck and Richard Nadeau, alternatively, find that "cognitive Madisonians," voters who intentional split their ticket for partisan balance, comprise about 20 percent of the electorate.[34] Regardless of cause, divided government serves as the most visible sign of aggregate voter incoherence and institutional structures that do not allow for the easy translation of voter preferences into policy outcomes.[35] Under a system of divided government, what are the institutional incentives for political compromise? And how are elected officials held accountable for collective outcomes?[36]

The practical effect of divided government is to make the presidency symbolically more important, as legislators and citizens look to the president to act decisively to solve problems. Accountability rests primarily on the shoulders of the president with any spillover into the Congress landing in the laps of members of the president's political party.[37] Accountability in Congress is more accidental than intentional and, barring a high-profile scandal, is almost completely divorced from actual institutional performance.

In the U.S. Congress, there is only a small and diffuse penalty for collective failure. Members of Congress succeed because they are on the right side of the issues, not because they were part of process that actually solved problems, crafted landmark legislation, or worked across the aisle to forge compromises on substantive policy matters.[38] Minnesota Republican Michele Bachmann may have never been a serious contender for the 2012 Republican nomination, but the fact that she briefly emerged post–Herman Cain as the Republican alternative to Mitt Romney (with little or no legislative accomplishments to her credit while a U.S. Representative) is illustrative of the problem. In 2008, President Barack Obama was similarly criticized for his lack of legislative accomplishment, a fact he acknowledged in a jab at Florida senator Marco Rubio during his remarks at the 2013 White House Correspondence Dinner: "The guy has not finished a single term in the Senate and he thinks he's ready to be president. Kids these days!"

Tea Party revolts against RINOs have made the situation worse. Running in increasingly safe districts in terms of partisan balance, incumbent Republicans often have to worry more about a challenge from their right rather than from the left. Indiana senator Richard Lugar's long and impressive record as a leading expert on U.S. foreign policy, for example, was insufficient to hold off a challenge from within his own party in 2012. Notably, in 2006, Lugar was named by *Time* magazine as one of the nation's best senators. Lugar's opponent, Richard Mourdock, ran against his foreign policy expertise and his willingness to work with the other side, including a ten-day trip with President Barack Obama, which earned Lugar the unfortunate moniker of President Barack Obama's favorite Republican. "Bipartisanship," Mourdock argued during the campaign, "ought to consist of Democrats coming to the Republican point of view."[39] Lugar's primary loss not only cost Republicans a much-needed Senate seat but also lost the U.S. Senate his substantive expertise.

One might think that the lesson for Republicans would be that winning partisan control of government is worth a little intraparty compromise. This is decidedly not the case. In December 2012, just a month after President Obama won reelection decisively, Republican speaker John Boehner began feeling pressure from the right wing of the Republican Party over his willingness to negotiate with President Obama on a deal to avoid the fiscal cliff. Absent compromise, taxes would revert to pre–Bush era tax rates and draconian and automatic spending cuts would be made to government services. The combined effect, economists argued, would be to send an already fragile economy back into recession. The conservative *Washington Times* raised the issue of whether Boehner should be reelected speaker,[40] while #FireBoehner quickly became a trending topic on Twitter. The compromise failed and Representative Boehner remained speaker.

Concurrently, South Carolina senator and Tea Party leader Jim DeMint exited the U.S. Senate to become president of the conservative Heritage Foundation. The jump from U.S. senator to conservative spokesman provides DeMint with a megaphone but without the inconvenience of being personally responsible for his decisions.[41] It frees him from having to vote on contentious issues that could have serious economic, social, and political consequences (like the fiscal cliff). Jim DeMint, of course, is not the first prominent politico to step down from office to pursue politics by other means. Former Alaska governor Sarah Palin left the governor's office to become a Fox News commentator and lecture circuit speaker. Not only was the pay better, but Palin was also freed from the constraints of actually having to govern.

The *Washington Post* described the significance of DeMint's retirement as follows: "DeMint's decision marks a monumental change from a not-so-long-ago era when abandoning a prime perch in the Senate to head a think tank would have been unthinkable."[42] The article further noted DeMint's willingness to back Republican challengers against Republican establishment candidates (including incumbents) without ever having passed a significant piece of legislation. One may fairly argue that President Barack Obama's victory over Hillary Clinton in the 2008 Democratic primaries was similarly made possible by the fact that he never had to vote on the use of military force in Iraq and was subsequently free to form ad hoc criticisms of the decision. Would Senator Obama really have voted against the resolution despite overwhelming public support?

More broadly, these examples highlight the central problem of contemporary American government. Congress has no collective responsibility for solving problems. Indeed, there is a reward for being an obstructionist; for being vocal on issues without being responsible for ensuring that problems are addressed, solutions are proposed, or policy is successfully implemented.

Notably, this is not a new criticism. In the not-so-distant past, Congress was structured in a way (i.e., through committees and subcommittees) that proved relatively efficient for addressing particularistic or local concerns but relatively ineffective at addressing long-term policy problems. This institutional structure provided an easy path to reelection—pay careful attention to constituencies through casework and frequent contact, bring projects back to the district, focus on work (via committees and subcommittees) that matters most to your district, and make sure to visit home often. Incumbent defeats during this period were relatively rare, with losses mostly reflecting political scandal or an unusual wave election. Even so, skilled incumbent politicians insulated themselves from national tides by heeding Tip O'Neill's advice that "all politics are local."

Newt Gingrich effectively changed the scope of congressional politics, nationalizing what used to be local races. The effect, however, has been felt primarily through changing institutional norms rather than through actual governance. Congress remains unable to address long-term concerns. Indeed, as Mann and Ornstein argue, the problem has grown worse as stronger political parties have enhanced the ability to block and obstruct policy but have not created more responsible governance or greater accountability for individual legislators.

THE FAILURE OF AMERICAN POLITICAL INSTITUTIONS

The natural impulse is to try to fix the American political structure, to enhance the voice of the public (broadly defined), and to limit the more narrow partisan concerns that drive our policy-making process. Consider, for example, a relatively simple solution: Get rid of congressional districts and elect the U.S. Congress based on proportional representation in a single national vote. Such a system would allow the majority to effectively govern by ensuring control over all of the policy levers of American national government. It would also be inherently more democratic in that it would reflect the popular will as expressed by a majority of citizens at the ballot box.

The trouble with such solutions, however, is that they fail to address more fundamental concerns about the nature of democratic governance. The mistake is to believe that the policy process is simply beset by an obstinate minority intent on obstruction. Certainly, that is the most visible and annoying symptom of the current malaise, but the cause runs much deeper and into the very marrow of democratic governance. The obstinate minority accurately reflects the opinions of a wide cross-section of the American public—a cross-section that on a different day, with only a slight change in the political winds, can fairly claim majority support. Perhaps even more to the point, political observers who see an obstinate minority in congressional Republicans also saw a Democratic minority too willing to roll over on the vote to use force in Iraq during the Bush administration.

The problem isn't that public opinion isn't represented in contemporary political arrangements or that public opinion is distorted by the participatory biases of democratic politics. The problem is that public opinion is represented too well and that it is contradictory, ambivalent, and unstable. Fragmented policymaking reflects a fragmented public. In fairness, the U.S. Constitution does provide an added burden to any sort of coordinated and consistent policymaking efforts, but this extra roadblock could easily be overcome with significant public commitment. Operating in the wake of the 9/11 terrorist attacks, the Bush administration found it easy to craft majority support for the ill-conceived Patriot Act. Obstruction was not the problem. Similarly, the federal deficit could easily be addressed if the American public showed even the faintest signs of being willing to endure the sacrifice of tax increases or significant cuts to entitlement programs.

James MacGregor Burns may have been wrong in identifying strong political parties as the solution to partisan deadlock, but his more general diagnosis, focusing on the need for strong, exuberant leadership, was right on the money. The puzzle is how to create leadership that can at once move beyond the restraints of democratic governance and the public's contradictory beliefs and expectations while simultaneously maintaining democratic accountability. This is no easy task. The solution, oddly enough, may be found in the philosophical ideas underpinning James Madison's constitutional design.

Madison recognized that the "consent of the governed" was critical to any successful political system, but he also feared a public inflamed by passion and willing to redistribute property or strip minorities of their political rights. His solution was to confine democratic inputs to the U.S. House of Representatives. The more aristocratic Senate would be well positioned to respond, but not accede, to public demands. Policy, Madison believed, should be guided not by public whim but by considered by reason, by the considered judgment of an educated, experienced, and aristocratic class. The president, two steps removed from public opinion—first by the Electoral College and then through selection by the House of Representatives—was thought to be a nonentity in this arrangement, a mere administrator of policy decisions made by the legislative branch.

Today, the democratic impulse infuses these institutions. The U.S. Senate is, arguably, more responsive to public opinion than the U.S. House of Representatives and the U.S. presidency because its singular nature is the most important policymaking institution in our constitutional structure. Only the U.S. Supreme Court remains uniquely and characteristically elitist. It is also, not coincidentally, our most respected and revered political institution.

It is, of course, too late to turn back the pages of the U.S. Constitution to 1789 and begin again, but it is worth asking this important question: Would we be better off if many of our most pressing political decisions were made not by "democratic" political processes but by panels of experts? Is it possible to recapture the philosophical underpinnings of Madison's constitutional design, in which democratic inputs influence but do not control the policymaking process, and in which government is based on the consent of the governed, but actual governing is left in the hands of elected trustees who make decisions based not on public whims but on a rich and deep understanding of the public's best interests?

NOTES

1. Alicia Cohn, "Trump Calls for Revolution, Blasts Electoral College," *The Hill's Twitter Room*, November 7, 2012, http://thehill.com/blogs/twitter-room/other-news/266423-trump-calls-for-revolution-blasts-electoral-college (accessed May 28, 2013).

2. Kristen Lee, "Republicans React to Obama Triumph with Anger, Gloom, and Calls to Fight," *New York Daily News*, November 7, 2012,

http://www.nydailynews.com/news/politics/republicans-react-obama-win-anger-gloom-calls-fight-article-1.1198334 (accessed May 24, 2013).

3. Dahlia Lithwick and Alex Lithwick, "Moving to Canada, Eh? Let Slate Help You Decide If It's Really for You," *Slate*, November 5, 2004.

4. Bill O'Reilly quoted in "The White Establishment is Now The Minority," Fox News, November 7, 2012, http://nation.foxnews.com/bill-oreilly/2012/11/07/bill-o-reilly-white-establishment-now-minority (accessed on September 22, 2013); Rush Limbaugh, "In a Nation of Children, Santa Claus Wins," *Rush Limbaugh Show*, November 7, 2012, http://www.rushlimbaugh.com/daily/2012/11/07/in_a_nation_of_children_santa_claus_wins (accessed on September 22, 3013).

5. Anne Coulter, *Treason: Liberal Treachery from the Cold War to the War on Terrorism* (New York: Three Rivers Press, 2003).

6. Specific wording is as follows: "In the next few years, an armed revolution might be necessary in order to protect our liberties." See *Belief about Sandy Hook Cover-Up, Coming Revolution Underlie Divide on Gun Control*, Fairleigh Dickinson University Public Mind Poll, May 1, 2013, http://publicmind.fdu.edu/2013/guncontrol/ (accessed May 24, 2013).

7. It is worth noting that there is some talk of changing the rules that would make it more difficult for Republicans to mount a filibuster. If history is any guide to the future, Democrats will regret the change in a future administration. This isn't to defend the filibuster, but only to remind readers that short-term considerations driving rules changes are often regretted in the future.

8. Clinton Rossiter, *The American Presidency* (New York: Harcourt, Brace & World, 1956).

9. David Frohnmayer, "Regulatory Reform: A Slogan in Search of Substance," *American Bar Association Journal* 66 (1980): 876.

10. Richard Neustadt, *Presidential Power: The Politics of Leadership* (New York: Wiley, 1960).

11. But as political scientist, William Howell has observed that presidents can act decisively in the absence of formal power and in the absence of buy-in from other political institutions. Presidential power is not just the power to persuade. See William Howell, *Power with Persuasion: The Politics of Direct Presidential Action* (Princeton, NJ: Princeton University Press, 2003).

12. Samuel Kernell, *Going Public: New Strategies in Presidential Leadership*, 4th ed. (Washington, DC: CQ Press, 2007).

13. Matthew Baum and Samuel Kernell, "Has Cable Ended the Golden Age of Presidential Television?" *American Political Science Review* 93 (1999): 99–114.

14. Sarah Kliff, "The Incredible Shrinking Presidential Address," *Washington Post (WonkBlog)*, January 24, 2012, http://www.washingtonpost.com/blogs/wonkblog/post/the-incredible-shrinking-presidential-address/2012/01/24/gIQAFXj7NQ_blog.html (accessed May 24, 2013).

15. Samuel Kernell and Laura Rice, "Cable and Partisan Polarization of the President's Audience," *Presidential Studies Quarterly* 41 (2011): 693–711.

16. Matthew Baum, "Preaching to the Choir or Converting the Flock: Presidential Communication Strategies in the Age of Three Medias," unpublished manuscript, http://www.hks.harvard.edu/fs/mbaum/documents/Baum_3Medias.pdf.

17. Amy Guttmann and Dennis Thompson, *The Spirit of Compromise: Why Governing Demands It and Campaigning Undermines It* (Princeton, NJ: Princeton University Press, 2012), 24.

18. Nolan McCarty, Keith Poole, and Howard Rosenthal, *Polarized America: The Dance of Ideology and Unequal Riches* (Cambridge, MA: MIT Press, 2006). The data are updated at http://voteview.com/polarized_america.htm (accessed May 24, 2013).

19. Bill Bishop, *The Big Sort: Why the Clustering of Like-Minded America is Tearing Us Apart* (New York: Houghton Mifflin, 2008).

20. Jamie Carson, Michael Crespin, Charles Finocchiaro, and David Rohde, "Redistricting and Party Polarization in the U.S. House of Representatives," *American Politics Research* 35 (2007): 878–904; Alan Abramowitz, Brad Alexander, and Matthew Gunning, "Incumbency, Redistricting, and the Decline of Competition in U.S. House Elections," *Journal of Politics* 68 (2006): 75–88.

21. Charles Bullock III, Donna Hoffman, and Ronald Keith Gaddie, "Regional Variations in the Realignment of American Politics, 1944–2004," *Social Science Quarterly* 87 (2006): 494–518; Earl Black and Merle Black, *The Rise of Southern Republicans* (Cambridge, MA: Harvard University Press, 2002).

22. One of the more intriguing arguments on redistricting is that voters are happier in uncompetitive districts because they value winning more than they value democratic competition. Lopsided districts, as Thomas Brunell argues, are subsequently good for democracy. See Thomas Brunell, *Redistricting and Representation: Why Competitive Elections Are Bad for America* (New York: Routledge, 2008).

23. Thomas Mann and Norman Ornstein, *It's Even Worse Than It Looks: How the American Constitutional System Collided with the New Politics of Extremism* (New York: Basic Books, 2012).

24. James MacGregor Burns, *The Deadlock of Democracy: Four Party Politics in American Politics* (New York: Prentice Hall, 1963).

25. Robert J. Samuelson, "The Deadlock of Democracy," *Washington Post*, November 1, 2004, http://www.washingtonpost.com/wp-dyn/articles/A14694-2004Oct31.html (accessed on September 22, 2013).

26. Burdett Loomis, ed., *The U.S. Senate: From Deliberation to Dysfunction* (Washington, DC: CQ Press, 2011).

27. From the Dirksen Congressional Center Robert H. Michel Papers, Speech and Trip File, December 8, 1980, http://www.dirksencenter.org/images/RHMichel/rhmleader1980.PDF (accessed May 24, 2013).

28. Peter Boyer, "Good Newt, Bad Newt," *Vanity Fair*, July 1989, retrieved form PBS Frontline at http://www.pbs.org/wgbh/pages/frontline/newt/boyernewt1.html (accessed May 24, 2013).

29. "The Long March of Newt Gingrich," *Frontline*, January 16, 1996, http://www.pbs.org/wgbh/pages/frontline/newt/newtscript.html (accessed May 24, 2013).

30. Thomas Mann and Norman Ornstein, *The Broken Branch: How Congress Is Failing America and How to Get Back on Track* (Oxford: Oxford University Press, 2006).

31. Mann and Ornstein, *It's Even Worse Than It Looks*.

32. Morris Fiorina, *Divided Government*, 2nd ed. (Needham Heights, MA: Allyn & Bacon, 1996).

33. Barry C. Burden and David C. Kimball, *Why Americans Split Their Ticket: Campaigns, Competition, and Divided Government* (Ann Arbor: University of Michigan Press, 2002).

34. Michael Lewis-Beck and Richard Nadeau, "Split-Ticket Voting: The Effects of Cognitive Madisonianism," *Journal of Politics* 66 (2004): 97–112.

35. John Coleman, "Unified Government, Divided Government, and Party Responsiveness," *American Political Science Review* 93 (1999): 821–35.

36. Robert Lowry, James Alt, and Karen Ferree, "Fiscal Policy Outcomes and Electoral Accountability in American States," *American Political Science Review* 92 (1998): 759–74.

37. Helmut Norpoth, "Divided Government and Economic Voting," *Journal of Politics* 63 (2001): 414–35.

38. Experimental work shows that independents may reward bipartisan approaches but not partisans. Members running in safe districts may subsequently act in ways that hurt the institutional image while benefiting politically. See Laurel Harbridge and Neil Malhotra, "Electoral Incentives and Partisan Conflict in Congress: Evidence from Survey Experiments," *American Journal of Political Science* 55 (2011): 494–510.

39. Kim Geiger, "Joe Donnelly Triumphs Over Richard Mourdock in Indiana Senate Race," *Los Angeles Times*, November 6, 2012, http://articles.latimes.com/2012/nov/06/news/la-pn-indiana-senate-result-20121106 (accessed May 24, 2013).

40. Henry D'Andrea, "Should a Conservative Congress Oust Boehner Over Fiscal Cliff Talks?" *Washington Times*, December 10, 2012, http://communities.washingtontimes.com/neighborhood/conscience-conservative/2012/dec/10/should-conservatives-oust-boehner-over-fiscal-clif/ (accessed May 24, 2013).

41. Of course, he also sees an estimated tenfold increase in salary.

42. Paul Kane and David Fahrenthold, "Jim DeMint Resigning from Senate to Lead Conservative Think Tank," *Washington Post*, December 6, 2012, http://articles.washingtonpost.com/2012-12-06/politics/35649614_1_de-mint-senate-conservatives-fund-republican-senate-candidates (accessed May 24, 2013).

6

FIRST, DO NO HARM

The fault, dear Brutus, is not in our stars,
But in ourselves, that we are underlings.

STEP 1: RECOGNIZE THE PROBLEM

People who know me well know that I like to take contrarian positions. It is part of what I enjoy about teaching and writing. You argue, press points, and play with ideas. You remain open to possibilities and follow your thoughts to wherever they may lead. So when I explain to friends and colleagues that I have been writing a book about the failure of American democracy, placing responsibility at the feet of the American public, the result is often quizzical, bemused expressions: "Is he serious? Is he just trying to provoke a reaction?"

Once engaged in conversation, I find most people share my concerns about the ability of democratic governance to solve our most pressing and persistent problems but misdiagnose the problem and offer exactly the wrong sorts of cures. In twelve-step programs, it is often said that the first step to recovery is recognizing the problem. This is only a half-truth. Problems are not solved through mere recognition. If it were only so, we would have no deficit: a problem easy to recognize but politically difficult to solve. Fixing problems requires action directed at the root cause of the illness; otherwise, the cure only treats the symptoms while the sickness grows deep beneath the skin. The alcoholic who realizes drinking is a problem but who switches from beer to bourbon is moving no closer to sobriety. Frustrated citizens who believe the solution to the partisan gridlock and government inefficiency is greater citizen engagement and involvement are similarly trying to put out a fire with can of gasoline. They are only making the situation worse.

Having said that, the first step to America's recovery is indeed recognizing democracy's flaws and imperfections. Democracy is not a one-size-fits-all solution to every problem, every failed system, or every bad decision. Democratic decision-making processes can—and have—made things worse. Democratic processes, while justifiably preferred for the representation of diverse interests, can (and do) lead to suboptimal decisions and inefficient decision-making. Anyone who has worked in an organizational culture that prizes democratic decision-making understands that decisions take longer and are often much worse than if they were made by the most knowledgeable and informed employees. On many decisions, expertise should be preferred over "common sense."

Like dysfunctional family relationships, democracy's pathologies are easier to see elsewhere. Elections in nations without adequate support for minority rights and procedural safeguards against majority governance, for example, are on Plato's short ride from democracy to demagogic leadership to tyranny. In the Middle East, democracy is no assurance against radical or extremist political groups winning control of government through fair, democratic, and open elections. Democratic processes can yield to decidedly illiberal governments. Even countries with long and storied histories of democracy (e.g., Greece) can vote themselves into fiscal insolvency by greatly outspending government revenues. Giving the people what they want rarely yields a balanced budget and is no guarantee of responsible governance, democratic peace, or economic prosperity. Writing in *The Guardian*, Slavoj Žižek described the growing dissatisfaction in former Soviet Republics this way: "In the glorious days of 1989, they equated democracy with the abundance of western consumerist societies; and 20 years later, with the abundance still missing, they now blame democracy itself."[1] Žižek further notes the dissatisfaction has been spreading to western democracies as citizenries increasingly recognize the failure of their democratically elected political elites. As the poet, writer, drinker, and scalawag Charles Bukowski once observed, "The difference between a democracy and a dictatorship is that in a democracy you vote first and take orders later; in a dictatorship you don't have to waste your time voting."

British member of Parliament Rory Stewart has similarly argued that advocates for democracy have oversold its virtues and, in doing so, have put it at risk. Democracy does not necessarily lead to more efficient or effective policy, and may not even make the material lives of democratic citizens better. Democratic governance, after all, is a messy, convoluted, and frustrating process. As Stewart observes, "The point about democracy is not that it delivers legitimate, effective, prosperous rule of law. It's not that it guarantees peace with itself or with its neighbors. . . . Democracy matters because it reflects an idea of equality."[2] (Stewart, it should be noted, was arguing for democracy, not because it yields better decisions or economic prosperity, but because it values political equality. Unfortunately, most advocates for more democracy do not recognize, or consider, the tradeoff.)

In contrast, authoritarian governments like China can have greater foresight in making long-term investments in science and education while pursuing long-term strategic nation building. In the United States, short-term budget constraints have yielded cuts in exactly those areas of spending that have the greatest long-term payoff, while long-standing problems that require short-term sacrifices remain unresolved. Democracy may well be threatening our long-term viability as a military, economic, and scientific super power.

Democracies are unquestionably better than dictatorships, but they can and do fail. They fail not only because despots seize political power through force but also because they fall under their own weight, unable to meet the unreasonable demands and unrealistic expectations of their citizens. Democratic citizenries can and have pushed for and supported undemocratic outcomes (e.g., limits on minority rights), undermining the very democratic principles that allow for public participation in public life. The long history of racial prejudice and segregation in the United States, for example, was endorsed by democratically elected officials.[3] Indeed, even today, candidates and campaigns use racial appeals (albeit implicit rather than explicit) to persuade undecided voters. Political consultants well understand the underlying political psychology: emotions move voters, not reasoning and certainly not intellectual appeals.

If the first step to recovery is recognizing the problem, the frustration and anger Americans express about their political system is a healthy sign. At least the public recognizes that the system is not working very well, even if too many citizens fail to see the gridlock and inefficiencies as the result of their own failure to place meaningful demands on democratically elected representatives. The problem, they believe, resides elsewhere—in Washington, DC, or in the state capitols of Sacramento, Albany, Springfield, or Baton Rouge. Or it is the fault of particular groups (none of which they happen to belong to)—the Tea Party, labor unions, right-wing conservatives, liberal socialists, or the more generically labeled "special interests."

The first step to recovery, then, is recognizing that the problem is not just in Washington. It is on Main Street, in the counties and towns that make up the Midwest, in the urban centers that define the Northeast, in rural Southern communities, and in the open plains and mountainous regions of the West. What happens in Washington cannot simply be sliced off from the rest of the nation as something foreign and remote or as something for which citizens bear no responsibility. What happens in Washington is a reflection (albeit an imperfect one) of who we are as a people. If we get the government we deserve, the challenge is not in replacing one set of officials with another; it is in demanding more and deserving better. Part of the solution is in understanding our role and limitations as citizens.

A Caveat

I need to take a moment to clarify. This book is not intended to be an argument against democracy in every size, shape, and form. Government should be based on the consent of the governed and every citizen should have the right to vote. This is no argument against the Fifteenth, Nineteenth, or Twenty-Sixth Amendments. The public does reasonably well in answering relative simple questions about whether the country is moving in the right direction, and this is a role the public should continue to play. The central question raised here does not lend itself to a binary choice between democracy and no democracy, but rather asks how much democracy and in what form. Where does democracy improve decision-making? And where would other decision-making structures work more effectively?

Our natural tendency is to believe democratic processes are always better than other forms of decision-making—even if, intuitively, we know this is not true. Consider, for example, our often-stated desire to have government run more like a business. The subtext is obvious, though not at all embraced or accepted when made explicit—government should run more like hierarchically structured corporations that are almost universally autocratic when it comes to decision-making.[4] The reason government cannot run like a business is simple: because government is not a business and because government leaders are not empowered to make decisions in the long-term best interests of the public. Elected officials cannot fire the citizens who elected them.

The American presidency may the most powerful office in the world, but the American president lacks the discretion the late Steve Jobs had to make decisions about the future of Apple. The iPhone would have been difficult to develop by a government-led enterprise because government has to be attentive to special interests and public inputs. Apple was, of course, motivated by a vision of how best to serve its potential markets, tested its products to gauge audience reaction, and, ultimately, was held accountable by the marketplace, but Steve Jobs maintained enough autonomy and independence to exercise real and meaningful leadership, which leads to this inescapable point: *If we want government to be more efficient, we must empower our elected representatives to make decisions based not our immediate wants or needs but on our long-term best interests.*

Government must be held accountable for its decisions, but that accountability should be based on whether our elected representatives have effectively solved our most pressing and persistent problems and not whether they have staked out the right position on issues they do little or nothing to resolve. Dogmatically opposing all tax increases while advocating for military interventions in Iraq and Afghanistan, for example, is as at least as fiscally irresponsible as any variant of tax and spend liberalism. Similarly, using social security and Medicare as a political hammer for defeating Republicans while failing to address the long-term fiscal solvency of these programs may make for good politics, but it is bad policy.

STEP 2: COMMITTING TO CORRECTIVE ACTION

Beyond mere recognition of the problem, the second step to recovery is committing to creating a more effective and viable political system and to a constant and ongoing reform of the American political process. Winston Churchill famously declared, "Democracy is the worst form of government, except for all those other forms that have been tried from time to time." Churchill's famous but unfortunate quote came after saving Europe from fascism but losing an election at home. The quote is routinely and regrettably used as an apology for the status quo, a resignation to imperfection—that the current system, while flawed, might be the best we can do. It does little good to recognize a problem only to realize you are helpless when it comes to identifying or acting on possible solutions. If this is the best we can do, why change?

Public cynicism about possibilities of meaningful reform is well justified. Real change often fails to materialize as the forces favoring the status quo dig in and defend the existing system. When reform does occur, it often leads to unintended consequences that must be undone by future reforms. Good intentions may not lead directly to hell, but they are certainly no guarantee of a more efficient or more responsible political system.

Consider the current process for selecting presidential nominees put in place by the McGovern-Fraser reforms following the 1968 Democratic Convention. These reforms were designed to increase the representativeness of national conventions and to ensure that delegate counts were proportional to a candidate's actual support in presidential primaries. They had the unintended consequence of increasing the length and expense of presidential campaigns by increasing the number and importance of presidential primaries. Absent McGovern-Fraser, it is unlikely that candidates would be traversing through the Iowa snow more than a year before the actual election.

Similarly, in the 1970s, Congress passed sweeping campaign finance reforms designed to limit the influence of "fat cats" in the political process. These reforms gave way to legally recognized political action committees (PACs) and a form of institutionalized corruption via campaign contributions from labor and business PACs. The reforms have been slowly whittled away through precedent, administrative rulings, and court decisions to the point that "fat cat" contributors matter more today than perhaps at any other time in American political history. The widely deplored *Citizens United* decision was simply the last straw in a crumbling regulatory regime already weakened by noncompliance (e.g., Barack Obama opting out of public financing in 2008) and concerted efforts by Democrats and Republicans to exploit loopholes in campaign finance regulations for partisan political advantage.

Decrying unintended consequences, however, is no excuse for inaction or for a meek and passive acceptance of the status quo.

That argument would not hold water in other policy areas and it should not hold sway when it comes to institutional reform. Most people, for example, would not accept the argument that cracking down on one form of drug use (cocaine) increases other types of drug use (crystal meth)—even if it is unquestionably true—as an argument for not trying to stop the illegal drug trade. Working to ensure a political system that is based on the consent of the governed while also adequate to the task of addressing long-term problems will unquestionably succumb to the law of unintended consequences. The solution, however, is not inaction. It is more action, an ongoing commitment to making the process better by seeking the right balance between the competing demands of efficiency and responsiveness.

STEP 3: DO NO HARM

Writing in *Federalist No. 51*, James Madison made the following observation: "If men were angels, no government would be necessary. If angels were to govern men, neither external nor internal controls on government would be necessary." We might add a corollary: If governing could exist separate from human nature, we might be able to devise a perfect and durable system of government that never needed reform. Because governing is an inherently human endeavor, all political structures and processes are eventually corrupted through practice and precedent and need reform and renewal.

Despite the Tea Party's misguided beliefs in original intent, the U.S. Constitution was neither divinely inspired nor perfected in its original manifestation. Not only does it specifically recognize slavery via the Three-Fifths Compromise, but it also intentionally left out the Bill of Rights. Its durability is due not to its inspired wisdom but its intentional ambiguity, its flexibility in allowing for the possibility of growth and transformation within a loosely defined institutional framework. The argument against the enumeration of political rights in a written Bill of Rights, for example, was that such an enumeration would incorrectly suggest that our rights were limited to those specifically detailed in the Constitution, a position ironically and directly at odds with contemporary purveyors of original intent.

The need for reform at a general level, however, is not a suitable argument for any specific set of reforms. To say that the system is broken is not the same as saying we have discovered the cure. This leads to our third principle rooted in the Hippocratic Oath: first, do no harm.[5] To achieve this end, we must take care to articulate a set of principles that should guide reform efforts.

First, reform might be oriented toward increasing the *responsiveness* of elected officials to their constituents. Calls for more democracy or returning commonsense values to Washington often rest on this important principle. Indeed, responsiveness as a value has great cultural resonance in American politics and is the underlying principle guiding most political reform movements. If only our elected representatives would heed the wisdom of the typical citizen, or so the logic goes, government would function more effectively. As I have argued throughout, the result is a system that is overly responsive to democratic inputs but collectively irresponsible. In a pluralistic democracy in which the practice of politics occurs primarily through group activity, this often means the system is overly responsive to pressures from well-organized and well-funded political groups that are best positioned to take advantage of democratic channels of influence. Greater responsiveness, ironically, makes the system more responsive to the most active and engaged citizens rather than to the collective "best" interests of the population.

Second, reform might be oriented toward increasing *responsible* decision-making. Responsible governments may be more or less responsive to public inputs but have the authority, autonomy, and independence to make decisions and address long-standing and persistent problems. Responsible governments, for example, would not risk a downgraded credit rating over an inability to raise the debt ceiling. Nor would they walk over a fiscal cliff because they have carefully calculated that once over the cliff compromise and negotiation will be politically more feasible. While democratic governments can be responsible, democratic decision-making processes do not necessarily lend themselves to greater responsibility. Indeed, the opposite is often true: having to go before the voters and explain policy decisions often means punting on long-term problems to avoid short-term and politically costly sacrifices (growing budget deficits) or making irresponsible decisions for politically motivated reasons (the decision to use force in Iraq).

Finally, reform can be directed at improving *collective accountability*. Our current political system is designed such that political accountability resides with the individual representative and his/her ability to reflect local opinion. The result is that individual representatives can be politically successful even as political institutions are failing. The most obvious manifestation of this is in the clichéd but accurate truism that we love our individual representatives even as we hate Congress as an institution. Now imagine if accountability were structured to reward collective responsibility and members were rewarded or punished based not on their individual position-taking but on the ability of Congress as an institution to effectively address long-term budget deficits. This leads us to a simple proposition: The goal of reform should be to enhance responsible decision-making while improving the collective accountability of the political system. It should not be improving the responsiveness of elected representatives to their local constituencies.

Proposals aimed at improving responsiveness without enhancing responsibility or accountability launch us down the slippery slope of dissatisfaction, democratic reform, and eventually greater dissatisfaction. That is, they will only make the problem worse.

The Fallacy of Direct Democracy

We live in a world where digital democracy is a very real possibility, where elected representatives could be replaced by popular democracy and ordinary citizens could vote on each and every issue. Why do we need elected representatives when they have proved inadequate to the task of actually governing? Why not put the power directly in the hands of the people? This would be democracy in its purest form and would ensure that policy followed the wishes of the public as expressed in real time and without the filters of elected representatives or news media interpretation and analysis.

As much as most people claim to believe in democracy, this proposal is generally met with a universal cringe. They begin with technical objections (e.g., what if the system for counting votes was hacked?) but quickly realize the problems run much deeper and are much more substantive. The average person does not have the time, the interest, or the capacity to understand the intricacies of health care policy, the federal budget, or foreign policy. Despite our expressed love of democracy, do we really want our neighbors voting on whether to send troops to a foreign country they cannot find on a map?[6] Do we want our co-workers deciding on federal government spending priorities when they grossly overestimate the amount of money spent on foreign aid, welfare, and virtually every other area of government spending? Now consider that subtle manipulations of policy choices (e.g., framing, question order, and question wording) can have profound impacts on citizen responses. Taken to its logic extreme, the folly of direct democracy is fully exposed.

Quickly, most people realize the value of representative government. We elect representatives for a simple reason: so they may govern in our place, so that they may spend the necessary time and energy to learn the details, the complexities, and the nuance underlying critical policy decisions. To govern effectively requires substantive knowledge, procedural understanding, a commitment of time and resources, and an ability and willingness to compromise. The need for compromise is especially acute in Madison's constitutional structure, in which no single branch of government is able to act effectively without the consent of others. And yet our political system is currently configured in ways that make compromise exceedingly difficult (and often impossible), that bind the hands of elected officials to constituent sentiments and organized interests in ways that make governing more challenging and partisan gridlock more likely.

The obvious solution so runs against our cultural instincts for democratic governance that it is nearly impossible to make out amid the fog of voter frustration and anger. In an age of declining trust, we need to find ways to entrust and empower our elected representatives to make decisions and exercise meaningful leadership.

The anger visibly rising in the redness of his face, a friend I frequently talk politics with asks the million dollar question: "You are telling me we need to place more trust in the crooks and liars in Washington?" Indeed.

Democracy Without Limits

Too often, the blame for political failure falls on our current slate of elected officials, as if trading Barack Obama for George W. Bush or Ronald Reagan for Jimmy Carter will cure all that ails American democracy. Even worse, it is as if our representatives and senators magically appeared in the U.S. Congress and state legislatures throughout the country without having actually been elected "by the people." This common refrain is paraphrased as follows: *The problem is these people get into office and never want to leave. What we really need are term limits to get some regular people in there instead of these professional politicians.*

Advocates for term limits are correct that members of Congress are increasingly professional and hold onto elected office with a fierce and relentless tenacity. The problem, however, is not the professionalization of politics or the individual politicians who routinely win election (and reelection), but rather what these politicians must do to win in the first place—the promises they must make and, regrettably, try to keep—and their ongoing efforts to be responsive to their constituencies.[7] They are successful for a reason: they give their constituencies what they want.

Our politicians may be disingenuous, some are unquestionably corrupt, and others are self-serving and dishonest, but they are, on the whole, no worse than the politicians of our past. Instead, they have better tools and resources at their disposal for understanding the demands, preferences, and needs of their constituents. For better or (mostly) for worse, they are more responsive to those constituents and supporters necessary to ensure their reelection.

The argument for term limits is essentially an argument against democracy: *Please get rid of the professional politicians who do such an excellent job representing their local constituencies that they can never be beaten. In their place, please bring in a set of amateurs who might do the right thing for the country by unintentionally misrepresenting their local constituencies.*

Advocates for term limits do get half of the equation correct: reelection pressures often work against serving the broader public interest, as incumbents focus narrowly on local reelection constituencies and on short-term election cycles rather than on long-term problems. If you want to understand what really needs to be done to address deficits, climate change, partisan gridlock, or a host of other problems, ask former or retiring members of Congress. Freed of reelection pressures and no longer worried about reprisals from special interest groups and the ideological fringe of their political parties, they have the ability to speak the truth. Remove democratic politics and you get closer to responsible governance.

Despite this obvious advantage, term limits are a bad idea because the problem is about not only who is winning office but also the incentive structures that guide representatives' policymaking decisions while in office. Representatives represent their *local* constituencies' *short-term* preferences very well. What is missing is the representation of the collective and a longer view, asking citizens to endure short-term sacrifice for long-term gain. The empirical research on state legislative term limits reveals significant issues in their adoption and implementation, including the loss of legislative professionalism, an increase in individualism and showboating, and a loss of institutional power relative to the executive branch. [8]

- A 2011 study of gubernatorial term limits found that reelection-eligible governors tried harder and were more competent than term-limited governors. The result was higher economic growth in states with governors who were not term limited. [9]
- A 2012 study of state legislative term limits in Missouri found that term limits reduced the level of knowledge in the legislature and weakened the state legislature relative to the executive branch. The author of the study, David Valentine, concluded that term limits "achieved none of the sponsors' principal objectives" and had significant negative consequences. [10]
- A study evaluating the effect of state legislative term limits over the fifty states concluded that term limits result in legislators who are more likely to follow their own conscience and less likely to follow constituent opinion, a potentially positive outcome. [11] In a separate article, however, these authors found that term limits increase individualism in legislatures and decrease the incentives for cooperation. While term limits did orient legislators more toward the state than local constituencies, the evidence suggests that the result was position-taking and showboating. That is, they made legislatures less responsive to district opinion but did little or nothing to improve collective accountability or institutional responsibility. Finally, there is some evidence to suggest that term limits decrease citizen knowledge of their state legislators by increasing legislative turnover, thus reducing an important lever for political accountability and an important link between citizen and representative. [12]

No, the fault is not our in our elected officials; it is in us, in our inability to live up to the unrealistic demands of democratic governance. The reasoning public that serves as a foundation of democratic theory is a façade, an unrealistic and untenable ideal. It is not entirely our fault as citizens as it is ingrained into our DNA. As human beings, we are subject to cognitive biases that lead us astray, that make us misperceive the nature of our world, and that leave us holding tightly to beliefs that cannot be supported by logic or evidence. Perhaps even more troubling, when we stumble across the inefficiencies, conflict, and compromise that define democratic decision-making, we turn away. We may say we believe in democracy, but we opt for entertainment over a presidential address and reality television over the nightly news. We are, as a citizenry, too often willfully uninformed and misinformed.

If too much democracy is at the root of our discontent, more democracy will not cure government paralysis. We get the government we deserve, paralyzed by gridlock, wrapped in indecision and polarized politics. Calls for greater democracy subsequently end badly, repeating a cycle of greater democratization, growing frustration, and reform. Nowhere is this more apparent than in the belief that term limits will help solve the problems inherent in professionalized career-centered politics. Laid bare, the problem is that our professional politicians represent us too well.

Reducing the Costs of Democratic Participation

Ever since Anthony Downs famously calculated that the individual costs of voting outweighed any policy benefits that might accrue if a preferred candidate were to win election, scholars and reformers have been looking to reduce the costs of registration requirements and making voting more convenient. As a result, voting and registration are now more convenient for routine voters, but the connection from registration requirements to voter turnout, citizen engagement, and participation is less clear.

Motor voter legislation, allowing for voter registration at state departments of motor vehicles, and early voting provisions appear to have had only small or insignificant impacts on voter turnout.[13]

Voting by mail experiments have similarly eased the costs of voting but have had, at best, small effects on voter turnout and little effect on the composition of the electorate.[14] When turnout has increased, it appears to reflect mobilization efforts on behalf of candidates, parties, and outside groups, and not legal changes making registration procedures less difficult. The simple act of asking someone to vote remains one of the most powerful mechanisms for increasing voter participation. Perhaps for these reasons, voter identification requirements have been found to have a small effect on voter turnout but have not—as feared or hoped—changed the composition of the electorate.[15]

Implicit in efforts to reduce the costs of voting is the unquestioned assumption that greater participation improves the performance of democratic governance. This is decidedly not the case. Voter turnout, for example, tends to be higher during periods of economic dislocation and voter dissatisfaction. "I'm mad as hell and I am not going to take it anymore" is a powerful mobilizing force,[16] though, notably, so are more positive emotional responses like hope and enthusiasm.[17] Regardless, voters are often influenced to participate not by a reasoned call to action but through emotion-based campaign appeals and social pressures.

Voter turnout is often read as the pulse of electoral politics, an indicator of the overall health of democratic governance. There is good normative reason for this. More robust voter turnout indicates a population able and willing to engage in the political process, to believe that their participation matters, and to have buy-in into the political system. Low voter turnout, particularly among historically disenfranchised groups (e.g., African Americans, Hispanics, and other immigrant populations), is a signal that democratic governance is not working as it should or that it is only working for some segments of the population.

Because the American political system is a pluralistic rather than a majoritarian democracy and because elected representatives respond to those voters (and groups) necessary to ensure their reelection, participatory biases have real and meaningful consequences on who benefits from policy-related decisions. It is no accident that politicians tread lightly around social security and Medicare for fear of angering active and engaged senior citizens or that the effective enfranchisement of African American voters as a result of the Voting Rights Act of 1965 resulted in policy more responsive to the concerns of African American voters. Individual participation may be insufficient for swinging an election, but the question of who votes has important consequences for policy responsiveness.

Practically speaking, however, higher voter turnout does not translate into more effective governance. Policy-related decisions do not suddenly become easier when voters participate in stronger numbers; in fact, policymaking can become more trying and divisive if participation is driven by ideological polarization, anger and frustration, or even heightened expectations unlikely to be realized by the realities of governance. Higher voter turnout makes governing easier only when voters send clear, unambiguous signals about what they want out of government. Rarely is this the case under our current institutional arrangements.

A More Educated Citizenry

For almost a decade now, I have been part of *Louisiana Public Square*, a locally produced television program and an ongoing experiment in deliberative democracy. Once a month, guests are recruited to have a conversation on an issue and to ask questions directly to policymakers. In an age of increasing polarization, the show serves as a healthy reminder that most people are fairly reasonable, not particularly ideological, and oriented toward practical and effective solutions. For me personally, the show serves as an elixir that counteracts my natural tendencies toward cynicism and distrust. Bringing a randomly selected group of people into a room to have a conversation gives one hope that the solutions to our most pressing problems are not completely out of reach and political compromise remains possible.

On one point, however, the show is almost comical. No matter what the topic or the context, education is almost always offered as a solution. It is the proverbial hammer in search of a nail. From a normative standpoint, it is hard to disagree: When is a more educated population ever a bad thing? In political science, the evidence is unequivocal—a more educated population is more involved, more engaged, and more ideologically consistent. If we think of democracy as a political system, better inputs should naturally yield better outcomes.

Unfortunately, education is not a panacea: a more educated population does necessarily lend itself to democratic consensus. As an academic, the easiest and most readily available evidence to this point can be found in dysfunctional faculty governance. As Henry Kissinger reportedly observed, "Academic politics are so vicious precisely because the stakes are so small."[18] PhDs practicing deliberative democracy will not result in easier decision-making; indeed, the ease of decision-making may be inversely related to level of education within the group as lines harden around relatively minor but "principled" disagreements. The result is often prolonged conversations and a reluctance to make decisions in the absence of consensus.

More generally, more informed citizens generally have more strongly held beliefs and hold onto these beliefs with greater tenacity. As we learned in the discussion of motivated reasoning, the willingness to reject new information often increases with education, as more politically knowledgeable citizens are also more equipped to counterargue with new messages or to find holes in new (or existing) evidence. Recent research suggests that ambivalence rather than cognitive ability is the key to evidence-based reasoning.[19] Second, in terms of decision-making, information does not necessarily lead to agreement in values, general orientations toward government, or specific policy options. Stated differently, the issue space between Democrats and Republicans does not narrow as education increases but instead expands. Third, over time, increases in formal education in the United States have not yielded a more effective political system or a less divided electorate.

It is fair to argue that this reflects fundamental issues in primary and secondary education, specifically the decline in the importance of civic education and basic political knowledge, but this is a different problem calling for a different solution: not more education but better education, presumably focused more on citizenship and an understanding of basic rules and procedures that define the American political system. Indeed, one of the most fundamental shortcomings of American public opinion is the failure of citizens to understand and appreciate democratic decision-making, the need for political compromise, and the unruliness and inefficiencies inherent in these processes. Democracy is messy and not clean. Because of this failure, citizens disapprove of democratic processes even as they profess their love of democracy.

Overall, a more educated citizenry can (and should) be valued for its own sake as it should translate into a more engaged citizenry with more coherent and consistent political preferences. But education is no magic bullet and provides no guarantee that democratic institutions will function more effectively or that ideological and partisan disagreements will suddenly diminish. To work effectively, the political system must be able to effectively translate democratic inputs into policies that, in turn, effectively address long-standing and persistent problems.

Stay in College

In 2000, George W. Bush won the presidency while losing the popular vote. His victory was made possible by the Electoral College, a much-maligned and, arguably, antiquated political institution designed to put distance between presidents and public opinion. That distance has almost entirely disappeared, as presidents are routinely measured by short-term fluctuations in their approval ratings and presidential power is closely connected to perceptions of popular support.

Since 2000, there has been a steady chorus of calls for a constitutional amendment replacing the Electoral College with a national popular vote. Indeed, when it comes to electoral reform, only term limits are more popular than proposals to abolish the Electoral College. A Gallup Poll conducted in January 2013, for example, found that 63 percent of Americans would support abolishing the Electoral College, compared to 71 percent who supported term limits.[20] Support for term limits and for abolishing the Electoral College serve as excellent examples of areas where the preference for "more democracy" is intuitively appealing but empirically flawed.

Moving to a national popular vote would unquestionably make presidential elections more democratic, but it would not instill greater legitimacy in election outcomes, nor would it make national government more efficient or effective. Highly competitive elections decided by very narrow margins almost always succumb to questions of fairness. Were votes counted correctly? Were there efforts to suppress the votes of minorities through arbitrary enforcement of identification standards and long lines? Were votes bought with "walking money" used as part of field operations during last-minute get-out-the-vote drives? It is the competitiveness, rather than the rules, that makes an election controversial. Narrow elections breed discontent. Had Al Gore narrowly won the 2000 presidential election based on his popular vote showing, the outcome would have likely been no less controversial.

Consider a system based on a national popular vote in which four well-funded candidates ran for the presidency and the winner received 26 percent of the vote while two of the remaining candidates received 25 percent of the national vote and the last-place finisher received 24 percent. Such an outcome would yield little confidence in the winner. Indeed, it is possible that the least-preferred candidate would win the presidency. In state primary elections, least-preferred candidates often emerge out of competitive primary elections. Perhaps the most dramatic example is Louisiana native and former klansman David Duke. Duke made it into statewide general election contests for Louisiana governor in

1991 and U.S. senator in 1989 by emerging out of crowded primary fields.[21] In doing so, he embarrassed the national Republican
Party and the state of Louisiana. Replacing the Electoral College
with a plurality "winner-take-all" election for the presidency might
encourage third parties and independent candidacies, subsequently expanding the range of political debate, but it might also open
the door to extremists able to secure just enough voters in a
crowded field to win an election.

Consequently, any proposal to replace the Electoral College
with the popular vote would also need a provision for a runoff
election or alternative voting (or instant runoff voting) to ensure
winning candidates receive popular support. A runoff election
would mean that at the end of an already extended campaign
season, Americans would be asked to vote one more time. Because
no candidate won 50 percent of the vote, this would have been the
case in the 1968, 1992, 1996, and 2000 presidential elections. It is
unclear how an additional campaign would have affected the outcome of these elections, but runoff elections at the state level
generally have lower voter turnout, and front-runners and incumbents are more likely to win.[22] Runoff elections do not solve the
problem of the least acceptable candidate making it into the runoff because they attract intense but shallow support. In a three-
candidate race, a candidate with an electoral ceiling of 34 percent
can make it into the runoff even if they have little or no chance of
winning the general election.

The instant runoff, or alternative voting, offers what at first
glance appears to be an attractive alternative by allowing voters to
rank their preferences for the available candidates. Under the scenario outlined above, the last-place finisher (with 24 percent of
the vote) would be eliminated in the first round of voting and their
votes would be reallocated to their second choice. This elimination
of candidates would occur until a winning candidate could be declared. Instant runoff voting (IRV) is intuitively appealing and
avoids the costs of an additional election campaign. Unfortunately,
it is also not free of perverse outcomes. Imagine, for example, a

scenario with three candidates—a Libertarian, a Republican, and a Democrat—and the following set of assumptions:

- In a two-candidate race, the Republican would defeat either the Libertarian or the Democrat.
- In a two-candidate race, the Democrat would defeat the Libertarian.
- In a three-candidate race with instant runoff voting, the Republican is eliminated first and the Democrat wins the election despite being the least-preferred candidate.

One additional criticism of the Electoral College bears mentioning: the tendency of candidates and campaigns to focus almost exclusively on crucial "swing states" instead of campaigning nationwide. States written off as solidly in the Republican or Democratic column receive little campaign activity, while voters in these states may be even more inclined to decide their vote doesn't matter. While this is fair criticism, it is a misreading of the fundamental nature of American political campaigns. Targeting voters by geography is one of the key tasks of any successful campaign. Were the Electoral College to disappear tomorrow, targeting would continue to occur, but the focus would be on localities rather than on states. Areas of the country that are safely Republican or Democratic would continue to see little campaign activity, while swing areas, now defined in terms of counties and metropolitan areas, would continue to be the focus of campaign activity.

Overall, despite its flaws, the Electoral College performs reasonably well. In most elections, it produces a relatively clear winner—even when no candidate wins a majority of the popular vote—and winning candidates have to build a wide base of political support extending far beyond any given region. Even in the divisive 2000 campaign, the Electoral College served to diffuse a potential crisis by focusing attention on the recount within a single state. Imagine the havoc that would have been wreaked by a national recount across all fifty states. The perceived failures of the Electoral College have less to do with an antiquated institutional structure and more to do with a divided electorate and a highly competitive election. The popular vote will do nothing to alter this and could make it worse.

NOTES

1. Slavoj Žižek, "The West's Crisis Is One of Democracy as Much as Finance," *Guardian*, January 16, 2013, http://www.guardian.co.uk/commentisfree/2013/jan/16/west-crisis-democracy-finance-spirit-dictators.

2. Rory Stewart, "Why Democracy Matters," TED Talk, October 2012, http://www.ted.com/speakers/rory_stewart.html (accessed May 25, 2013).

3. Those officials were elected with African Americans effectively disenfranchised, though many officials still ran on overtly racist platforms in the aftermath of the Voting Rights Act of 1965.

4. I realize that people can point to more democratic cultures within business organizations that have been integral to a corporation's success. Even so, democratic decision-making is not the rule in corporations.

5. Notably, the Hippocratic Oath does not actually contain this phrase.

6. No offense to my own neighbors, who are smart, civic minded, and politically engaged.

7. This passage owes much to Thomas Patterson's excellent work, *Out of Order* (New York: Knopf, 1993).

8. Thad Kousser, *Term Limits and the Dismantling of State Legislative Professionalism* (Cambridge: Cambridge University Press, 2005).

9. James Alt, Ethan Bueno de Mesquita, and Shanna Rose, "Disentangling Accountability and Competence in Elections: Evidence from U.S. Term Limits," *Journal of Politics* (2011): 171–86.

10. David C. Valentine, "The Impact and Implications of Term Limits in Missouri," Missouri Legislative Academy, Institute of Public Policy, Harry S. Truman School of Public Affairs, September 2012, http://ipp.missouri.edu/files/ipp/attachments/12-2012_term_limits_final_sept._2012-3.pdf.

11. John Carey, Richard Niemi, Lynda Powell, and Gary Moncrief, "The Effect of Term Limits on State Legislatures: A New Survey of the 50 States," *Legislative Studies Quarterly* 31 (2006): 105–34.

12. John Carey, Richard Niemi, and Lynda Powell, "The Effect of Term Limits on State Legislatures," *Spectrum: Journal of State Government* 75 (2001).

13. Steven Knack, "Does 'Motor Voter' Work? Evidence from State-Level Data," *Journal of Politics* 57 (1995): 796–811; Robert Stein, "Early Voting," *Public Opinion Quarterly* 62 (1998): 57–80; Robert Stein and Patricia Garcia-Monet, "Voting Early But Not Often," *Social Science Quarterly* 97 (1997): 657–77; Adam Berinsky, "The Perverse Consequences of Electoral Reform in the United States," *American Politics Research* 33 (2005): 471–91.

14. Adam Berinsky, Nancy Burns, and Michael Traugott, "Who Votes by Mail?" *Public Opinion Quarterly* 65 (2001): 178–97.

15. M. V. Hood and Charles Bullock, "Much Ado About Nothing? An Empirical Assessment of the Georgia Voter Identification Statute," *State Politics and Policy Quarterly* 12 (2012): 394–414.

16. Nicholas Valentino, Ted Brader, Eric Groenendyk, Krysha Gregorowicz, and Vincent Hutchings, "Election Night's Alright for Fighting: The Role of Emotions in Political Participation," *Journal of Politics* 73 (2011): 156–70.

17. Ted Brader, "Striking a Responsive Chord: How Political Ads Motivate and Persuade Voters by Appealing to Emotions," *American Journal of Political Science* 49 (2005): 388–405; George Marcus and Michael B. Mackuen, "Anxiety, Enthusiasm, and the Vote: The Emotional Underpinnings of Learning and Involvement During Presidential Campaigns," *American Political Science Review* 87 (1993): 672–85.

18. Woodrow Wilson is credited with a similar remark, as is William Sayre.

19. Howard Lavine, Christopher Johnston, and Marco Steenbergen, *The Ambivalent Partisan: How Critical Loyalty Promotes Democracy* (New York: Oxford University Press, 2012).

20. Lydia Saad, "American Call for Term Limits, End to Electoral College," *GallupPolitics*, January 18, 2013, http://www.gallup.com/poll/159881/americans-call-term-limits-end-electoral-college.aspx (accessed May 26, 2013).

21. The Louisiana primary system is unique in that candidates compete across party lines for a spot in the general election. If a candidate wins 50 percent in the primary, no general election is held. For federal

offices, Louisiana now uses closed primaries, but the blanket primary remains in place for state elections.

22. Charles Bullock and Loch Johnson, *Runoff Elections in the United States* (Chapel Hill: University of North Carolina Press, 1992).

7

AMERICA'S RECOVERY PLAN

There lies a point at which Democracy is impossible because
the people are too enterprising and active minded to let others
do their political thinking for them, and still too ignorant and
narrow to do their own thinking with success.
                                                    —C. H. Bretherton[1]

Too much democracy kills democracy.
          —From a June 18, 2012, story in *The Times* (London)
          on a vote in Switzerland to hold several national and local
                                                    referendums each year[2]

STEP 4: DEVELOPING A RECOVERY PLAN

In *It's Even Worse Than It Looks*, Thomas Mann and Norman
Ornstein argue that the dysfunction of contemporary American
politics is rooted in a mismatch between parliamentary-style political parties and a constitutional system designed to thwart majority
action. The institutional framework of American politics, created
out of fear of majority rule, allows a committed and ideological
minority to effectively shut down the political system. The Republican Party's willingness to risk credit default for ideological rea-

sons is symptomatic of this mismatch and the deep dysfunction of contemporary American politics.

The dysfunction runs much deeper. The Republican Party's willingness to risk credit default was not an irrational decision free of political considerations. Taking into account their base constituency and weighing the political and economic consequences of not raising the debt ceiling, Republicans decided to hold their cards and play their hand rather than fold. In doing so, they were responsive to their constituency—Republican voters most critical to their long-term political success (or failure) who wanted something done to reduce government spending and government debt. This was not a failure of one rogue political party bucking Madison's constitutional design; it was a democratic failure rooted in the best efforts of a political party to represent its core constituencies and act on the preferences of its supporters. If Republicans failed, so, too, did democratic governance.

Congressional Republicans may have misread public opinion and failed to understand that they, rather than President Obama, would be blamed for the ensuing partisan gridlock. The misreading of public opinion, however, is more evidence of this point. Misreading public opinion presumes trying to read it in the first place. The problem was not that Republicans ignored voter preferences but rather that they attempted to act on an immediate concern without fully accounting for the inherent contradictions in these preferences. Cut spending but not on anything that actually costs money. Or as an oft-quoted sign declared, "Keep the government out of my Medicare."

The larger problem is this: The political system is not unresponsive to citizen preferences (as is commonly believed) but is instead overly responsive. As a consequence, elected officials have too little leeway to adopt a long view, make decisions, and solve political problems. The result is wholesale frustration, as citizens perceive a political system that is not working to address the nation's most pressing and persistent issues. The mismatch is compounded (1) by a revolution in communication technologies that have transformed the political system from the mass democracy created and fostered by mass communications directed at median voters into a system defined by targeted appeals to narrow slices of the electorate; (2) by economic and policy shifts that have exacerbated income inequality; and (3) by political changes that have led to more ideological political parties and greater partisan polarization. For better or worse, we cannot unwind the hands of time to undo these shifts but must instead adapt our political institutions and processes to these new realities.

America needs a recovery plan.

Developing such a plan requires that the proposed solutions effectively address the actual—and not the perceived—problems. The root cause of our dysfunction resides in the following observations:

1. Our political system asks too much from a citizenry not up to the task of democratic decision-making. This is not the fault of citizens but reflects shortcomings in our ability to process information and reach the "best" possible decisions. Nor is this new. This has always been the case, but the democratic deficit becomes more troubling and dangerous in an age of instant information and immediate and ongoing feedback. As stated before, too much democracy can kill democracy.

    This is not to suggest that citizens should have no role in the political process. Our political system should be based on "the consent of the governed," but the system also needs to account for the very real limitations of democratic citizenries. The American political system, which divides authority into legislative, executive, and judicial powers and into state and federal authority, blurs policymaking responsibility, thus increasing the cognitive burden on citizens by making it more difficult to attribute responsibility.

2. Our political system gives too little discretion and too little leeway to political elites. To adopt a long view and effectively address long-standing and persistent problems, political elites need more authority, greater discretion, and less over-

sight. Contemporary elites are limited by a political system that punishes anyone suggesting short-term sacrifices for long-term investments. The result is fiscally irresponsible policy decisions, as government cuts taxes without corresponding spending cuts. We simultaneously fight wars and cut taxes without ever acknowledging the budgetary consequences. Generic Republican calls for spending cuts rarely, if ever, go to where the federal money is actually spent—defense and entitlements—and subsequently are best seen as political rhetoric divorced from reality.

3. Our political system places the mechanism for political accountability at the local level, ensuring representatives and senators are responsive to local reelection constituencies and not national constituencies. Senators and representatives represent their constituencies very well, but the larger national view is often lost. The executive is the only branch of government that can claim to speak for the nation.

4. Over the last several decades, policy decisions have led to growing income inequality and a shrinking middle class. This was no accident, nor was it a result of inevitable and predictable economic cycles; it was instead a consequence of the participatory biases inherent in democratic decision-making. The decline in the middle class threatens the stability of the political system.

Ask Less of Citizens

In his inaugural address in 1961, John F. Kennedy found the perfect words to encapsulate the idealism of the 1960s: "Ask not what your country can do for you—ask what you can do for your country." Kennedy's oft-quoted remark was a call to action, a call to citizens to bear responsibility for their country and their fellow citizens. Asking less of citizens runs against the grain of all that we have been taught (but perhaps not learned) about our responsibilities as citizens in democratic society. The contradiction, I would argue, is more apparent than real. Nevertheless, for our system to thrive, we need citizens to be less involved.

One of the curiosities arising out of an unquestioning and unwavering belief in democracy is the reflexive opinion that elections are the best mechanism for selecting public officials or deciding important issues. The result is a ballot long on choices and short on information. Most of the scholarship on voting behavior focuses on American national elections, in which information is relatively plentiful. Even in these elections voters fall far short of the democratic ideal. So what happens as one moves down the ballot, selecting between barely recognized names for political offices whose responsibilities are unclear? How does one vote for coroner? Does it matter if a coroner is a Democrat or Republican, a libertarian or a socialist?

As an aside, coroners sign death certificates and look for the cause of death, including determining whether the death merits additional investigation. They are generally not required to have a medical degree or any specialized training. The result is not without consequence. Elected coroners reported 15 percent fewer suicides than unelected medical examiners. The cause of the discrepancy is the social and political pressures created by the electoral process.[3]

Citing V. O. Key's famous dictum that "the voters are not fools," voting behavior scholars frequently argue that citizens rely on heuristics and cues to make reasonably good decisions with limited information. A voter relying on partisan affiliation, for example, can be reasonably certain that a Republican candidate is more conservative than the Democratic alternative. The availability and reliability of cues, however, lessen as citizens move down the ballot and make decisions on a host of issues (initiatives, state constitutional amendments, and local propositions) and elected offices for which they likely do no not know who is running and have little (or no) idea about what the office does. In 2010 Harris County, Texas, for example, voters had to decide between 250 candidates for 142 offices, including 72 judicial races. Harris County may be an outlier, but the long ballot is the norm rather than the exception. Across the United States, there are over five hundred thousand elected officials working in more than eighty-seven thousand local governments (including states, cities, townships, school boards, and special districts). Citizens adapt by using heuristics that may or may not be useful guides to decision-making. Being listed first on the ballot, for example, may be worth as much as 5 percent of the vote in low-information elections.[4] Attractive candidates and candidates with better vocal quality (defined in terms of having a low pitch) are evaluated more favorably than unattractive candidates and candidates with lesser vocal quality.[5] While this sort of decision-making may be rational at some level, it falls far short of even the most liberal interpretations of democratic theory.

Now add in the frequency with which Americans are asked to go to the polls. In Louisiana, voters routinely go to the polls more than five times in a single year for a wide range of political offices, local propositions, and constitutional amendments. Many of these elections are low visibility, receive little or no news coverage, and generate little voter interest and low voter participation. Asking voters to vote less often on broader choices would improve the level of citizen engagement and provide voters with more meaningful input. This is certainly what Madison would have meant by the consent of the governed, not the politico overly responsive to election constituencies on narrowly drawn issues.

With this in mind, I offer the following suggestions:

- Reduce the number of times voters are asked to go to the polls. There is no reason to vote more than once in a given year.
- Reduce the number of elections on the ballot. Citizens should give broad direction to government through relatively simple decisions. Are we heading in the right direction? More complicated decisions should be left to elected officials. Offices that are ill defined or poorly understood should be appointed rather than elected.

- Eliminate primary elections. Let the political parties decide who their nominees will be. If they make bad decisions, they will be held accountable in the general election.

Give Leeway to Political Elites to Exercise Real Leadership

When democratic politics fail, we often turn to unelected commissions to find solutions. Ask yourself this: How many of the problems that appear intractable in our contemporary political environment could be solved by a commission or a corporate CEO empowered to make meaningful decisions? Of course, there is a reason these unelected commissions (generally made up of retired politicians and unelected experts) succeed where elected officials fail. They are free from the political pressures that limit the range of potential solutions and the possibility for compromise. They are able to do the right thing without worrying about the consequences for their next election or how the decision affects the partisan balance in Congress or the president's approval rating.

Reducing the political pressure allows these commissions to focus on solving the problem at hand. There is less showboating, less overheated partisan rhetoric, and fewer appeals to ideological constituencies and organized interests. Even when these commissions fail, they often move the conversation forward. The National Commission on Fiscal Responsibility and Reform (Simpson-Bowles), for example, was created by President Barack Obama to define proposals for addressing ongoing budget debates regarding taxes, spending, and deficits. While the commission ultimately failed to transform the budget-making process, it at least provided a framework for addressing ongoing budget deficits and has served as the reference point for future negotiations. The model of allowing bipartisan expert panels to propose solutions that then must be voted on by the U.S. Congress in their entirety is one potential approach for achieving more coherent policy decisions.

Figuring out a way to empower elected officials to make these decisions—independently of commissions—is an even better solution. For this to work, we must turn conventional wisdom on its head. In an age of declining political trust and growing cynicism, we need to empower elected officials to make difficult and unpopular decisions (e.g., raising the retirement age, reducing defense spending, and/or cutting social security and Medicare benefits). In an age of instant information, we need less (as opposed to more) transparency. Closed-door meetings and backroom deals have deservedly drawn the condemnation and ire of political journalists and reformers, but openness and transparency exert their own costs.[6] Conversations are less honest and less productive when aspiring politicians know that every utterance can potentially be used as a thirty-second ad in their next campaign. This is not to suggest that politicians are lying whenever they are speaking on record, but rather that speaking on the record limits what they might say and the possibility for a meaningful exchange. Constantly playing for the camera—and often speaking to a narrowly defined partisan audience—means less focus on solving problems.

Imagine, for a moment, a televised conversation between the most liberal and most conservative member of the U.S. Senate. The conversation would gravitate between the unpleasant (as the senators talked over each other in highly partisan crosstalk) and the irritating (as the senators stuck dogmatically to their talking points, saying very little of interest). Now imagine if those same senators had a conversation behind closed doors. Pleasantries would likely be exchanged and then there would be a real conversation on where agreement might work and where disagreement was inevitable. This second conversation might end no more productively, but is there any doubt that it would be more forthright and more honest? Indeed, the greatest potential threat to undermining the exchange would come out of a fear of leaks—that what was said behind closed doors might somehow become public.

The consequence for public opinion is ironic: increasing transparency and openness can simultaneously increase cynicism and distrust. This point has been made most pointedly by Elizabeth Theiss-Morse and John Hibbing, who find that the public recoils at exposure to legislative politics.[7] The more people see democracy in action, the less they like it. Harvard political science professor Lawrence Lessig similarly observes that openness rooted in good intentions can have negative consequences. Disclosure of campaign finance data, for example, has not made voters more informed about the effect of campaign contributions on elections or legislative behavior but has instead increased cynicism. Similarly, Craigslist made information more readily available but had the unintended consequences of undermining classified ads, one of the economic staples of daily newspapers. As Lessig observes,

> How could anyone be against transparency? Its virtues and its utilities seem so crushingly obvious. But I have increasingly come to worry that there is an error at the core of this unquestioned goodness. We are not thinking critically enough about where and when transparency works, and where and when it may lead to confusion, or to worse. And I fear that the inevitable success of this movement—if pursued alone, without any sensitivity to the full complexity of the idea of perfect openness—will inspire not reform, but disgust. The "naked transparency movement," as I will call it here, is not going to inspire change. It will simply push any faith in our political system over the cliff.[8]

Our politics will remain dysfunctional as long as most of the conversations remain in the public eye. Openness is not a synonym for candid conversations, nor does it lead to better decisions or greater public buy-in. Clearly, there must be accountability in decision-making and adequate protections against corruption, conflicts of interests, and incompetence, but overly scrutinizing elected officials limits the range of debate, closes off the conversation, and makes meaningful change and compromise less likely.

This leads to the following suggestions:

- Utilize nonpartisan and unelected commissions to propose legislation, requiring the U.S. Congress to vote up or down on the proposals.

- Create opportunities for legislators to have closed-door meetings so as to encourage a frank discussion of political issues.

Restore Collective Accountability

One of the myths of contemporary politics is that redistricting is the principal cause of partisan polarization. Redistricting has certainly played a role in the partisan dysfunction in the House of Representatives. Elected from more partisan districts, representatives are, not surprisingly, increasingly partisan. But the polarization of the contemporary American political scene—at least at the elite level—extends far beyond the House of Representatives and into the U.S. Senate, where redistricting provides no traction as a viable explanation.

Even so, the winner-take-all plurality nature of U.S. House and Senate elections remains an important consideration because of how it narrows the focus of representation to local concerns and, even more narrowly, to local reelection constituencies. Legislative accountability is rooted mostly in local considerations and only indirectly and weakly in institutional performance.[9] Elected representatives can contribute little or nothing to drafting legislation, crafting political compromises, or addressing important issues, and still easily win reelection. Indeed, as long as their votes and issue positions align with their local constituencies, they will likely be reelected until they engage in personal malfeasance or decide to retire. Legislators become vulnerable primarily through scandal or by having the misfortune to win election in one of approximately forty to sixty marginal congressional districts or the handful of competitive U.S. Senate seats in any given election.

Now imagine working for a company in which you could be routinely promoted even as the company failed to make a profit, in which individual productivity was not rewarded, but vocally advocating for (or against) specific policy proposals was highly valued. Most observers would quickly recognize this as a failed business model and a poorly designed corporate structure.[10] In the ideal corporate setting, individual productivity should drive performance and individual reward should be tied to overall company performance. One might fairly argue that this is the model that weakened U.S. manufacturing, as union contracts created disincentives for innovation and initiative in the workplace, or that undermined corporate performance by guaranteeing lucrative CEO compensation packages even in the event of company-wide failure.[11] It is certainly the model that defines the relationship of elected representatives to the U.S. Congress. Individual success is almost completely divorced from institutional performance.

The more general point is this: incentives drive behavior, and the incentive structure in the U.S. Congress makes dysfunctional behavior more likely. Writing in his landmark work *Congressmen in Committees*, political scientist Richard Fenno observed that there are three sets of incentives that guide congressional behavior: (1) reelection, (2) power within Washington, and (3) good public policy. In his later work *Senators on the Campaign Trail*, Fenno added progressive ambition as a fourth incentive.[12] Because reelection is paramount to these other incentives, it drives behavior and decision-making. Political scientist David Mayhew similarly described members of Congress as "single-minded pursuers of reelection."[13] For many observers, the pursuit of reelection is the problem: remove the electoral incentive and the system will markedly improve. However, this only captures half the equation. If we remove reelection as an incentive, what replaces it? The solution lies not in eliminating electoral incentives but in tying individual electoral success to institutional performance.

This requires fundamentally rethinking the structure of accountability in American politics. Collective accountability in the American political system falls almost entirely on the presidency. Perhaps ironically, presidents are held accountable for system-level performance even in areas where they have little or no power and even when circumstances are largely beyond their control. A bad economy, for example, may reflect bad policy decisions, external shocks (e.g., problems tied in to the global economy), or inevitable economic cycles. Congressional accountability for collective outcomes runs indirectly through presidential performance and has little to do with representative performance. Democrats running in marginal districts in 2014, for example, can fully expect their opponents to tie them as closely as possible to President Barack Obama regardless of their actual voting record or performance in office. Democrats running in safe districts will, in the absence of scandal, remain safe.

In a partisan era with majority control of the U.S. House and Senate often in play, it is fair to argue that there is some measure of collective accountability in partisan swings. Unfortunately, because collective accountability is tied to presidential performance and only loosely to congressional performance, there is little incentive for solving collective problems. Not working with the president and ensuring the system becomes mired in gridlock potentially creates the necessary conditions for partisan wins in midterm election years. There is an obvious risk in that a political party can become viewed almost entirely as an institutional roadblock, as was the case for Republicans in 2012. This risk, however, has to be placed in the context of the six-seat gain in the U.S. Senate and sixty-three-seat gain in the House of Representative during the 2010 midterm elections, when Republicans were no less obstinate and no more cooperative. If there is a price to play for political obstinacy, there is also a very strong reward structure.

The problem of collective accountability is made even more striking when one considers that Democrats won the national popular vote in 2012 for the U.S. House of Representatives but did not win majority control of the chamber. Unlike the 2000 presidential election, in which Al Gore bested George W. Bush in the popular vote but lost the presidency, this decidedly undemocratic outcome yielded few cries for institutional reform. No one called out for the equivalent of replacing the Electoral College with a national popular vote. Indeed, hardly anyone noticed. Yet here lies one of the central failings of American democracy: in an election year when President Barack Obama's campaign efforts benefited from a Republican brand weakened by congressional obstructionism, Speaker of the House John Boehner maintained his party leadership post despite his party winning fewer voters than the opposition. The absence of collective accountability should be appalling.

This outcome was not the result of gerrymandering, the intentional drawing of districts for partisan gain, but instead reflects an inherent bias in the process of creating congressional districts.[14] The geographic distribution of votes—with Democrats located in relatively compact urban areas and Republicans located in more rural areas—creates a structural bias that favors the Republican Party. The result is that Democrats receive fewer seats than would be expected based on their vote totals because too many Democratic votes are wasted in heavily Democratic districts. Notably, this occurred even in states where Republicans and Democrats shared responsibility for drawing congressional districts. In Pennsylvania, this effect was magnified by intentional (and effective) partisan gerrymandering. Democrats won eighty-three thousand more votes than Republicans in U.S. House races, but the Pennsylvania delegation remained heavily tilted to the right, with thirteen Republicans and five Democrats.[15]

The solution resides in a relatively simple fix: move away from single-member "winner-take-all" districts and toward larger and more encompassing multi-member districts with proportional representation. On Election Day, citizens would cast a vote for a political party and seats would be allocated by states according to the proportion of the vote received by the respective political parties. Consider, for example, a state with ten House seats and a seventy-thirty partisan split. In this scenario, the majority party would control seven seats while the minority party would control three. Under our current system, the outcome would depend entirely on how the districts are drawn and on how the votes are distributed across geographically defined districts.

Broadening the base of electoral competition from local districts to states would increase competition, move the conversation away from localized concerns, make individual votes more meaningful, tie the success of individual politicians to institutional performance, and reduce the power of incumbency. It would have the added advantage of ending the costly, protracted, and politically divisive redrawing of district lines. Curiously, the adoption of single-member districts resulted from concerns that states, relying on multi-member districts but without proportional representation, were not adequately representing the views of their constituents and were effectively minimizing minority concerns. By requiring the drawing of individual districts, it was argued, the vote would more closely approximate opinion within the state. Moving from individual districts to proportional representation would move the system even closer to this intent. Because there is nothing in the U.S. Constitution requiring single-member districts, this would not require a constitutional amendment, though the hill to proportional representation is still steep. Specifically, it would involve three steps: (1) a majority vote in the U.S. House and Senate to repeal legislation passed in the 1842 Apportionment Act banning multi-member districts and in 1967 banning multi-member congressional districts; (2) state legislatures would have to agree to proportional representation (and to give up the power to draw individual district lines); and (3) the legislation would have to survive any constitutional challenge that multi-member districts were created to dilute minority voting rights.

If legally the solution is relatively simple, politically this may prove challenging. Single-member districts are culturally ingrained into the political culture—as is the idea that representatives should represent local constituencies. An alternative would be to add a set number of representatives to the U.S. House (forty to sixty) to be selected based on the national popular vote. Since the Apportionment Act of 1911, the size of the U.S. House has been set at 435. There is no reason that it should remain this size. Increasing the size of the House of Representatives to include national representatives would add an important measure of collective accountability, even if it kept intact the current districting process.

Finally, one can imagine a scenario in which citizens cast ballots for or against the U.S. Congress. A negative vote would disqualify current members from seeking reelection. Individual members would suddenly be required to pay greater attention to institutional performance. While such a scenario is unlikely, it illustrates the importance of incentives to political behavior. If members of Congress are highly responsive to reelection pressures (and they are), the solution resides not in removing the incentive entirely but in recasting it to create mechanisms of collective accountability.

Rather than a set of solutions, I would offer these alternatives:

- Replace single-member winner-take-all congressional districts with multi-member districts with proportional representation; OR
- Add forty to sixty seats to the House of Representatives to be given to the political party winning the national congressional vote.

Reducing Participatory Bias and Economic Inequality

Individual votes may not matter a great deal in a democracy with approximately 130 million voters. The odds that an individual vote would decide a presidential election, for example, are infinitesimal. Yet the political system is remarkably responsive to groups of voters and organized political pressure. Senior citizens, for example, exert considerably more influence over the policymaking process and receive more in-group benefits than college students because they participate at a much higher rate. The participatory bias that defines American politics does not end at voting. Indeed, it is even more pronounced through other forms of participation, including campaigning, direct contact of public officials, attending meetings and events, and contributing to favored candidates and political parties.

As a result of these biases, the American political system is overly responsive to democratic political inputs, but these inputs rarely (if ever) reflect the broader public interest. This is an important and notable paradox: democratic governance does not simply reflect majority sentiments but instead responds to the loudest, best organized, and most effectively presented voices. The public opinion that affects democratic politics is a distorted public voice. Throughout American political history, different groups have had notable and disproportionate influence over the political system. Labor unions exerted a powerful influence over policy throughout the New Deal era. Their power was rooted in organization and the ability to turn out union members who voted en bloc for preferred candidates. Despite the obvious flaws of corruption and political intimidation, unions connected economic success to working-class prosperity. The decline of labor unions severed this link.

When union leaders failed to deliver the voters, unions declined relative to business organizations, a reality reflected in Democratic Party efforts to seek corporate backing during the 1980s and Bill Clinton's endorsement of NAFTA over union objections in the 1990s. Over the last several decades, business organizations have become more numerous, more active, and more powerful. The *Citizens United* Supreme Court decision, which recognized corporations as "persons" for the purposes of the First Amendment, reflected, but did not define, this reality. Economic policy, as a result, has been designed to encourage business growth and development and not at ensuring working- or middle-class prosperity. Indeed, working-class prosperity is largely treated as a fortunate by-product of economic growth (even if the empirical evidence calls into question this relationship).

Participatory bias is a reality of democratic politics. An open and fair political system ensures that some voices will speak louder and some organizations will be more effective than others. Yet the nature and consequences of participatory bias are not a given and can be directly affected by reform. Asking citizens to participate less, for example, reduces the information burden on individual voters and (perhaps paradoxically) increases political involvement. This involvement may be shallow, but it would also be wider and more directly connected to how citizens make decisions. Here is a rule that captures the paradox: fewer votes equals more voters.

Similarly, increasing collective accountability means that each vote has clear and direct consequences on policy. Citizens who vote for hope and change, for example, but get four years of partisan gridlock are understandably frustrated. But what if their votes led to meaningful policy shifts? What if they could be assured the winning political party would have the capacity to enact its legislative agenda? Empowering elected officials to make meaningful decisions and increasing collective accountability would also help to reduce participatory biases in politics.

Participatory biases could be further minimized by reducing the influence of money over the political process. Given the history of Supreme Court decisions (e.g., *Buckley v. Valeo* and *Citizens United*), it is not clear that serious campaign finance reform can ever be realized. Or, alternatively, that once realized, it would not be undermined by a future court decision or by political actors actively undermining the intent of reform for political advantage. Lost in Democratic Party lamentations over *Citizens United* and the subsequent rise of conservative super PACS is this simple reality: President Barack Obama effectively ended post-Watergate campaign finance regulations when he opted out of public financing in 2008 because it gave him a short-term political advantage over John McCain.

Political scientists are quick to note that money is no guarantee of an election win. This is unquestionably true but largely irrelevant. Money drives the American political system. It affects candidate behavior, from the strategic decision to run (or not run) down to tactical decision of when, where, and how to employ messaging strategies, and it also affects the relative influence of individual citizens. Individuals who can, Sheldon Adelson–style, give $70 million always get their phone calls returned.

Interestingly, Adelson broke the record for contributions in a single election cycle set by George Soros in 2004. Both men spent on behalf of losing causes: Adelson to defeat Barack Obama in 2012, Soros to defeat George W. Bush in 2004. A critic might fairly argue that this proves that money does not buy elections. Money is certainly no guarantee, but this claim misses the larger point. The pervasive importance of money in the political process ensures that contributors have greater political influence than non-contributors over policy decisions, just as policy favors older citizens (relative to younger citizens) because they vote at higher rates.

This has unquestionably been the case from the American founding to present day, but ineffective campaign finance regulations and the massive loopholes created by the *Citizens United* decision have amplified the power of money over the political process. Examined through a historical lens, contemporary American politics looks less like the post-Watergate era, which attempted to reduce the role of money in the political process, than the Gilded Age, when money drove the political process.

The most effective mechanism for decreasing participatory biases would be a system of public financing that ensured that money did not exaggerate the voices of wealthy individuals and well-financed political groups. Under such a system, the currency of democracy would be votes and organization rather than contributions. The influence of a vote would not depend on the ability of the voter to write a check but on the ability of the individual to persuade others to vote in similar fashion. Thanks to Supreme Court precedent and political practice, however, wholesale reform remains unlikely.

Absent such wholesale reform, the campaign finance system could be redesigned in ways that encourage greater accountability, political mobilization efforts, and retail politics. Limits on contributions to political parties could be lifted, thus encouraging contributors to give directly to political parties rather than to unaccountable super PACs.[16] Unlike special interest groups, political parties have an incentive to fund challengers (thus increasing competition), are more inclined to spend money on mobilization efforts, and are ultimately held accountable for their decisions. Political parties win or lose control of government, and thus have an incentive to moderate if they become too extreme, to rethink the nature of their coalition in the wake of a defeat, and/or to seek out different types of candidates. Losing political parties innovate, while winning political parties attempt to rerun their last successful campaign.

Republicans have, fairly or unfairly, received the lion's share of the blame for the increased polarization of contemporary politics. Such simplistic attributions of responsibility miss important distinctions within the Republican Party. Mainstream Republicans, focused on winning elections, recognize the need to broaden the base, build coalitions, and adjust issue positions to better appeal to a changing electorate. The distortion has come from outside groups (specifically, the Tea Party) exercising the levers of democracy to affect party nominees and party positions. How much better would our current political system function if mainstream Republicans were able to effectively control partisan nominations? How much better would the political system function if campaign funding flowed through the political parties and to the candidates rather than from super PACs to television ads?

CONCLUSIONS

Confronted with crisis, the American political system too often resorts to a familiar but misguided refrain: more democracy. Democracy is the reflexive but incorrect solution applied to every failure of government. The result is greater inefficiency and increased frustration. The actual solution runs against our every instinct as citizens socialized in democratic norms and values: less democracy and more leadership.

This is not a call for ending democracy in every shape and form. Nor is it a call for philosopher kings or benevolent monarchs. Government should be based on the consent of the governed and that consent is best given through free and fair elections in which every citizen is eligible and encouraged to vote. There is little reason, however, for citizens to vote five or more times in a given year on issues they do not understand, for candidates they barely recognize, or for political offices whose responsibilities are unclear. There is a paradox here: reducing the number of elections, shortening the ballot to a few meaningful choices, and tying elections more directly to policy outcomes would likely reinvigorate democratic participation.

Not addressing the failure of democratic governance has significant consequences. Government gridlock is the result of a system that is overly responsive to citizens placing contradictory demands on government. Republicans working to make President Barack Obama a one-term president through ongoing and relentless opposition were fairly representing the voters who put them into office. This was not a failure of democracy; it was a manifestation of democracy serving to derail effective governance.

More spending and fewer taxes may make little or no sense from a fiscal standpoint, but this contradiction fairly captures where most Americans stand on budgetary policy. Keep delivering entitlements, fighting wars (as long as we are winning), and cutting taxes. While citizens may express concern about deficits, they provide no clear path for reducing government spending or increasing government revenue. Balancing the budget, they believe, can be done just by eliminating wasteful spending and foreign aid.

Assessing the budgetary landscape, former Obama administration budget director Peter Orszag identified democracy as the problem and called for automatic policies and depoliticized commissions to make decisions that would effectively address deficits.[17] Similarly, in a rare moment of honesty for a politician, North Carolina governor Bev Perdue similarly opined that "I think we ought to suspend, perhaps, elections for Congress for two years and just tell them we won't hold it against them, whatever decisions they make, to just let them help this country recover."[18]

The larger problem of the democracy is the almost universal unwillingness to make short-term sacrifices to address long-term needs. How do we address long-term problems when our vision is limited to a two-year (or four-year) election cycle? How do we ensure that we are investing in science and technology so that our position as military and economic superpower is not threatened by our own shortsightedness? To make these decisions, our elected officials need more rather than less leeway. They need the ability to meet behind closed doors, to forge compromises, and to act in the best interests of the country without the constant surveillance of the Internet age or the ongoing threat of a thirty-second ad going viral. The ironies are abundant:

- Too much democracy yields ineffective governance.
- Too much openness and transparency creates political incentives for position-taking and showboating and disincentives for solving problems.

The larger threat is that inefficient governance increases voter frustration. As the only official who has a national constituency and who is held accountable for collective outcomes, the American president is subject to a natural temptation to exceed his constitutional authority. The temptation grows during periods of crisis, when presidents can exceed their constitutional authority with public support. The contemporary political environment, with the backdrop of an ongoing fiscal crisis, invites this expansion of authority and provides a potential pathway for a demagogue to undo our constitutional republic.

This threat is admittedly overstated. More than likely we will—as we are prone to do—continue to muddle through our crises. Nevertheless, recent efforts by Republicans to change the Electoral College so that votes reflect congressional districts rather than states should sound alarm bells. The goal of these reforms is to make it more likely that Republicans are elected without popular support. More troubling, they reflect growing disregard for the legitimacy of the political system and a desire to rig the system for favorable political outcomes.

James Madison understood the need for balance in institutional arrangements. His constitutional design reflected the need for public input (which he called passion) but an even greater need for reasoned judgment. In Madison's design, the public voice would be heavily filtered through institutional structures that ensured the consent of the governed but discouraged democratic control over policy outcomes. Contemporary politics has lost that balance, and now tilts too heavily toward the public's passions and away from reasoned judgment. The solution to our current dysfunction resides not in more democracy, but in less. It resides not in the commonsense solutions or the wisdom of the average voter, but in effective leadership and technical expertise. To get there, we must think in ways that run against our cultural norms and embrace the unconventional idea that democracy is not always the only or best solution. Sometimes what we need is leadership and expertise.

Now is one of those times.

NOTES

1. C. H. Bretherton, "Too Much Democracy," *North American Review* (1927): 646–53.

2. Seventy-five percent of voters rejected the idea, recognizing that too much democracy can be a bad thing.

3. Joshua Klugman and Gretchen Condran, "The Role of Medico-Legal Systems in Producing Geographic Variation in Suicide Rates," http://sites.temple.edu/klugman/files/2012/11/Klugman-et-al-forthcoming-SSQ-The-Role-of-Medico-Legal-Systems-in-Producing-Geographic-Variation-in-Suicide-Rates.pdf (accessed May 25, 2013).

4. David Brockington, "A Low Information Theory of Ballot Position Effect," *Political Behavior* 25 (2003): 1–27.

5. William Hart, Victor Ottati, and Nathaniel Krumdick, "Physical Attractiveness and Candidate Evaluation: A Model of Correction," *Political Psychology* 32 (2011): 181–204; Cara Tigue, Diana Borak, Jillian O'Connor, Charles Schandl, and David Feinberg, "Voice Pitch Influences Voting Behavior," *Evolution and Human Behavior* 33 (2012): 210–16.

6. News organizations are, of course, not very transparent in how they make editorial decisions regarding what stories to cover or how to cover them.

7. John Hibbing and Elizabeth Theiss-Morse, *Stealth Democracy: Americans' Beliefs about How Government Should Work* (Cambridge: Cambridge University Press, 2002); John Hibbing and Elizabeth Theiss-Morse, *Congress as Public Enemy: Public Attitudes toward American Political Institutions* (Cambridge: Cambridge University Press, 1995).

8. Lawrence Lessig, "Against Transparency," *The New Republic*, October 9, 2009, http://www.newrepublic.com/article/books-and-arts/against-transparency# (accessed May 26, 2013).

9. David Jones, "Partisan Polarization and Congressional Accountability in House Elections," *American Journal of Political Science* 54 (2010): 323–37.

10. Complaints against tenured faculty often fall into this same category. What is the incentive for productivity when it is nearly impossible to be fired? In my experience, there is no question that incentive structures play a role in academic performance, but this reflects as much on the absence of a carrot (raises in good years are often at or just above the rate of inflation) as on the absence of a stick.

11. In fairness, one might argue that this is the model at most universities.

12. Richard Fenno, *Congressmen in Committees* (Boston: Little, Brown, 1973), and *Senators on the Campaign Trail: The Politics of Representation* (Norman: University of Oklahoma Press, 1996). See also Ronald Keith Gaddie, *Born to Run: Origins of a Political Career* (Lanham, MD: Rowman & Littlefield, 2003).

13. David Mayhew, *Congress: The Electoral Connection* (New Haven, CT: Yale University Press, 1974).

14. Nicholas Goedert, "Not Gerrymandering, but Districting: More Evidence on How Democrats Won the Popular Vote but Lost the Congress," *The Monkey Cage*, November 15, 2012; Jowei Chen and Jonathan Rodden, "Unintentional Gerrymandering: Political Geography and Electoral Bias in Legislatures," *Quarterly Journal of Political Science* 8, no. 3 (2013): 239–69.

15. Griff Palmer and Michael Cooper, "How Maps Helped Republicans Keep an Edge in the House," *New York Times*, December 14, 2012, http://www.nytimes.com/2012/12/15/us/politics/redistricting-helped-republicans-hold-onto-congress.html?pagewanted=all&_r=0.

16. James Regens and Ronald Keith Gaddie, *The Economic Realities of Political Reform: Elections and the U.S. Senate* (Cambridge: Cambridge University Press, 1995).

17. Peter Orszag, "Too Much of a Good Thing: Why We Need Less Democracy," *The New Republic*, September 12, 2011.

18. Z. Bryon Wolf, "Too Much Democracy? A Modest Proposal from N.C. Gov. Bev Perdue," ABC News, September 28, 2011.

NO-WIN ELECTIONS AND THE
FUTURE OF AMERICAN DEMOCRACY

An Afterword

The 2014 midterm elections were a resounding victory for the Republican Party. Not only did Republicans win control of the U.S. Senate from a beleaguered and "hollowed out" Democratic Party,[1] they extended their control of the U.S. House of Representatives from 234 to 247. So much so that it is now hard to imagine a Democratic House majority until after 2022 when district maps will be redrawn to match 2020 census populations shifts. Republicans also made significant and historic gains in state legislatures assuring a strong farm team of experienced elected officials for future congressional elections and control over the often overlooked but critically important arena of state politics. At the state level, Republicans will be well-positioned to push conservative initiatives, including restrictions on abortion access and state tax reform. So given an overwhelming and decisive Republican victory, how exactly are these no-win elections?

To answer this question, consider a simple model of representation where voter preferences are articulated during elections and expressed via the selection of representatives who, once elected enact policy. The model assumes that voters have clear

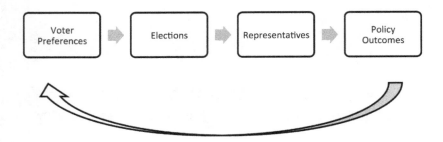

enough preferences (1) to inform policy on the front end (via prospective voting) OR (2) to hold elected officials accountable on the back end (via retrospective voting). But what if neither of these assumptions holds? Elections would do little to align public sentiments with policy outcomes. Instead of serving as a pressure valve for the political system, elections would add to growing citizen frustration while making the process of governing more difficult. The result would be a downward spiral of citizen disaffection, cynicism, governing efficiency, gridlock, and dysfunction. The 2014 midterm elections are case study in this dynamic. They did little to realign public preferences with public policy. Even worse, they created conditions likely to lead to greater partisan polarization, dysfunction, and gridlock. American voters voted (once again) for what they have repeatedly said they do not want.

THE 2014 MIDTERM ELECTION CONTEXT

We can begin by considering the context of the 2014 elections. The public mood going into the election might be best described as deeply unsettled, marked by economic uncertainty, dissatisfaction with President Obama and the direction of the country, and growing frustration with Republicans and Democrats in Congress. In terms of partisan implications, the signals were initially mixed, indicating a potential anti-incumbent pox on all parties and working to the disadvantage of Republican and Democrat incumbents alike. Each of these signals, however, needs to be interpreted within a larger environment of political polarization and fragmentation. Republicans were deeply unsatisfied with President Obama while Democrats found Republican congressional leadership loathsome. Independents either sided with Republicans or found other things to worry about.

Economic Uncertainty: Since 2009 when Barack Obama assumed office, the economy has slowly and consistently improved. Unemployment rates declined from 10 percent in November 2009 to approximately 6 percent just prior to the 2014 midterm elections. Despite this relatively good economic news, wages and incomes remained relatively stagnant and the gap between rich and poor continued to grow. The middle and working class, squeezed by rising prices and stagnant wages, remains deeply uncertain about their economic future and specifically about Barack Obama's stewardship over the U.S. economy. Going into the election, President Obama's approval for his economic performance were subsequently in the low forties. Whatever improvements there might be in the overall economy, middle-class and working class Americans were feeling little of the benefit and President Obama was getting little or no credit.

The economic uncertainty that defined the 2014 midterm elections highlights two failings of the American public: (1) The tendency to attribute too much responsibility to the president in a system of separated power and checks and balances; and (2) Widespread misunderstanding of the economy to the point that perception matters far more than actual (and measurable) economic conditions. First, public misunderstanding of the process—presidents are really not all that powerful—makes it far easier than it should be for the opposition party to tie public discontent to the president's party. Unlike the U.S. Congress, U.S. presidents are saddled with collective responsibility, even for events or conditions beyond their control. Indeed, public misunderstanding is so great that it is possible for a committed opposition party to undermine presidential leadership on the one hand and then use public frustration rooted in presidential effectiveness against the president's party during the next election. Republicans did this to great effect during the 2014 midterms.

Second, the public is also poorly informed about economic conditions, grossly overestimating unemployment and inflation and unable to define even basic economic terms. As a result, public opinion on the economy is highly contingent on elite interpretations of economic conditions and those interpretations have grown increasingly partisan and polarized. As long as there is economic uncertainty, elite partisan cues—and not actual economic conditions—drive economic perceptions.

Dissatisfaction with President Obama and the Direction of the Country: Economic uncertainty carried over into President Obama's overall approval rating and perceptions about whether the country was heading in the right direction. Going into the election, President Obama's approval rating stood at 44 percent, a troubling sign for Democratic candidates, especially in those states with competitive Senate elections where Obama's approval ratings typically dipped below the national average. Democratic House and Senate candidates subsequently opted to keep their distance from President Obama throughout much of the campaign while Republicans worked hard to connect their Democratic opponents to the unpopular Democratic president. This general dissatisfaction was further reflected in growing concern about the direction of the country. Just over 1 in 4 Americans said the country was heading in the right direction while more than 6 in 10 said the country was heading in the wrong direction.

Frustration with Republicans in Congress: Public dissatisfaction was not, however, focused exclusively on President Obama or the Democratic Party. Approval ratings for Congress, always fairly low, were abysmal (averaging between 10–15 percent) just prior to the 2014 midterms. Similarly, "Republicans in Congress" rated below President Obama and Democrats in Congress: Only 21 percent of Americans approved of "Republicans in Congress" while 29 percent approved of "Democrats in Congress." The Republican Party also consistently rated as "less favorable" than the Democratic Party. Indeed, just one month prior to the election (on October 9), Gallup reported that Republican Party favorability had sunk to just 28 percent, the lowest party favorability since Gallup began tracking party favorability numbers in 1992.

Looking just at public opinion then, neither party was particularly well positioned to "win" the 2014 midterm elections. Indeed, it was very possible that the election might turn into a bipartisan anti-incumbent wave with incumbent Republicans like Kentucky Senator Mitch McConnell potentially losing alongside Democratic incumbents.[2] The defeat of House Republican Majority Leader Eric Cantor in a primary election against a little known and under-funded George Mason University economics professor appeared to be the canary in the coalmine, signaling that public dissatisfaction ran equally strong against leaders of both political parties. As it turned out Republicans were able to use the campaign to effectively redirect public frustration toward Democratic candidates but this redirection of public angst was by no means preordained. Indeed, one of the troubling aspects of the election cycle was that widespread dissatisfaction had no natural target and there appeared to be no natural release valve for public frustration and anger over partisan gridlock and dysfunction. Imagine, for example, a voter concerned about the economy and the future of the country, unhappy with President Obama's leadership, and distrustful of congressional Republicans. Where would such a voter go? What candidates would she support?

NO-WIN ELECTIONS

The answer is that these voters mostly stayed home, leaving the election to those intensely partisan voters who cared most deeply about the election outcome and who had the most clearly defined and ideological viewpoints. On Election Day, just 36 percent of the voting eligible population showed up to vote, the lowest voter turnout in 72 years. The last time voter turnout reached these depths was 1942 when the United States was in the midst of World War II. The midterm electorate—older, whiter, and wealthier than the electorate during presidential election years—typically favors the Republican Party. This built-in advantage can be offset when short-term factors favor the Democratic Party but in 2014 the short-term context favored Republicans.

The Republican Party, particularly the Republican Party leadership, was neither particularly well-loved nor respected going into the election cycle; but, in American politics, accountability typically begins and ends with president's party. As a result, partisan Republicans turned out in greater numbers than Democrats to voice their disapproval of President Obama and the Democratic Party and "won" the election. Their victory, however, provided no real guidance for policy and will likely further agitate rather alleviate public frustration. In this respect, the American public voted for exactly what it did not want: More polarization, more gridlock, and more dysfunction.

Consider, for example, health care reform. If there was a single issue that drove Republican voters to the polls it was anger over the government's expanding role into health care and the "private" relationship between patients and doctors. The anger was fueled by Democratic failures (1) to adequately prepare the public for the possibility that at least some individuals would, in fact, lose their health care despite President Obama's promises to the contrary; and (2) the failed roll-out of the healthcare.gov website which damaged to public perceptions of President Obama's leadership and competence. Yet, if health care reform was broadly unpopular especially among Republican voters, a number of the specific provisions enjoy widespread public support. Most Americans support provisions allowing children to stay on the parent's health care plans until they reach age twenty-six, protecting individuals with "pre-existing" conditions so that they are not denied coverage, creating health exchanges to help lower the insurance costs, and expanding Medicaid to cover more of the working poor. In fact, the only provision of health care reform that a majority of Americans do not support is the mandate requiring individuals to purchase health insurance. Further complicating any effort to repeal health care reform is preliminary data indicating fewer

Americans are uninsured and that health-related expenditures are declining rather than increasing. Despite its administrative glitches, health care reform appears to be working.

Contradictions in opposition to the health care law in the abstract and support for law's specific provisions exist because much of the public is uninformed or misinformed about policy and the political process. Within the context of health care reform, the public is typically unaware of the laws more positively evaluated provisions, imagining health care reform as something different than an aggregation of the individual provisions they mostly support.

More broadly, the public remains widely uninformed about politics. According to an Annenberg public opinion survey conducted in September 2014:

- Only 36 percent of Americans could name all three branches of government, 35 percent could not name a single branch of government.
- Only 38 percent of Americans knew the Republican Party controlled the House of Representatives, 17 percent said the Democrats, and 44 percent said they did not know.
- 38 percent of Americans knew Democrats controlled the Senate, 20 percent said the Republicans, and 42 percent said they did not know.

That Republicans "won" the midterms by capitalizing on widespread public dissatisfaction has to be placed within this specific context of policy and process-related ignorance and misinformation. In an election in which control of the U.S. Senate would be decided, 61 percent of Americans either did not know or were misinformed about which political party controlled the chamber. A comparable 62 percent did know or were unsure which party controlled the House of Representatives. In the face of such widespread misinformation, accountability is, at best, an illusion. Consider that despite widespread dissatisfaction with both political parties and with Congress as an institution, 95 percent of House incumbents and 85 percent of Senate incumbents won reelection.

This is the first and perhaps most important lesson to be drawn about no-win elections. Structurally, our political system provides little choice for voters dissatisfied with the status quo, particularly when both Republicans and Democrats are culpable for political dysfunction. The problem is made worse by an electoral system that draws congressional districts in ways that assures voters have little say over actual governance. Throughout much of the country, there was no meaningful election for voters to express their discontent. In U.S. House elections, just 25 of 435 districts were considered toss ups just before the election and only 19 seats actually changed hands from the Republican Party to the Democratic Party. Republicans won 16 seats held by Democrats, while Democrats won 3 seats held by Republicans. Seen in this light, the story of the election should not be defined as a Republican victory but as an exercise in democratic failure. Widely distrusted political institutions remained unscathed despite overwhelming public frustration. Even worse, the election endorsed and extended the political dysfunction voters claimed to have grown weary of.

RECONSIDERING DEMOCRACY

The argument I presented in the book (and continue to present) is that democracy—or at least our conceptualization of it—is part of the problem. The irony is that the more democratic we make our political process, the less democratic it becomes and the more difficult it is to translate voter preferences into policy outcomes. The reasoning is logically quite simple but normatively challenging: Our conceptualization of democracy requires more of the average voter than she is willing (or able) to give, thus leaving "democratic" political processes to partisan activists and ideologues. Consider, for example, a local government considering a new development. In order to assure public buy-in, they hold a series of meetings asking for public input. The meetings are attended not by average (or typical) citizens but by residents most directly affected by the development and by activists on both sides of the issue. The decision to seek public input yields not a more democratic outcome but one biased in favor of activists who also happen to be more ideological, wealthier, and better educated. The creation of a more democratic process resulted in a more biased and less democratic outcome.

The common lie, too often believed by voters, is that representatives go to Washington and lose touch. Nothing could be further from the truth. Representatives are not ignoring their districts or the voters' districts. They are representing them quite well; or at least the active and engaged citizens who vote for them, volunteer for campaigns, contribute money, and show up at public meetings and events. The problem is not with our representatives but in how we expect voter preferences to translate into representative decisions. The process of drawing congressional districts minimizes political competition and encourages representation as position-taking by placing representatives in clearly defined Democratic or Republican districts. In such a district, there is little political incentive for crafting policy, reaching compromise, or otherwise solving problems as satisfying the base means towing the party line. The result is that our system is very responsive to constituent views but lacks collective accountability and fails to translate public opinion (broadly defined) into policy outcomes. Representatives, in this system, are unlikely to lose as long as they faithfully reflect their constituents' views by staying on the right side of the issue, even if this means getting anything done. In fact, playing a visible policy making role can be counter-productive as constituents see policy-makers as compromised insiders.

The good news is that there are solutions. They begin with acknowledging that our conceptualization of democracy needs work. Democracy should not always be defined by open political processes, particularly where those processes do little or nothing to further democratic governance. Even when open processes are not willfully manipulated and undermined by activists and special interests, they often yield to the most extreme views and loudest voices. This is not democracy but a bastardization of it.

We can further acknowledge that representation should not be defined as the aggregation of local preferences where local is defined by computer-generated district lines. Such a system might have worked at one time, but in contemporary politics, the selection of voters is too sophisticated and the drawing of districts too precise. Able to select their voters, political parties have colluded to create politically homogenous districts, stacked to assure little or no competition and providing little or no incentive to listen to the other side. Creating economically, politically, ethnically, and racially diverse districts would also help to create a politics of negotiation and compromise.

We should also acknowledge that our political system needs to be infused with collective accountability. Congress has always been structured such that individual members could succeed politically even as the institution grew increasingly unpopular, but what was once a curiosity is now a pathology. Where members once succeeded despite congressional failure, at least some members now strategically create failure in order to succeed. Rather than becoming pariahs within their parties for undermining democratic political institutions and obstructing the policy-making process, they are instead elevated into presidential contenders and possibilities.

Finally, we must acknowledge that this is not a Washington problem created and perpetuated by professional politicians, it is problem created and perpetuated by "we the people." We create the conditions under which "no-win" elections yield a clear and decisive victor. In doing so, we reward the gridlock, partisanship, and dysfunction, we claim to hate and we assure that we get more of the same.

NOTES

1. Dan Balz, "Two Midterm Elections Have Hollowed Out the Democratic Party," Washington Post, November 8, 2014, available at http://www.washingtonpost.com/politics/two-midterm-elections-have-hollowed-out-the-democratic-party/2014/11/08/0366c60a-66c9-11e4-9fdc-d43b053ecb4d_story.html accessed on January 15, 2015.

2. McConnell ended up easily winning reelection, though much of his "success" is blamed on an ineffective Democratic opponent.

INDEX

and, 32, 45n37; length of
presidential campaign, 122–123;
micro-targeting and, 40–41;
nominations, 30, 33–34, 45n30,
171; overreactions to losses,
135–139; permanent campaign,
34–35, 36; predictions on, 124–125;
"truth" vs. belief and 2012
campaign, 124–126. *See also*
campaign finance; *specific
candidates*
elections, reducing number of,
196–197, 209–210
Electoral College, 19, 183–187
electoral process, 19–20, 30–31. *See
also* party system
elites: elite democratic theory and
failure of, 51–54; giving leeway to,
197–200; "iron law of oligarchy"
thesis and, 38–41, 84; Jefferson on
natural vs. artificial aristocracy,
17–18, 25; Key on choice and, 58;
manipulation by, 40–41, 91; social
distance and, 53
emotional appeals, 89–90
emotional attachment to belief, 56, 61,
127
engagement of citizens: digital media
and, 117–119, 128, 142;
disengagement, 47–48, 55–57;
education and, 181–183; elite
manipulation and, 40–41;
misinformation and, 128; never-
ending campaign and, 67–68; news
media and, 120–121; public
ignorance, 3–4, 7, 24, 90–93; voter
turnout and reducing costs of
participation, 179–181. *See also*
psychology, rationality, and
decision-making
engineering of consent, 51, 68
Enlightenment model of reasoning, 10
entitlement spending, 37
evangelicals, 88
executive branch. *See* presidency

fact-checking, 124
fairness, 61, 85, 110, 111, 184
The Federalist Papers (Madison,
Hamilton, and Jay), 15, 17, 22–23,
28–29, 172
Federalists, 22–23
Fehrnstrom, Eric, 88
Fenno, Richard, 201
filibusters, 139, 150, 160n7
financial crisis of 2008 (Great
Recession), 96, 98
Fiorina, Morris, 58, 153
First Amendment freedoms, 24
fiscal irresponsibility, 170
Founding Fathers. *See* constitutional
design and democracy
Fox News, 104, 105–106, 114, 120
Frank, Thomas, 55, 88
Franklin, Benjamin, 15, 41
Freud, Sigmund, 47, 48–49
Frohnmayer, David, 140–141
Fukuyama, Francis, 95–96, 97

Gaudet, Hazel, 55
Gerry, Elbridge, 17, 23
Gilded Age, 54
Gilens, Martin, 83–84, 95
Gingrich, Newt, 35, 145, 151,
152–153, 156
Godin, Seth, 116
Gore, Al, 2, 9, 32, 117, 184
Great Recession (financial crisis of
2008), 96, 98
gridlock, institutional: compromise as
negative, 143–144; congressional
polarization and rancor, 148–157;
effects of divided government,
153–154; ideological realignment of
parties and, 144–146; limits of
presidential power and, 140–143,
146–147; public opinion and, 147,
157–159; reactions to election
defeats, 135–139; redistricting and,
144; Republicans blamed for, 192.
See also polarization, partisan

9 781442 247505